Studying Law

To my mother and father

Studying Law

Fourth Edition

Phillip H Kenny, LLM
Solicitor, Professor of Law and Head of School of Law,
University of Northumbria at Newcastle

Butterworths
London Edinburgh & Dublin
1998

United Kingdom	Butterworths, a Division of Reed Elsevier (UK) Ltd, Halsbury House, 35 Chancery Lane, LONDON WC2A 1EL and 4 Hill Street, EDINBURGH EH2 3JZ
Australia	Butterworths, a Division of Reed International Books Australia Pty Ltd, CHATSWOOD, New South Wales
Canada	Butterworths Canada Ltd, MARKHAM, Ontario
Hong Kong	Butterworths Asia (Hong Kong), HONG KONG
India	Butterworths Asia, NEW DELHI
Ireland	Butterworth (Ireland) Ltd, DUBLIN
Malaysia	Malayan Law Journal Sdn Bhd, KUALA LUMPUR
New Zealand	Butterworths of New Zealand Ltd, WELLINGTON
Singapore	Butterworths Asia, SINGAPORE
South Africa	Butterworths Publishers (Pty) Ltd, DURBAN
USA	Lexis Law Publishing, CHARLOTTESVILLE, Virginia

© Reed Elsevier (UK) Ltd 1998

A CIP Catalogue record for this book is available from the British Library.

First edition   1985
Second edition   1991
Third edition   1994

ISBN 0 406 09329 6

Printed by Butler & Tanner, Frome and London

Visit us at our website: http://www.butterworths.co.uk

Preface

This edition is written at a time of almost hectic change in the legal world. The Labour Government is poised to make major changes in the legal system which will greatly affect the professions. Reform in many areas of the administration of justice is long overdue and it is to be hoped that radical and beneficial changes can be made. Will there soon be joint legal education for barristers and solicitors? Will a new and fair foundation be laid doe providing access to justice for the poorer sections of society? What will be the effect on our lawyers and courts of the accelerated development of the European Community? These are all questions to which the readers of this edition will see existing answers unfold as they embark on their own study of law. One thing is certain: a strong and well-trained legal profession will remain a fundamental safeguard of civilised democratic life. The challenges and complexities which lawyers will go on facing will continue to intensify and with this growing challenge the satisfaction and personal reward of studying law will also intensify. This is a tremendous time to begin the study of law and become one of the lawyers of the new millennium.

Professor PH Kenny
April 1998

v

Contents

1 Choosing law

Law is one of the most popular subjects for undergraduate study. Law degree courses are very many times over-subscribed and the entry standard is quite high. Yet it is very commonly said by law teachers that students choose law with very little idea of the real nature of the years ahead. The whole of this book, although intended to be a companion for those embarked upon their career as law students, contains information, and opinions, which should help the would-be student. The bulk of students intend to qualify as solicitors and a much smaller proportion as barristers. In forming a judgment as to either of these options, the material which follows detailing the system of examinations, training and apprenticeship will be of some value. Perhaps there is some insight to be gained by reading books of a biographical or autobiographical nature about life in 'the profession'. Personally I doubt if these often romanticised accounts are of much value for this purpose. Again, whereas the shelves of public libraries are well stocked with texts about successful members of the judiciary there is little to convey the real atmosphere of day-to-day life in solicitors' offices or even at the junior Bar.

There is no substitute for getting into an office or a set of chambers, 'getting stuck in' and seeing 'what is really going on'. There is growing willingness both at the Bar and in solicitors' offices to take students on for a short period so that they can have a look at the kind of career in prospect. At the Bar this will be unpaid, and in a solicitors' office, no or little pay can be expected for a summer's placement of this kind. Indeed, it would be surprising if the case were otherwise. In both cases, particularly in a solicitor's office, the student may be asked to undertake menial tasks such as making tea for his principal or delivering forms, briefs or correspondence or collecting forms from the law stationer. The prospective lawyer who shrinks from providing this kind of assistance will not make a good colleague. Solicitors, like God, love a cheerful volunteer. It should not be overlooked, either, that this vacation experience may assist greatly in the later obtaining of a training contract in a solicitor's office or pupillage in a barrister's chambers.

As with employment at most levels in the legal profession, there is no clearly-established machinery for providing places for trainee solicitors and self-help is necessary in this area.

If you have family or social contacts in the profession, this will obviously help. But there is no reason why you should not approach firms of solicitors directly and ask if they have temporary vacation work available, explaining your reasons. You will meet with some rebuffs but if you persist you will eventually succeed and may obtain an entry to a firm which eventually leads to a place in a training contract.

In a sense, though, the first thing you need to discover is what it is like to study law — not what it is like to practise law. Although there are no exact statistics, a reasonable guess might be that a quarter or even more of law graduates do not become law practitioners as such.

If you wish to gain some idea of the material which you will read on a law course at college, there are many preliminary works on legal topics which you will find helpful to read.

It is important in doing this to go further than material written at a very general level for laymen — you do wish after all to obtain an insight into the work involved in studying for and obtaining legal qualifications.

Some examples may be given of the books which you could read which will both stimulate and test your enthusiasm for legal study. *Freedom, the Individual and the Law* by Professor H Street is an excellently clear and thought-provoking account of the individual and his civil liberties. *Consumer Law and Practice* by Lowe and Woodroffe is an equally valuable introduction to a totally different area. If you wish to obtain a foretaste of a more theoretical side of legal studies there is *The Idea of Law* by Professor D Lloyd — although this is very heavy-going in parts. *The Proof of Guilt* by Professor G Williams is a thought-provoking series of lectures on the criminal prosecution. A more general but highly thought of introductory book is *An Introduction to Law* by P Harris.

By and large, wide preliminary reading is not advised before you embark upon a law course at college. The reading referred to is suggested to help you make up your mind whether you will enjoy the type of study involved in a law course, and not to lay any foundation for the course. Law teachers, whether teaching on a degree course or teaching law as part of another course, assume that the student has no particular knowledge at the start of the course. An uncluttered but critical mind is more important than any preconception as to the subject matter to be studied.

Many newspapers contain daily law reports. These are a little mysterious at first to the ordinary reader. However, familiarity will lead to understanding and enjoyment. As you will see, the stuff of English law is in great part the decisions of the law courts — and the daily law reports in the quality newspapers are often the harbingers of momentous legal developments. Similarly, important trials are reported in considerable detail and should be followed. The issues they deal with will often be raised at interviews at a law school. Current debates such as the legal position of persons on permanent medical life-support are not ones on which an interviewer would expect you to be familiar with the last word in legal philosophy. But, a would-be lawyer will show an intelligent interest in such topics and be able to engage in healthy debate.

For the reasons above, law teachers are often not enthusiastic about the value of 'A' level law as a preliminary to its undergraduate study. This is largely a hang-over from the not so distant past when 'A' level law consisted of a superficial treatment of large areas of law. This is not now the case, and there are valuable books and materials produced for the 'A' level student. Consequently, I would not see any great harm in a would-be student attempting this particular 'A' level in order to test his enthusiasm and aptitude for the subject. To this, two warnings should be given: first, there is, particularly amongst older law teachers, a residual suspicion about 'A' level law. Secondly, the student himself proceeding to degree level should not assume that his qualification will give him a flying start. On the contrary, he should be extra cautious to avoid any muddled or damaging preconceptions.

Choosing a college

There are now more than 90 universities and other colleges where students are able to take a first degree in law. Some of these degrees are called Bachelor of Laws and some are called Bachelor of Arts. No difference between the content or the quality of these degrees is indicated by the different title. In addition to the straight law degree there is now a wide range of opportunities to study law together with other subjects — social science, languages or business studies. It is not proposed to give any guidance on how to choose between individual colleges and their styles of degree. Opinions will differ widely and no one person's advice could suit the tastes of widely differing students. In terms of passing professional examinations later, there is probably some slight advantage in selecting a straight law degree. But, the opportunity of studying some other much-liked discipline perhaps for the only time in one's life should not be discarded lightly. Appendix 1 of this book lists the current providers of law degrees. Some small comment is given on each. Readers should note in looking at this two things — firstly, that the list will of necessity in a short compass be incomplete as new courses are developed from time to time and, secondly, the contents and standing of individual courses will vary also.

Advice that can usefully be given is to take the process of selection seriously. A not too ancient (1983) *Sunday Times* survey indicated that the geographical location of a city was the prevalent factor in student choice. There are other important criteria.

(i)   Obtain prospectuses — study them carefully — do they tell you anything about the quality of the educational experience you can expect?

(ii) Compare syllabuses — are they developing? — are contemporary issues given reasonable but not undue prominence? eg computer skills should be expected to play at least a small part in legal education.

(iii) Take the opportunity to visit one or two colleges. Ask by letter for an appointment with a relevant member of staff — course leader, tutor, or whatever. Try to evaluate the reception you are given and work out how it reflects upon the institution.

In the last resort, as you will be aware, entry is very competitive and no student has an unrestricted choice. But, the more you inform yourself on this process of matching your aspirations to an available place, the more you will improve your chances of ultimate success.

Completing UCAS applications

The system of allocating places is through the Universities Central Council on Admissions. You may select up to eight. No preferences are permitted. The first step is to ascertain the level of entry requirements for colleges in which you have an interest. There is a small book — *Degree Courses Offers* by B Heap—which may be of help. You must have a realistic appreciation of your own abilities. Entry levels to law degree courses at universities are now very varying. Some require a number of grade As; other courses can be very much lower with mixed degrees reaching the level of a mixture of Cs and Ss or even lower. Can a sensible strategy be worked out to maximise your chances of ending up with an offer which you have matched with your own examination performance? It may, for example, make sense to include in your choices a mixed degree which will still enable you to qualify as a lawyer, but have a lower entrance requirement. You may hold two offers until after the examination results have been published in the summer. This is a great advantage to the candidate and the opportunity for security which it gives should not be thrown away. The number of applications for law places are such that in very many years no places will be available in the 'clearing' systems that operate after the 'A' level results for candidates who have failed to meet the grades of their offers. However, the more likely scenario is that there will be places available at some law schools. Rarely will it be sensible to turn down a place in the chance of improving your A levels. Work hard on your degree and do well and the whole world of law still lies before you.

Applicants give a very great deal of thought to the information to include about themselves in the application form. Statements explaining why law courses are chosen and showing strong career motivation may be helpful. Details of work experiences in legal areas should also be included. Beyond these rather obvious points the applicant should try to demonstrate a wide range of interesting occupations and achievements — to capture the readers' attention. Bear in mind in doing so that such matters may be subject to gentle probing at an interview. The simple truth though is that the main factor regarded by admissions tutors is examination performance and predictions. Nothing on your form tells so much as the achievement produced by sound consistent work.

Preparing for an interview

Some law schools invite applicants for interview and some do not. Amongst those who do use interviews for selection the interviewers' purpose will be very similar. The interviewer will be interested in establishing enthusiasm and commitment and also aptitude for legal study. The student should demonstrate that a definite choice has been made to study law and that this arises from a discovery of relevant information about law and legal careers. Some knowledge about the career(s) in mind and the routes to qualification should be demonstrated. As mentioned above, familiarity with current issues relevant to law in the newspapers should be shown. You will read about issues such as euthanasia, self-government for Scotland, our constitutional position in Europe. If you are used to debating these topics vigorously with friends, parents and teachers then you will expect to do well in an interview at law school. The interviewer is interested in your general awareness of issues but will not expect detailed or technical knowledge. An ability to reason, to respond to critical argument and to reflect intelligently is what is required.

Some law schools may use a more specific aptitude test. This is an example:

Assume that English criminal law states the following rules:

'1   Murder is the intentional killing without lawful excuse of another person.

2   Manslaughter is the killing by culpable negligence of another person.'

Explain if the following fall within these rules:

(a)   Adam shoots a gun at Bertram and misses Bertram but kills Cedric.

(b)   Damion believes that God has ordered him to kill his wife Ethel and does so.

(c)   Frederick parks his car on a hill and sets the hand-brake so that the car rolls forward while he is away and kills a child crossing the road.

(d)   Gertrude who is pregnant is angry with her husband who neglects her.
She throws herself downstairs and suffers a miscarriage.

Such a test may be given to you by way of questions in an interview or
in writing as an addition to the interview. The first guidance is do not be
flummoxed into rushing into a confession of stupidity or babbling
incoherence. Take your time.

I do not myself think that such 'technical' interviewing is of any real
assistance. But, your interviewer does and you must respond accordingly.
First, understand that the interviewer has limited goals. You are not
expected to understand the law on murder or manslaughter. You are
expected to be able to understand the rule which is stated and restate why
the scenario posed is a problem and venture some solution, eg: as to question
(a) you might reply –

> Murder requires the guilty to intend to kill someone. The problem is do you
> have to intend to kill the person you actually kill. It seems equally criminal
> to me to kill one person while you are trying to kill another; *or*

as to question (d) –

> I do not know from the question whether Gertrude was trying to kill her
> unborn baby or not. If she had no such intention to kill it then I do still think
> that the issue of manslaughter has to be considered. What I do not know is
> whether the law regards the unborn baby as a 'person' for the purpose of
> manslaughter or murder. I think it might depend on how long she had been
> pregnant …

Here, of course, the interviewer would very much like to argue with you
about the age when a foetus becomes a person. Again, no knowledge of the
actual detailed law need be shown — but, you must be willing to take up a
sensible position, defend it and argue rationally. Try this yourself with
problems (b) and (c) — perhaps using a friend or parent as the 'interviewer'.

Also in the interview you are bound to be asked if you have any questions
to ask the interviewer. I have found it has a negative effect if interviewers
ask questions which are clearly answered in the information they have
already been sent: neither need you strain to ask clever questions. If you
really have no gaps in your required information you can say that you have
found that the information supplied in the departmental brochure,
prospectus or whatever has answered your questions. Some interviewers
(somewhat unfairly) will ask if you have any other offers or even what your
intentions are. The fairness or sensibleness of this strategy is not really open
to you to pass sentence on. An interviewer can turn you down unfairly and
you will never know. I would simply reply to the effect that at present you
are keeping your options open but very much like [the interviewer's

university] and hope to receive an offer. Of course, if you definitely no longer wish to go there you must, we hope, resist the chance to reply impolitely!

The variety of law degrees available

It has been suggested already that students often choose their college for reasons unconnected with the content of the particular course in mind. Nevertheless, there are now quite substantial differences between some of the main kinds of course on offer and a general description of them will be attempted. Do not, however, read this part of the text as a 'good course guide' — what is intended is a description of the styles of course available, and it is for the student to choose between them if the opportunity to do so is available.

Four-year law degrees

In England and Wales there are three four-year sandwich degrees in law. One is at Brunel University, another at Nottingham Trent University, where there is also a three-year law degree of the traditional kind. The third is at Bournemouth in Dorset. Each of these degrees include periods where students are placed in some relevant area of legal practice.

The philosophy behind this development in legal education is self-evidently sound. The quality of understanding of law in the classroom is very likely to be much improved where it is complementary to involvement in law in action. The value of the experience is much dependent on the enormous effort which staff expend in finding suitable placements and also on the ungrudging effort students put into making their placements work and performing the tasks which they are given.

The overwhelming drawback of the three existing sandwich degrees is that they last for four years as opposed to the normal three years. The periods spent on placements during these degrees can, at most, be counted towards six months of the two-year training contract required for qualification as a solicitor. It cannot count towards the one-year pupillage required of barristers.

Students wishing to qualify as solicitors must decide whether the 'sandwich' element in the degree is sufficiently attractive to counter-balance the reduction in length of the two-year training contract to eighteen months. There are many solicitors' firms who are not willing to take trainee solicitors for a shorter period than the full two-year training contract.

Four-year 'exempting' law degrees

At the time of writing there is one four-year exempting LLB degree in existence. This is at the University of Northumbria. An exempting law degree is one which completes the usual three-year LLB programme but also exempts the student from requiring to take a legal practice course in order to become a solicitor or where the student may alternatively pursue a programme which provides complete exemption from the bar vocational course. This means that at the end of the degree the graduate is both a law graduate and entitled to be called to the bar. Thus, a student completing the four-year LLB at the University of Northumbria in Newcastle has no further examinations to take before entering a training contract to qualify as a solicitor or being called as a barrister. This course qualifies for a mandatory grant for all four years. Students at Northumbria University may also choose to complete a traditional three-year degree if they chose.

The exempting degree is described further below. It combines the learning of academic law with the development of legal skills such as drafting and advocacy. It includes participation in work with real clients in a law office run as part of the Law School. Because this approach to law is so clearly advantageous many Law Schools are preparing to follow in Northumbria's footsteps when they are able to do so.

The traditional three-year law degree

Of the 60 or so degrees in law available the preponderance are overwhelmingly *traditional* in style. It is not easy before your law studies commence to describe exactly what this means — although it will be quite clear to those who have experienced legal education.

The traditional pattern of a law degree involves studying for all, or nearly all, of each of the three years. Subjects comprise 'proper' law subjects as opposed to complementary subjects such as economics, social science or philosophy. Even the most undiluted degrees will usually contain at least one subject which does not involve the analysis of legal rules. This is jurisprudence. Jurisprudence, as a subject, involves the study of law from the standpoint of other disciplines — for example, sociology or more traditionally, philosophy, or perhaps from a historical or anthropological viewpoint. Questions are addressed such as: What is the definition of law? What is meant by a legal obligation? Is there any minimum content to a system of laws? Is civil disobedience ever justifiable? What is the relationship between law and morality?

The remainder of the degree will then consist of a number of subjects, each having as its content one area of law and studied from the standpoint of critical analysis of the pertinent legal rules. This is what most law teachers would describe as the study of law properly so-called.

Until twenty years ago, law degrees were surprisingly uniform in their content and followed this traditional pattern. The advantage of attending a law course following this model is that you learn a great deal of law and you have every opportunity to develop skills of legal analysis. On the whole, and this may strike you as a somewhat philistine approach, graduates from such courses are better equipped to, and do, perform better in professional examinations than their counterparts from the less traditional law schools. Nowadays, the breadth of subjects available to students and the opportunity for students to study complementary areas has grown in virtually all law schools. Examples (and purely examples) of law schools following the traditional model on their full-time three-year law degrees are:

Nottingham University and Nottingham Trent University;
Bristol University and the University of the West of England;
Leeds University and Leeds Metropolitan University.

These examples are given so that when you obtain prospectuses you will have some point of reference — they are not claimed to be either the best or the worst examples or extreme examples of either type.

For the very many students who have made up their minds irrevocably to join the profession, they will find congenial numbers of like-minded colleagues on the traditional law degree course and find its contents satisfactory for their purposes.

Non-traditional law degree courses

There are a number (rather small) of three-year law degree courses which have largely eschewed the traditional approach in favour of what is seen by them as a more intellectually stimulating framework of study. The hallmark of this approach is the phrase 'law in context'. An example may clarify. Contract law can be studied as a set of rules — for example: How are contracts made? What formal requirements are there for a valid contract? What are the legal remedies for breach of contract? It may also be studied in other ways, such as: How effective are the legal remedies theoretically available? How are contract disputes disposed of by negotiation and settlement? Yet another approach would be to ask what systems of political and economic thought are reflected in our contract law. How are the functions carried out by contract law in our state carried out in a Marxist economy?

The possibilities of broader approaches to legal study such as those indicated above are enticing. Examples may be found in the syllabuses of Warwick University and Kent University at Canterbury — the latter having a distinctive interest in Marxist legal theory.

You will find it valuable to obtain prospectuses from the contrasting traditional and non-traditional law schools indicated. When you obtain prospectuses from many law schools you will note individual syllabuses with a gradual shift of emphasis towards the 'law in context' approach. Many law schools will now contain syllabuses preponderantly traditional in emphasis, but by no means exclusively so.

It can be said with certainty that the growing heterogeneity of legal study has enriched legal scholarship and helped to develop a much more questioning approach to the law. In the wake of stimuli to their thought processes most law schools have added new subject areas — welfare law and labour are now commonplace. Housing law, immigration law and the law of discrimination can also be found. In commercial areas, too, there is a healthier diversity of study — maritime law, international contract law, the law of the European Economic Community, intellectual property law, ie copyright and patent, have each found their niche here and there.

The picture is now fairly diverse and the description of the *traditional and non-traditional* models is easily pilloried as crudely unfair. But it will help give your ideas some focus as your mind numbs following the perusal of many prospectuses. Do not be afraid when you attend for an interview or on an open day to ask searching questions. Is it more important for your undergraduate course to maximise your chances in subsequent professional examinations, or for you to seize the opportunity for more radical study of the legal system?

In talking to a very large number of students who are thinking of studying law it has frequently struck me how wide is the range of possibilities and how very little the would-be student knows about each. In this edition I have tried to list each of the places offering law degrees (or CPE/Diploma in law courses). I would recommend prospective students to obtain and read the prospectuses of a large number of colleges before exercising choices. If time and opportunity permit it is worth attending several open-days, especially those where it is possible to meet existing students and chat about the reality of life as a law student.

Mixed degrees

There are very great opportunities now to study law as a part of a degree. If you wish to obtain exemption from the first stage of the solicitor's or barrister's professional qualifications, then it is necessary to study what are called the six core subjects: tort, contract, equity and trusts, land law, constitutional and administrative law, and criminal law. This, however, leaves potentially half your degree available for non-legal studies.

Even if you are taking a law degree as opposed to a mixed discipline degree, there is very often the opportunity to take one or more non-law options. This may be an important factor in selecting a course. Stimulating subjects for lawyers, such as criminology, sociology and economics, are frequently offered as a small part of a law degree and someone who will spend the remainder of his or her adult life in the practice of law has much to gain in the way of openness of mind from their study. A mixed degree gives an even greater opportunity for the systematic pursuit of some other discipline.

There is a range of colleges where law can be taken as part of a mixed degree. Some of those courses open the door to very interesting law-related careers. There are, for example, many opportunities in European government, and nowadays in private practice, for the lawyer-linguist.

A glance at Appendix 1 will show that there are many opportunities to study on mixed degree courses. Recent developments are in accountancy and business areas. Combining these areas with the study of law makes a great deal of sense for the future lawyer. It gives a background to the lawyer's understanding of the business world which should prove most useful.

Two-year law degrees

Buckingham University, which is privately financed, offers a two-year degree in law. The three-year pattern for a degree is not hallowed by reason but simply enshrined in tradition. In the author's opinion, there is a substantial loss to students in forgoing the steadier intellectual maturation process of a three-year degree. This is largely a matter of intuitive feeling and you can certainly gain a year by taking the two-year degree which is recognised by both the Law Society and the Council of Legal Education. It must be made clear that because this is a private university this will be a more expensive path to follow.

Other two-year law degrees are coming into existence, for example, at Hertford University. Such a course may represent a cheaper and quicker method of obtaining a degree. It has no other merit.

Student life

Wherever you undertake to study law, there will be a broadly similar pattern to the course provided. There will be a certain number, four or five, of law subjects studied at one time or in one year. These nearly always form very separate items of study. There will be formal lectures in each subject — one hour, two hours, more usually, and occasionally three hours in a week. Then, for each subject there will be small group classes — seminars, tutorials, problem classes — where you will discuss legal problems which have already been prepared by the class. The proportion and frequency of these vary quite a lot from college to college and year to year of a course. At any time, however, you will expect to have less than fifteen hours a week in the lecture or seminar room and very often ten hours or less in a week. The rest of your time is your own. This is the fact that above all invests the study of law with its distinctive character and discipline.

In the 'taught' part of the course you accumulate a somewhat shapeless mass of information — statements of law, opinions, and a large number of references. The study of law consists of the sum of your efforts to make order out of this apparent chaos. Much time must be spent in your study and in the law library aiming first at reducing the areas of law involved to a comprehensible pattern and then in following up references to critical materials — whether in decided case law or in the masses of secondary material produced by academics in journals, monographs and textbooks. This private study involves a disciplined use of time.

The organisation of study time

The modern student most often comes to the study of law fairly directly from his 'A' level studies. The sixth form will have given the student a foretaste of private study. There is, nevertheless, a big divide to cross. Many students find the challenge of organising their time insuperable. At the beginning of the academic year June seems far away, there is much else to do other than study, and anyway the course is three years long. These are tempting siren calls. It is the writer's personal experience that a workmanlike timetabling of one's efforts is the most effective way of overcoming this. The proponent of the more free-and-easy approach to the academic life will decry this philistine approach — and it is admitted that not all students will prosper under the same regime. But, it is strongly urged, the sensible student is one who knows for certain whether he is working or not working, who knows when work is finished and is ready for the other activities that student life offers so richly.

How hard to work

The work of a law student is creative. It involves a constructive re-ordering of material, considerable effort at comprehension and the development of highly-pronounced critical faculties. It is a dull student who thinks that work of this kind can be valuably pursued without break or recreation. Seven to eight hours of time *spent working* in a day means a very long working day. Certainly the sum of hours in a week *spent working* cannot usefully exceed 50, at least for lengthy periods of time. For the student of good average ability not aiming for academic stardom a working week of 40 hours will be more than adequate.

Two riders must be added to this dogmatic advice. First, the times suggested are inclusive of lectures and seminars. Secondly, the concept of *time spent working* is used very deliberately. What is important is not so much the exact quantification of time spent working as the realisation that there must be a clear division between work and recreation so as to maximise the effectiveness of the former.

It has always been a source of great puzzlement to the author that some able students fail from the beginning of the course. All students selected for entry onto law degrees have the ability to pass. They have simply to decide how well they wish to do and work accordingly. Those who fail are very rarely the ones having the best time outside the lecture-room. The lesson is to enjoy both sides of university life — but not quite to the full.

Women in the law

It is scarcely necessary, perhaps not even proper, these days to include such a heading. Quite a long time ago when the writer was a student, one-third of his undergraduate class was women. Yet, the proportion in the professions has remained much smaller and in the judiciary and comparable posts, say, for example, university professors of law, the proportion is surprisingly small. This says more for the tradition, organisation and life-style of the professions than it does for the ability (or otherwise) of women lawyers.

It is a regrettable, but probably undeniable, fact that the majority of members of the legal profession are prejudiced about nearly everything about which it is possible to harbour prejudice — often in a charmingly courteous and self-deprecatingly apologetic way but, nevertheless, decidedly prejudiced. It is equally a fact that, especially for the neophyte, long hours and full commitment are needed — and there are obvious difficulties for young married women in maintaining the continuity which may be necessary to achieve, for example, a partnership in a solicitor's practice.

The writer's experience is that women are as able as men at all facets of legal work and find some of the demands of study less of a trial than their male counterparts. Perhaps the knowledge that the legal profession has not thrown its arms open too wide encourages only the more committed to persevere but, for whatever reason, there is little doubt that women candidates out-perform men as often as not. In short there is no reason whatsoever for a woman student not to assume she can compete on an absolutely equal footing in any branch of the profession and, on this demonstrably certain premise, she should and doubtless will proceed undaunted.

The words quoted above were written for the first edition of this book in 1985. It is to be hoped that neither the reader nor the profession is offended by their continued inclusion and I leave both to judge as to their accuracy.

Access to the professions

The cost of qualification as a lawyer is returned to at length in the separate chapters dealing with qualification as a solicitor or barrister. As the reader will see in detail there, the time taken to qualify is long and the student will inevitably occur some expense from their own or another's pocket. I have to say with very great regret that it is now, in general, harder for a person from a not well-off background to enter the profession than it was in my own youth. It is to a vigorous entry from all parts of our society that the legal system must actively look for its future health. Future chapters will help to explain some of the sources of financial support that can be tapped. In addition, at the time of writing, new part-time routes of entry to the profession are being planned. Nevertheless, the message should be clear — the years of training will mean for all except a fortunate minority a level of financial restraint and even sacrifice. Some might suggest that this is a character building experience — what is undeniable is that this beneficial effect of the reduced availability of student grant is spread very unevenly throughout society.

2   English law and the English courts

English law and the English courts

English law consists of a very large body of case law and an enormous amount of statute law — the collective name for Acts of Parliament. In addition there is now a body of European law to consider. The purpose of this chapter is to introduce the nature of English law and give an overview of the English court structure. Many other countries in the world have a system of law which is modelled on or derived from ours. What all these systems have in common is a system of law based upon precedent — this is the essential nature of the common law system.

Common law

The expression common law like many words used by lawyers has a number of different meanings. An unusual meaning nowadays refers to the time when England was not such a unified country as it is now. Common law in this context refers to the system of law applied by the King's courts throughout the whole country. As English law developed the common law came to be applied through a number of Royal Courts of Justice. Alongside this application of the common law in the courts the King still permitted suitors to apply to his Council for particular justice or relief from unfairness. This part of the royal prerogative came to be exercised by one of the King's principal servants, the Lord Chancellor, and the court in which it was exercised came to be known as the Court of Chancery. Common law in one usage, thus, means the rules applied in the common law courts as distinct from the more flexible rules applied in the courts of chancery.

It is the common law courts which developed the system of precedent which is such a feature of English law.

A system of precedent is one where the decision in one case can bind a court in another case. The doctrine of precedent is a very special feature of

English law. It means that the study of law involves to a very great extent the study of case law. Nowadays the amount of statute law that is law contained in Act of Parliament is also very great but the ability to deal with case law is still the hallmark of a really good common lawyer. To understand how to deal with case law it is first necessary to understand the structure of the courts.

Court structure

This is explained in outline by the figure below.

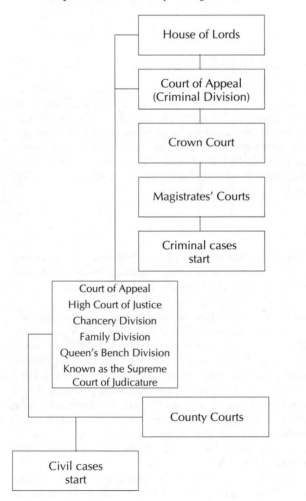

One useful working division of cases of the courts is into civil and criminal cases. The diagram shows the different courts in which civil and criminal cases begin. The final appeal in each may be to the House of Lords. Although this had its origins in the role of Parliament as a court it is now in effect simply the ultimate court of appeal, its members being the Law Lords — the most senior judges appointed to that office. These are known as Lords of Appeal in Ordinary. There are presently ten of these. The most senior judge is the Lord High Chancellor who may, and sometimes does, sit in the House of Lords.

Below this is the Court of Appeal. It has two divisions — the civil division and the criminal division. The President of the criminal division is the Lord Chief Justice. The President of the civil division is the Master of the Rolls. This rather odd title has become the title of the most senior civil judge by historical accident. The 'Rolls' referred to are the rolls of parchment on which court records were formerly kept. The record of solicitors entitled to practise is also known as the roll and the Master of the Rolls has titular responsibility for this.

The Court of Appeal is a part of what is known as the Supreme Court of Judicature. In 1873 the existing courts were reorganised by the Supreme Court of Judicature Act. The courts of first instance (that is, courts in which cases commence) became known as the High Court of Justice.

For convenience the High Court is divided into divisions which deal with different types of work and High Court judges in practice belong to one of these divisions. The present divisions are:

*   Queen's Bench Division, which deals with general civil cases such as personal injury, medical negligence, libel and contract disputes;
*   Chancery Division, which deals with company law cases, disputes involving trusts and trustees, bankruptcy and wills and probate;
*   Family Division, which deals with marriage, divorce and children.

The senior judge in the Queen's Bench is the Lord Chief Justice. The senior judge in Chancery is the Vice-Chancellor. The senior Family judge is the President of the Family Division.

The previous divisions of the High Court since the Judicature Act are as follows:

Divisions of the High Court since 1875

1875–1880	Chancery Queen's Bench Common Pleas/Exchequer* Probate**
1881–1971	Chancery Queen's Bench Probate**
1972+	Chancery Queen's Bench Family

* The work of these two courts was merged in the Queen's Bench Division.
** These dealt with Probate, Divorce and Admiralty. Probate was transferred to Queen's Bench(1) and Admiralty to Chancery.
+ The present division of work derives from Sch 1 to the Supreme Court Act 1981.

Precedent in the English courts

The rules of precedent mean that decisions of the House of Lords bind all the inferior courts. The House of Lords also regards itself as bound to follow its own previous decisions in most cases. The decisions of the Court of Appeal are in the same way binding upon itself and inferior courts. Decisions of the High Court also have value as precedents. Beneath these are the inferior courts, the decisions of which rarely find their way into a law report and which are not formally binding upon any other courts.

English judges do not give succinct judgments which announce 'the rule I am laying down in this case is ...' They give quite long judgments running for several pages. The lawyer has to determine from this what precise rule is laid down by the case. This rule is referred to as the *ratio decidendi* of a case. This expression is the Latin for *the reason for the decision*.

New laws are in fact made by the judges in laying down new precedents. This process is described as follows:

It is to be observed, however, that many specific questions are perpetually occurring, in which the rule of the common law does not happen to be fixed by any known decision, and that these are disposed of by the judges in the manner that they think most comfortable to the received rule in other analogous cases; or if there be no such analogy to guide them, then according to the natural reason of the thing; though (in defence to the principle already referred to, that the opinion of the judge is not to make the law, but only ascertain it), their determination always purports to be declaratory of what the law *is* and not of what it *ought* to be ... judicial decisions are the principal and most authoritative evidence, that can be given, of the existence of such a general custom as shall form a part of the common law. The judgment itself, and all the material, ie formal proceedings previous thereto, are carefully registered and preserved ...

It has been uniformly considered to be the duty of those who administer the law, to conform to the precedents thus established. For the scale of justice is not intended to waver with every new judge's opinion (which would be productive of intolerable inconvenience), but when in any case the law has been solemnly declared and determined, what before was uncertain, and perhaps indifferent, is now become a permanent rule, which it is not in the breast of any subsequent judge to alter or vary form, according to his private sentiments; he being sworn to determine, not according to his own private judgments, but according to the known laws and customs of the land; not *delegated* to pronounce a new law but to maintain and expound the old one.*

* These extracts are from *Blackstone's Laws of England*, one of the most influential law books ever written and first published in 1765.

Often in giving judgment a judge will make a statement as to what the law would be in facts similar but not identical to the case before the court. This statement of law is *obiter dicta*. This means it is said by the way — that is not strictly relevant to the case in hand. The rule which binds other courts is the *ratio* of the case. What is referred to as an *obiter* or as an *obiter dicta* does not bind other courts. An example may help follow this: suppose a taxi driver called Clarke is kidnapped by the Irish Republican Army and forced at gun-point to drive his car into the Royal enclosure car park at Ascot and leave it there to explode where it kills an innocent bystander. Clarke may be charged with murder and eventually an appeal in his case heard by the Court of Appeal. Then the Lord Chief Justice might say 'it is no defence to murder for Mr Clarke to say he was under threat of his own life'. This could well be a version of the *ratio decidendi* of that case. The Lord Chief Justice might add 'nor would it be a defence if the threat was to Mr Clarke's wife or child'. That statement would be *obiter dicta* as clearly not necessary for the decision in Clarke's appeal (doubtless you will have your own strong views on these two alleged statements of law and when you study criminal law you will find whether either of these statements I have put in the mouth of the Lord Chief Justice is correct).

A great deal of the skill of a common lawyer is in identifying correctly the ratio of a case which tells you how one case will be applied in another. When a judge in a case does this he is said to *follow* the previous case. If a higher court wishes to depart from the rule (laid down in an earlier case) then it may *disapprove* it and *overrule* that decision. If it thinks a case lays down a rule which is not binding on the present facts then it may *distinguish* the previous case. If we return to the mythical case of *R v Clarke* then we may see how it could be applied in *R v Jones*. In this case Jones has killed a politician by shooting after being told that his wife Mrs Jones is held a hostage by the IRA and will be killed herself if he does not kill the politician.

Here Mr Justice Wright says 'I must consider the case of *R v Clarke* which says that a threat to the accused cannot be a defence to murder. I can *distinguish* that case because the threat here was not to Jones but to Mrs Jones. The Lord Chief Justice in *R v Clarke* said a threat to another cannot be a defence either. If that was a decision of a lower court I would *overrule* it as I find it repugnant to reason. However, it is not a part of the Court of Appeal's decision in *Clarke* and was *obiter*. Accordingly I am not bound to *follow R v Clarke* at this point. The view of the distinguished Lord Chief Justice is obviously of *persuasive* and not *compulsive* authority and therefore …'

In reading this you should note that a view of a judge which is not binding is referred to as *persuasive*. If it is a view stated deliberately after thought and after the point is argued before the court it may be given appropriate weight. The law report will tell you whether the court gave its judgment on the day of the argument or after adjourning for some days or weeks to consider the point. A judgment given 'off the cuff' is referred to as *ex tempore* and one after a delay for thought as *reserved*. The report in such a case may indicate *cur. adv. vult*, which is short for *curia adversari vult*, which is Latin for 'the court wished to deliberate over the matter'.

The divisions of law

There are many ways of dividing up the huge areas of law and it is helpful for the student to know these at an early stage:

Public and private law. The expression public law covers the area of law involving the state. It may include conflicts between the individual and the state or the laws which govern government processes. The subjects which fall within public law in the law degree are public international law (concerning conflicts between states; constitutional law; judicial review (a very dynamic area of law concerning the circumstances when the courts will intervene to protect the citizen from improper exercise of power by or on behalf of the state) and criminal law.

Private law covers the areas of law which govern disputes and legal relationships between individuals. Typical subjects in the curriculum are contract, conveyancing, land law and the law of torts.

Common law and equity. The expression common law has been discussed above. Here we use it to mean the areas of law developed by the common law courts. The two most important of these for all students are contract and tort. The meaning of the first of these is quite obvious. Torts is the area of law concerned with remedies by one person against another in respect of injuries or loss wrongfully caused. Torts include such matters as libel, slander, nuisance, negligence and trespass. Tort and contract are together the two basic subjects in which students study the development of case law. Contract itself is the basis of many other legal subjects.

The expression equity refers to the system of rules and principles developed by the court of chancery. It includes wide remedial principles that allow the courts to protect individuals from strict common law rules. For example, a person may sign a contract when under unfair pressure from another. A child may give property to an overbearing relative. A pupil may be cheated in effect by a svengali-like teacher. To assist in such cases equity has developed a whole area of doctrine known as undue influence. Its operation is powerfully illustrated by the case of *Lloyd's Bank v Bundy*.

This case concerned a farmer who had mortgaged his farm to Lloyd's Bank in order to help out his son whose business had run into trouble. The case was introduced as follows by Lord Denning the Master of the Rolls:

Broadchalk is one of the most pleasing villages in England. Old Herbert Bundy was a farmer there. His home was at Yew Tree Farm. It went back for 300 years. His family had been there for generations. It was his only asset. But he did a very foolish thing. He mortgaged it to the bank. Up to the very hilt. Not to borrow money for himself, but for the sake of his son. Now the bank have come down on him. They have foreclosed. They want to get him out of Yew Tree Farm and to sell it. They have brought this action against him for possession. Going out means ruin for him.

Then in coming towards a decision Lord Denning attempted to sum up the relevant rules of equity which could be applied and made this famous statement:

Gathering all together, I would suggest that through this instance there runs a single thread. They rest on 'inequality of bargaining power'. By virtue of it, the English law gives relief to one who, without independent advice, enters into a contract on terms which are very unfair or transfers property for a consideration which is grossly inadequate, when his bargaining power is previously impaired by reason of his own needs or desires, or by his own ignorance or infirmity, coupled with undue influences or pressures brought to bear on him by or for the benefit of the other.

Applying this generous principle of equity the Court of Appeal was able to assist Mr Bundy and prevent Lloyd's Bank obtaining possession of his farm.

Equity also includes the detailed law dealing with trust. The idea of a trust has been defined as follows:

A trust ... is the relationship which comes whenever a person called the trustee is compelled in Equity to hold property, whether real or personal, and whether by legal or equitable title, for the benefit of some persons (of whom he may be one and who are called *cestui que trust*) or for some object permitted by law, in such a way that the real benefit of the property accrues, not to the trustees, but to the beneficiaries or other objects of the trust. (*Keeton Law of Trusts* p 5.)

Equity thus includes the detailed rules of law dealing with the management of trustees. However, as exemplified in *Lloyd's Bank v Bundy* it has a wider function described as follows:

Equity is not part of the law, but a moral virtue, which qualifies, moderates, and reforms the rigour, hardness, and edge of the law, and is a universal truth; it does also assist the law where it is defective and weak in the constitution (which is the life of the law) and defends the law from crafty evasions, delusions, and new subtleties, invented and contrived to evade and delude the common law, whereby such as have un-doubted right are made remediless; and this is the office of equity, to support and protect the common law from shifts and crafty contrivances against the justice of the law. Equity therefore does not destroy the law, nor create it, but assist it.[*]

Criminal courts

In criminal cases there is a division between cases which are tried before a jury in the Crown Court and cases which are tried before a bench of magistrates in the magistrates' court. The former is called a trial on indictment and the latter a summary trial.

The indictment is the formal statement of the crimes of which the defendant is accused. The defendant is first brought before the magistrates who decide whether there is a case for him to answer. If there is the defendant is committed for trial to the Crown Court. There the accused is tried upon the indictment before a judge and jury. The parties in a criminal case are ordinarily the Crown Prosecutor and the accused and cases are entitled *R v Smith* (or whatever is the name of the accused). Sometimes the prosecution is taken over by the Director of Public Prosecutions in politically important, very grave or difficult cases. In this case the title of the case will be *DPP v Smith*.

A right to a trial before a jury of twelve lay persons is regarded as one of the great bastions of English freedom. The trial is in public. Any prospective law student would benefit from watching such a trial. If you go to your local Crown Court to do so there will be pinned up a list of the cases in each court. You should be able to find an usher (court servant) who will tell you in a more helpful way what is 'on' in each court. You may be drawn to a notorious crime such as a rape or murder. These, however, often run to quite long trials. Ask the usher to direct you to a trial which will last only a half day or so, such as a shop–lifting case. Here, you will be able to watch the whole procedure of a trial and learn more than ten thousand words in a book could tell you.

The trial is each time an absorbing drama conducted with a measured formality that heightens the excitement. From the time the jurors swear their oath 'To try the several issues tried between our sovereign lady the Queen and the Accused' until the foreman of the jury announces the verdict there is an unfailing tension in the court.

A trial in the magistrates' court is considerably less of a drama. The ceremonial dress and procedure are absent. The three magistrates try the case assisted by a legally qualified clerk who sits in front of and below them. Once more the proceedings are public and a session or two observing the

---

[*]   Per Sir Nathan Wright LK in *Lord Dudley and Ward v Lady Dudley* (1705) Prec Ch 241, 244.

process is worthwhile. You will readily be able to contrast in your own mind the strengths and weaknesses of each of the two trial systems.

Which is fairer to the accused? Which is more apt to discover (if such can ever be known) the real truth? What changes would you suggest to either of these ritual processes?

The civil trial

The two main courts are the High Court of Justice and the County Courts. The High Court is situated in the Royal Courts of Justice in The Strand in London. It is open to the public and will inevitably be visited by the student of law. The High Court sits also 'on circuit' outside London. There are County Courts in most important towns and they are also open to the public.

A civil trial is much harder to follow than a criminal trial. Much information is contained in the pleadings. These are the formal statements of the plaintiff's claim and in the defendant's response to that claim. The aim of the pleadings in a case is to define sharply the issues between the parties so that the trial itself can focus on these. A typical statement of claim is reproduced on p 24 showing a claim or breach of contract. It is followed on p 25 by the defence which is filed in reply.

The civil trial is usually in front of a judge alone. The judge has the benefit of the formal pleadings prepared by the parties. There will be the statement of claim, a detailed defence to this and then further pleadings to narrow down the issues between the parties. There may also be agreed statements of evidence such as reports from expert witnesses.

The lawyers

The lawyers whom you will see when you visit these courts are divided into two groups — solicitors and barristers. The nature of the two professions and how you join them is the subject of Chapters 10 and 11. Solicitors deal more with work outside court and barristers in general with representation of the client in court. In court he is an advocate and when at his best fulfils this description of the role of an advocate given by the great criminal advocate Lord Birkett:

> The first quality beyond all others in the advocate, whatever his particular type of advocacy may be, is that he must be a man of character. The Court must be able to rely on the advocate's word, his word must indeed be his bond; and when he asserts to the Court those matters which are within his personal knowledge, the Court must know for a surety that those things are as represented. The advocate has a duty to his client, a duty to the Court, and a duty to the State; but he has above all a duty to himself that he shall be, as far as lies in his power, a man of integrity. No profession calls for higher

IN THE OLDCASTLE COUNTY COURT   Plaint No 94/2762

BETWEEN

Fred String Esq,
(trading as Quikflo)   Plaintiff

and

Jerry and Co Limited   Defendant

PARTICULARS OF CLAIM

---

1   The Defendant is a building and civil engineering contractor carrying on business at 27a, Marl Lane, Oldcastle.

2   By a contract in writing contained in correspondence between the Defendant and the Plaintiff dated July 12th 1997 and between the Plaintiff and the Defendant dated July 16th 1997 the Plaintiff agreed subject to the terms contained in the letter of July 16th 1997 to carry out certain works of plumbing and fitting at a new house under construction at Oldcastle.

3   The contract price for the said work was £320 plus VAT.

4   The said contract price was subsequently varied during the course of work because the Plaintiff had to carry out additional work as a result of the Defendant negligently and in breach of their specification hanging kitchen doors which opened inward instead of outward and the final contract price due to the Plaintiff is £400 plus VAT.

5   The Defendant has made payments to the sum of £200 only.

6   The sum of £260 remains owing to the Plaintiff AND THE PLAINTIFF CLAIMS THE SUM OF £260 and interest on the same until payment or judgment.

Dated this   day of   1998

To the Registrar of the Court
and to the Defendant

Poly Tyne & Co
1 High Street
Oldcastle
Solicitors for the Plaintiff

IN THE OLDCASTLE COUNTY COURT

Plaint No 94/2762

BETWEEN

Fred String Esq
(trading as Quickflo)

Plaintiff

and

Jerry & Co Limited

Defendant

DEFENCE

---

1. Save that the Defendant admits that the Plaintiff was engaged to carry out works of plumbing and fitting at Oldcastle the Defendant denies the Plaintiff's claim and each and every part thereof.

2. The said contract in writing between the Plaintiff and the Defendant was contained in the letter of July 12th 1997 and not as alleged in paragraph 2 of the Particulars of Claim and the said Contract price was £280.

3. The Defendant denies that the additional work carried out in accordance with the Contract between the Plaintiff and the Defendant or as a result of the Defendant's lack of care or failure to comply with their specification.

4. Further and in the alternative the contract was a fixed price contract in the terms of the said letter of July 12th 1997 and no payment is due for unforeseen work undertaken by the Plaintiff.

5. Further and in the alternative the sum of £200 was paid to and accepted by the Plaintiff in satisfaction of all claims under the said contract.

6. Further and in the alternative the said sum of £200 was paid to and accepted by the Plaintiff in satisfaction of all the Plaintiff's said claims under the contract and in return for a waiver of all claims by the Defendant and Mrs Madge Lowrie as to the Plaintiff's defective performance of the said contract.

Delivered this   day of   1998

Wear, Old & Company
Solicitors
Oldcastle

To the Registrar
and the Plaintiff

standards of honour and uprightness, and no profession, perhaps, offers greater temptations to forsake them; but whatever gifts an advocate may possess, be they never so dazzling, without the supreme qualification of an inner integrity he will fall short of the highest. In the conduct of any case, whether it be in the Magistrates' court or in the House of Lords, the advocate must have made himself master of all the facts; he must have a thorough understanding of the principles and rules of law which are applicable to the case of the ability to apply them on the instant; he must gauge with accuracy the atmosphere of the Court in which he pleads and adapt himself accordingly; he must be able to reason from the facts and the law to achieve the end he desires, and he must above all have mastered the art of expressing himself clearly and persuasively in acceptable English.

The two major legal professions have existed in their present form since the nineteenth century. Solicitors comprise by far the larger profession, consisting of over 60,000 practitioners. There are fewer than 10,000 practising barristers. Solicitors practise in offices which are in town and city centres and suburbs all over the country. These are similar to the offices of other professional and commercial persons. The majority of barristers practise in London in or around one of the four Inns of Court: Gray's Inn, Lincoln's Inn, Middle Temple and Inner Temple. Barristers do not practise from offices but from chambers. There are barristers' *chambers* in most major cities but not outside these.

Barristers are sometimes referred to as the senior profession. This is because they act in something like a consultant role to solicitors. Presently barristers appear more commonly than solicitors in the higher courts. The right to appear in a court on behalf of another person is called a right of audience. Barristers dress in a traditional way — men wear black jackets, striped trousers, a gown and a wig; women wear a dark suit, a gown and a wig. This form of dress dates from the eighteenth century and at the present time is long overdue for reform.

Two newer professions in the law should also be mentioned. The first is Legal Executives. This developed in the post-war period as a professional organisation for persons working in solicitors' firms who carry out work as assistants to the solicitors. The profession is run by the Institute of Legal Executives and has a very demanding system of examinations encouraging specialisation in a variety of aspects of solicitors' work. The second is that of Licensed Conveyancers. These came into being in 1986 as a result of the government's view that there should be more competition in conveyancing. The profession is run by a statutory body, the Council for Licensed Conveyancers. It also has a scheme for examining would-be entrants to the profession.

3 The way law is taught

This chapter is concerned to describe law teaching. It should not lead you to forget that law is learnt more than it is taught. The most important part of the study of law is the effort and work that you make yourself and that you make largely on your own. But the lectures and seminars which you are given provide the essential framework for your study.

In many ways the format of lectures and the smaller group seminars and tutorials has remained unaltered for a century. Law teachers have been as conservative in their teaching method over the years as teachers of any other discipline.

There is always a danger that a method of delivering information, advice and explanation such as the lecture can become rather routine and dull. It is important that a continual effort is made to use the different forms of class lectures and seminars to the best advantage. Do not accept too readily a role as the passive recipient of instruction and allow the experience to flicker past your half-waking mind like a half-watched late-night film.

Lectures

'Lecture means a teaching period occupied wholly or mainly with continuous exposition by the lecturer' (Sir E Hale, *Report of the Committee on University Teaching Methods*, London University Grants Committee).

'A means of transferring information from the notes of the lecturer to the notes of the student without passing through the minds of either' (traditional definition of a lecture).

In most colleges, lectures are formal occasions. There are different types of lectures and exceptions to the rule but usually those attending are expected to listen and take their own notes without interrupting the speaker with questions at least until invited to do so, perhaps at the end of the lecture. However, some lecturers do encourage or allow questions and you will soon be familiar with the style of your lecturers, and whether they would prefer no interruptions at all, even to the extent of not asking them to repeat the name of a case you did not hear.

Why lectures?

You may wonder what is the value of a lecture. Lectures, as implied above, are usually monologues by the lecturer, generally twice a week for 50-60 minutes on any one subject. They are quite often a one-way process, your role being passive and your participation limited to attendance and note taking. You may feel that attendance is not particularly beneficial, and that you could do as well reading a textbook or copying up somebody else's notes. Lecturing is sometimes portrayed as an unnecessary activity, a relic from the days when textbooks were rarer, and the lecture would have been an opportunity to communicate essential knowledge to a large number of people at one time. Lecturers obviously vary as much in style and quality as must do any other professional group — perhaps more so as the role encourages a certain independence, even eccentricity, of approach.

Looked at from the lecturer's viewpoint, it is not possible to satisfy everyone. The student's requirements themselves vary from those who prefer an accurate set of notes which means the lecturer must speak mostly at dictation speed throughout, or make it clear what to write down, to those who would rather listen and make only outline notes, gathering the material and going through the sources for themselves. What should the student expect to *achieve* from lectures?

A collection of notes. The second part of this chapter contains a lengthy discussion of note-taking. Many law students become a little obsessed with taking a verbatim record of their lecturer's golden words. Notes are important in lectures but not to the exclusion of intelligent thought. It might help to enumerate briefly what note-taking can achieve.

(i)   It provides a body of material which can be used later to assist in seminar work and later still in preparing for examinations. All but the hopeless cases will expect to supplement their lecture material quite considerably for the latter purpose. A 'good set of notes' has a value in helping organisation of thoughts and in providing a psychological prop, but is not sufficient in itself for any but the barest of passes. Even with this aim in mind, a more valuable, useful record will be achieved if you concentrate on clear headings, sub-headings and brief simple points.

(ii) The record you keep of lectures provides a valuable indication of the real syllabus. Law syllabuses tend to be drawn in an indiscriminate way, including, in theory, the entire contents of very large areas of law. Lecturers will inevitably leave out parts of the given syllabus or place huge emphasis on some parts and little on others. It is wise to pay close regard to this.

(iii) The lecturer will provide frequent reference to decided cases, learned articles and other sources of valuable information and critical comment. Some lecturers give exact references, others give clues — eg 'there is an article on this worth reading by Professor Rogers in CLJ'. In either case the references are meant to be followed up — the different style reflects different degrees of belief in the amount of effort one can expect of students. If tempted into indolence, remember that lecturers refer you to articles that have stimulated their interest, and topics in which they have a keen interest frequently find their way into examination questions.

(iv) In the same vein, the lecturer will attempt to bridge the gap between the printed textbooks and the present state of knowledge. The law in nearly every field is developing rapidly. There is an ever-increasing deluge of decided cases, reforming statutes and law journals. Inevitably, student textbooks come to be quite out of date in the intervals between editions. The lecturer performs an invaluable role in making sense of all these indications of change. Sometimes, it may be felt academic lawyers place too much emphasis on 'the latest thing' in the way of case law. For the law students, however, the sieve provided by the lecturer between them and the welter of publications is essential.

(v) The lecturer will stimulate a student's interest, provide valuable background insight and impart to the student some of his or her own enthusiasm for the subject. This intangible set of benefits to be derived from lecturers is perhaps the most important. The lecturer will have strongly held, often controversial, views about the way the subject is and ought to be developing. These views expressed in a forceful and challenging way will assist the student in developing his or her own critical faculties.

Attendance. Apart from the reasons implicit in the above as to the benefit of attendance at lectures, it is quicker and easier to attend them yourself and make your own notes, than to copy by hand — or even, at some expense, photocopy — other people's. Other people's lecture notes are seldom as useful to you as your own. The style will be different, making them harder to assimilate. They may have missed essential points. Finally, the mere fact of having listened and written them yourself helps to familiarise you with the material and eases the learning process.

A minority of lecturers teach by means of handouts containing all the information they consider necessary to be retained from a lecture. Is there any point in attending the lecture itself so long as you learn the handout?

My advice would be 'yes' as hearing the area discussed, the explanations and the illustrations must cost less in effort for the same or better results than going through the work entirely alone.

Attendance at lectures and seminars is essential for a further reason which is hard to describe briefly. It lies in the nature of law. The law you study is a mass of statutes and case-law decisions. The essence of studying law is making shape and order out of this chaos. Things that are unclear can dramatically slide into focus when explained by someone who does already have a deep knowledge and profound understanding and above all is an enthusiast of the subject under discussion. The lecture is the place where systematic understanding can be greatly assisted and the enthusiasm of the student kindled.

It should not be forgotten also that while the lecturer has obligations as a full-time member of the faculty so does the student have obligations as a participant in the course. Education is a two-way process — and the giving and receiving are reciprocal. It is reasonable for lecturers to demand a high level of both attendance and participation. This, after all, is the purpose for which a place at college is accepted.

Equipment. You may think it too obvious to mention, but there are some students who use notebooks for taking lecture notes, whereas loose file paper is far more convenient. Your aim whilst gathering material from lectures or your own study, should be to produce 'a package'. This consists of placing all the information relevant to any one point in the same place, and the basis of this package will be your lecture notes (unless you are on a course where the lectures are not intended to supply the basic information relating to a topic, in which case you will have to rely on your own notes to form the basis of this package). You can then supplement the lecture with cases, notes on articles and apposite quotations by interleaving them on additional sheets of paper, or perhaps even cards. Such a package can then be used for course work, and can be easily used for revision rather than having to remember that there is a note on an article somewhere else or trying to look at several files or books at once. A level of organisation and planning is required — not as a rigid strait-jacket — but as a precaution against the evaporation of time and the dissipation of effort.

Note-taking. Effective note-taking is essential to maximise the benefit to be gained from most law lectures. If you are attending a 'one-off' lecture by a visiting speaker, you may prefer to sit and listen, and make any notes, if at all, afterwards. Equally, with an 'ideas' lecture, it may be sufficient just to sit and listen and some people do find it easier to understand and recall without the distraction of note-taking. However, law lectures have a weighty factual content, and are both fact and concept intense. It has apparently been proved by research that the average number of items that a person can hold in his short-term memory is seven, plus or minus two, and a law lecture containing less than seven points worth remembering would be most unusual. Therefore note-taking is necessary.

For the notes to be an effective aide-memoire, you must read through them soon after the lecture, not only from the point of clarifying exactly what you have written down but also to begin consolidation of the information. If possible, you should go over them several other times before revision so that when revising you are able to read through them as opposed to having to struggle through them painfully seeking comprehension.

In developing a system of note-taking these are helpful suggestions.

(a) You must develop your own system of abbreviations: particularly for the common terms on your courses. In this context, see the notes on the extract of the lecture; and also the comments on those notes (p 34).

(b) You must find a way of setting out your notes on the page that highlights the main points, so that when you read through them, or are revising from them, the main points stand out in divisions of paragraphs and sub-paragraphs instead of just presenting a page uniformly covered with writing. Cases should be underlined. For an illustration of how notes are taken and can be set out, see the notes from the extract of the lecture (p 34).

(c) You must be selective, and cultivate the ability to recognise information worth noting. Unless you are listening to a lecturer who makes it clear how much you should write down, the difficulty of what to note and what to leave out is a problem that totally defeats some students, even into their third year. It is certainly difficult to be selective when you are unfamiliar with a subject, its terminology, and in most cases the end result in the form of the examinations. The temptation is not to leave out anything in case it crops up again later. However, the endeavour to keep up with the lecturer and write down everything will in the long run lead to points being missed and critical gaps or mistakes in your notes.

The first step in being selective is to leave out repetitive material. Most lecturers repeat themselves, either directly or in slightly different words, to help make a point intelligible and emphasise it.

Secondly, unless necessary to aid comprehension, many hypothetical examples and illustrations can be omitted. The same point can be illustrated by several different factual situations which are merely meant to strengthen an explanation, and are not necessary to the theme of the lecture. For example, while mentioning unreasonable behaviour in family law, the lecturer might give many examples of different types of behaviour, but not related to any particular case, which could amount to unreasonable behaviour. Rather than try to note them all, it would be better to listen and appreciate the sense of what is being said.

If, however, the example were a 'what if' factual variation to a case, introducing slightly new facts to the type of cases already discussed, it might be well worth noting. There is such a hypothetical example in the extract from a lecture below. It extends the factual situations already discussed, and once again, where it is referred to as a point of some importance, it is likely to arise again in later discussion or questions.

Below is an extract from a lecture on 'what amounts to an offer in contract'. What the lecturer actually said is set out in full, and this is then followed by a set of notes on that lecture, as an illustration of one possible way of taking down and setting out lecture notes. At the end of these notes you will find some comments on the notes themselves explaining why particular points were noted, and the further work that should be done in preparation of 'the package'.

Extract from a lecture

After the somewhat brief introduction to the law of contract, I will start to look today at the ingredients of the basic idea I mentioned last — the phenomenon of agreement — and the premise that in English law this is judged objectively, an important point.

The starting point is the offer — most contracts (later on I shall look in more detail at the extent of generality of this statement), most contracts in any event are formed by an act of one party clearly identifiable as an *offer* to enter into a contract followed by an *acceptance* by another party of that offer.

What is an offer?
Before coming to a definition of 'offer' — if such can be formulated — I am going to consider the nature of the problem of distinguishing an offer from other statements and acts before formation of a contract. The situation in question typically is: parties who might or might not end up in a contract 'chaffering', as the cases put it, about the terms of the bargain they might make. Only part of what is said will be 'an offer' and the rest will be characterised as an 'invitation to treat'.

The first question to discuss then is how to distinguish an offer from an invitation to treat. A major difficulty in commencing this discussion has been the reluctance of the court to adopt a clear definition of an offer and then apply that to subsequent cases. I will start with a working definition. 'An offer is an expression of an intention to be bound contractually on certain terms.'

Taking this preliminary definition, let us look at an area where this invitation to treat/offer dichotomy has produced some debate — that is the situation of an 'offer' for sale of goods in a shop or an analogous situation.

Case law discussing the situation where a shop-keeper exhibits goods in a shop window with a price-tag seems consistent in holding that that is not an offer, but that the offer is made by a customer who offers to the shop-keeper or cashier the price of the goods which the shop-keeper is free to accept or not as he chooses. A fairly recent example occurs in the theft case of *Dip Kaur v Chief Constable* [1981] 2 All ER 430, concerning the purchase of a pair of shoes intended to be sold for £5.99 but incorrectly marked with the tag £4.99. The suggested rule was certainly the assumption. See eg the Chief Justice Lord Lane at p 432, referring to an offer made by the purchaser — *Dip Kaur.*

The *locus classicus* where this area was discussed is: *Pharmaceutical Society of Great Britain v Boots Cash Chemists Ltd* [1952] 2 QB 795; and this area has also given rise to a number of articles you might read eg Winfield in 55 LQR and on this point see pp 516-518, Unger in 16 MLR and also Kahn in 72 South African LJ 246.

The facts in the *Boots* case were as follows.

The shop was a self-service shop — drugs listed in the Pharmacy and Poisons Act 1933 were sold there. It was not lawful to sell these goods save under the supervision of a registered pharmacist (s 18(1)). Drugs were displayed and priced on a central island where customers would select them and place them in their basket. The customer then took them to a cashier's desk and paid for them and left the shop. The place where the money was paid was supervised but not the place where drugs were exhibited. The Court of Appeal accepted the decision and reasoning of the Lord Chief Justice Lord Goddard at first instance and he, [1952] 2 All ER at 456, stated quite clearly:

> It is a well-established principle that the mere fact that a shop-keeper exposes goods which indicate to the public that he is willing to treat does not amount to an offer to sell. I do not think I ought to hold that there has been a complete reversal of that principle merely because a self-service scheme is in operation.

Before considering further the validity of this decision in the light of a proposed definition of an offer, I will refer you to one or two other relevant authorities:

Fisher v Bell [1960] 3 All ER 394, QBD concerned the interpretation of the words 'offers for sale' in s 1 of the Restriction of Offensive Weapons Act 1959. The question was: when a flick-knife was placed in a shop window with a ticket with the words on 'Ejector knife — 4s.' had there been an offer for sale? The Court said no. Lord Parker CJ added, 'the display of an article with a price on it in a shop window is merely an invitation to treat'.

A case in an analogous area is *Partridge v Crittenden* [1968] 2 All ER 421. The same kind of reasoning was applied to the same effect to an advertisement in the magazine *Cage and Aviary Birds* which announced 'Bramblefinch cocks, Bramblefinch hens, 25s each'. (Again a criminal case, this time for offering for sale a live bird contrary to the Protection of Birds Act 1954.)

Before coming to the merits of these cases let us add to the plot a hypothetical example given by Winfield in the article referred to at p 518: 'even if the ticket on a clock in a jeweller's window were "for sale for £1, cash down to first comer" we still think that it is only an invitation to do business and that the first comer must be one of whom the jeweller approves'.

If we recall the preliminary definition of an offer with which I started —

an expression of an intention to be bound contractually on certain terms —
let us with that in mind look at the merits of the restrictive view of what is an
offer shown by the cases and supported so trenchantly by Winfield ...

Notes on the lecture

Agreement[1]

(Objective standard?)[2]

A.   The Offer[3]
      Most contracts formed by one prty mking an offer, fllwd by an accetpance
by ano. prty.
(i)   Distinction from other statements and acts before contract.[4]
Prties chaffer about terms: which part is an offer & which invtns, to treat (ie
preliminaries nt bng offers).
      — In distinguishing from invtn to treats crts are reluctant to give defn of
an offer and apply it to other cases.
Poss deftn = an expressn of intn to be bnd contractually on certn terms.
Distinction between invtn to treat & offer in sale of gds cases:
      Dip v Kauer v Chief Constable for   [1981] 2 All ER 430[5]
Theft case — prchse of pr of shoes. Price was 5.99 — one shoe wrongly
labelled 4.99
Crt assumed offer was by customer, see esp. Lord Lane at 432, see also
      Ph. Soc. of G.B. v Boots Cash Chemists Ltd [1952] 2 QB 795[6]
(also carticle in 55 LQR esp. pp 516-518
Unger 16 MLR
Khan 72 So. Af. LJ)

Self-service shop — listed drugs sold — unlawful to sell them except under
supervision of reg. ph. Displayed on central isaldn for cust to choose. Pd at
cashier's desk — desk was supervd by reg. ph.

C.A. upheld 1st inst. judgment of LC-J Goddard & Fllwd his reasoning (Note
[1952] 2 All ER 456).
Sd displaying gds is nt offer for sale. Particularly this rule wd nt be reversed
for self-service scheme.
      See: *Fisher v Bell* [1960] 3 All ER 731.[7]
Interptn of 'offer for sale' in s 1 Restctn of Off Weapons 1930 (repealed)
Flick-knife in shop window — ticket 'Ejector-knife 4s'.
Was this 'offer for sale' within 1959 Act?
Held Parker LC-J article in shp window with price on is merely invtn to treat.
Same reasoning applied in:
      Partridge v Crittenden [1968] 2 All ER 421[8]
Ad in mag — 'bramblefinch cocks, ditto hens 25s each'
Poss offence to offer for sale a live bird (Protectn of Birds Act 1934).
Winfield in 55 LQR at 518[9] says: 'For sale for £1 cash down to 1st comer' is
still an invtn to treat. 1st comer must be one of whom jeweller approves.
How does this sq with hypothetical deftn?[10]

Comments on notes

The numbers in these comments correspond to the numbers in the lecture notes.

1 The heading 'agreement' is approximately in the centre of the page. The lesson from this astonishingly significant statement is this: the lay-out of your notes *is* important. You will be trying to learn from them and this process will be considerably assisted by an eye-catching reasonable layout.

2 'Objective standard' is followed by a question mark to remember to seek further elucidation about this point, probably in tutorials.

3 Sub-heading 'A'. 'The Offer', being the first element discussed in agreements (see comment 1 above).

4 (i) indicates that this is the first point discussed in relation to offers; the numbering serves to distinguish it from other points about offers.

It seemed fundamental to note that offers must be distinguished from invitations to treat and that the courts are reluctant to give a definition of an offer. In the absence of a definition by the courts, it appeared worth noting the lecturer's definition, since, as is often the case with definitions, it was referred to again later in the lecture. Definitions tend to form a starting point and are frequently drawn into the lecture again later as a point of comparison. They are therefore worth noting.

5 Case name misspelt. You should correct this, as it can give the impression that you have not bothered to look up the references or any relevant texts. Gap left in the name as it was impossible to get it all down, and this could be filled in later. Reference particularly was made to Lord Lane's judgment at p 432. The main points of this, or any apposite quotations, can be noted on a separate sheet/postcard, and interleaved in the file in appropriate place.

The case names are indented and underlined to make them stand out. The references to cases are also taken down where possible. You obviously should not endeavour to learn them, but it expedites the work of preparing your 'package' (see above) if you have the references to hand.

6 The articles are noted as this is stated by the lecturer to be a *locus classicus*. These should be looked up, summaries made on a separate sheet/card of any points you wish to remember, together with any pertinent quotations. The quotations should be a matter of several phrases rather than lines long, as in this extract alone from one lecture there are six specific references and the task of memorising them all would be an intolerable burden. Therefore be selective, and paraphrase

the arguments. The fact that so much material has been referred to, and such emphasis laid on the case means that it may well recur in tests/ examinations/assessment and is worth spending time on (see hidden curriculum, p 29 above). Incidentally, the annotator failed to notice that Winfield's article was written prior to the *Boots* case.

7   On reading through the notes again after the lecture, it would be apparent that *Fisher v Bell* did not merit much further time. The lecturer did not place the same emphasis on it as the *Boots* case, and its main value would be illustrative. The greatest value that you would probably get out of it is in an examination where you are discussing this point and could say something along the lines: 'Another illustration is *Fisher v Bell* where the Court held that exhibiting a flick-knife in a shop window with a price tag does not amount to an offer for sale within the meaning of the relevant Act.' Therefore, do not waste time making a conscious effort to commit the details to memory. The reference in this was unclear and can be corrected.

8   Similarly, with *Patridge v Crittenden*. Further research and learning of the detail are unnecessary when you consider the possible use of the case. It is a later case than the *Boots* case and *Fisher v Bell*, but it seems from the lecturer's introduction not to make any new points.

9   A hypothetical example from Winfield, being a slight variation on the factual situations already discussed. Worth noting and reading later, and adding any important points in the article as past of 'the package'. (See above.)

10   This note, which in facts refers to the preliminary definition by the lecturer, is presumably going to be developed further in the next lecture. No indication is given on possible background reading before the lecture (see Chapter 5 on background reading).

Throughout the lecture notes, abbreviations were used. Although there are formal shorthand systems such as Pitman's or speedwriting, most student do not know these, and indeed using such a system as Pitman's it would probably be necessary to transcribe the notes. Therefore, abbreviations tend to be personalised, and those in the notes above were merely meant to be illustrative examples. As said before, you can adopt any system so long as you can read it back easily afterwards. Below are the full words for the abbreviations used in this text, together with some further suggestions:

prty,prties	party, parties
ano	another
fllwed	followed
invtns	invitations
nt	not

bng	being
crts	courts
reluctnt	reluctant
deftn	definition
poss	possible
intn	intention
bnd	bound
certn	certain
gds	goods
prchse	purchase
pr	pair
Ph. Soc.	Pharmaceutical Society
supervsn	supervision
cust	customer
reg. ph.	registered pharmacist
inst	instance
pd	paid
sd	said
wd	would
interptn	interpretation
restctn	restriction
off	offensive
shp	shop
ad	advertisement
mag	magazine
protectn	protection
sq	square
C-J	Chief Justice
L C-J	Lord Chief Justice
H of L	House of Lords
C.A.	Court of Appeal
H. Ct.	High Court
Co. Ct.	County Court
Mags.	Magistrates' Court
P.C.	Privy Council
M.R.	mens rea
D.M.C.	Donatio Mortis Causa
W.	Will
cqv	cestui que vie
T	tenant
L	landlord
V	vendor
P	plaintiff or, conventionally π
D	defendant or, conventionally Δ

The possible list is obviously immense, and with practice you will contrive your own shortforms and abbreviations.

Making a fair copy of lecture notes

This is probably unproductive using time better allocated to understanding your notes, reading around them and supplementing them with further material, towards the end goal of establishing 'the package' (see above). You should be aiming to take sufficiently good and clear notes during lectures to make it unnecessary to spend further time merely in rewriting the same material again. You may find it necessary to add to your notes if you had to leave a gap, or to correct small passages, but it should not be necessary to have to rearrange the whole fifty minutes' worth.

There may be circumstances, however, in which you feel it is desirable to rewrite all or part of the lecture notes. Before doing so, the following are points worth considering.

(a) Rewriting the notes can help you assimilate the material but it is advisable to go through the lecture soon after anyhow, and this would probably have the same effect.

(b) Was the lecturer's style unclear? Did he/she jump from point to point? Or speak quickly? With the result that it was impossible to take adequate notes? In this case it may be worth sorting out what you did manage to take down, adding your own material and rewriting the notes to form one comprehensible set. The criterion must be whether what you wrote down in the lecture was so bad it is a good use of your time to produce a fair copy, or whether you can make sense of what is left — even if somewhat messy — and simply add material of your own.

(c) Was the lecture intended to supply essential core material for your course? In other words, will you have to rely on the information contained in the lecture notes at some later stage, or can you achieve equally good results without referring to them again? If so, again, there is little point in making a fair copy, however inadequate they are.

Questions

There are several types of question you might want to ask during the course of a lecture:

(a) a request for repetition of a misheard word;
(b) an explanation of something you did not understand;
(c) developing further a point made by the lecturer.

It is impossible to advise you how any one individual lecturer will react to questions. Attitudes vary as to whether any questions at all are permitted, and as to whether a request merely to repeat a case name or statute will meet with a chilling response. The author recalls in an early contract lecture a student, asking for a point to be repeated, being told — 'I am not dictating a child's guide to the law of contract.' Students can expect a more helpful response from most people who have chosen to be law teachers! For the lecturer, questions interrupt the flow and thoughts, and with a large class this can be disruptive. You may find therefore that the atmosphere is quite formal, with questions only at the end, if then. On the other hand, some lecturers are quite willing to have a pause in the lecture, seeing the break as an opportunity to revive interest and attention.

Even where questions are allowed, you can consider whether the question is necessary. While appreciating the need for comprehensible notes, it can be irritating for the lecturer to have repeated requests for spellings of case names or of parties involved in a case. This is something that can easily be checked up later, if in doubt. Therefore, even where questions are permitted you should ask yourself whether it is something to which you can easily provide the answer yourself afterwards.

Seminars, tutorials, problem classes

The style, frequency and content of these classes is by no means constant. Typically, before each class a student is set a problem or an essay title and is required to either prepare the same for discussion or to write out a written answer. Some suggestions as to preparing written work are made below (Chapter 7).

A crucial question for students is the amount of time to spend on seminar preparation. Let us consider two simple examples of seminar topics.

(a) From contract law: 'The doctrine of promissory estoppel has driven a cart and horses through traditional contract theory.'

(b) From constitutional law: 'A government with a large majority in the Commons faces defeat in the House of Lords over a proposal to abolish the constitutional role of the monarchy.' Discuss the various implications of this proposal.

Each of these topics has in its way enough dimensions to form the subject matter of a separate book. Yet each might also form a question on a subsequent examination paper where the candidate has to answer five questions in three hours. It is helpful for the student to regard the seminar as both an educational experience in its own right and as part of a specific programme of preparation for the examinations. Given these twin aims it might be suggested that there is little point in a preparation for seminars in such a depth and quality as cannot be utilised in the examination. Certainly so far as the preparation of written work for seminars is concerned this is true — although wide-ranging reading is to be encouraged, the accumulation of notes made on obscure articles is not likely to be helpful.

Making the most of seminars

Students fail to take advantage of the opportunity seminars provide. Consider the following as a guide.

(a) *Preparation.* It is very annoying to lecturers when students 'do not bother' and attend seminars unprepared. No-one expects days of preparation to precede each seminar. For a typical seminar discussion of the kind mentioned above, four or five hours' preparation might be a norm. References given should be followed up, read, understood and the main points noted. If the seminar is to take the form of an oral discussion, the main points should be set out gathering arguments and references under suitable headings.

The students who prepare for a seminar by perusing lecture notes and then turning to them whenever they are asked to contribute are wasting their own and the lecturer's time. Everyone knows already the arguments and materials rehearsed in the lecture.

(b) *Contribution.* It cannot be overstated how important it is for students to make every effort to become involved in seminar discussion. During the seminar you have the opportunity to develop your nascent skills in oral argument. Putting forward an argument, you will be rebutted by lecturer or fellow-student and have the opportunity of rejoinder. Never sink into apathy. You can expect early on to find that your reasoning does not convince all your colleagues. Unfortunately there are a few lecturers — but you may well meet one — who revel in the demonstration of effortless intellectual superiority over their students. It is very important not to let the situation overcome you — in life as a lawyer you will often have to argue with people who appear to have greater forensic fire-power and from time to time with those who assume an intellectual strength because of their position instead of because of their argument. Argue tenaciously and forcefully when you have a good point to make; accept correction gracefully if your argument is shown to be false.

(c) *Make use of the tutor.* The lecturer in the seminar as elsewhere is the provider of a service. If you cannot understand something, if an explanation is confusing to you, if you would like to go over some ground again — ask the lecturer. If you require further elucidation, ask to see the lecturer at some other time or at the end of the seminar. You will find the overwhelming preponderance of lecturers welcome the chance to give further assistance.

4 Varieties of law teaching

The previous chapter has described what may be termed the 'traditional' style of law teaching. There are other approaches, each of which has possible advantages and possible difficulties. The purpose of this chapter is to describe the range of varieties of law teaching and give some idea of what the law student may expect to derive from each. No assertion is made that each law degree should contain such methods of teaching. The author's own preference is strongly in favour of change and innovation particularly as stimulating student interest. Law teachers are refreshingly individualistic and have widely differing views on this issue especially.

The case method

For very many years the dominant approach to law teaching in the United States of America, the case method, has had a small but persistent role in this country. In its classic form, the students use a set text consisting of extracts from a number of cases and perhaps other materials such as government reports, socio-legal studies and so on. This text will have been prepared with a view to its use in teaching through the case method. The best, and perhaps the only example in this jurisdiction, of a text that is especially designed to fulfil this requirement is Smith and Thomas *A Case Book on Contract*. There are casebooks in other subject areas (see Chapter 5) but not such carefully structured programmed texts. Armed with their casebooks the students are set a number of pages to digest *before* each lecture. Instructions in the lecture then takes the form of the lecturer posing questions — very frequently to a named student — and the development of this question and answer process, which in American jargon is called 'Socratic dialogue'. The strength of this method is in displaying to the student the processes of legal reasoning in a case-law subject. The students are forced into the considerable effort of finding the reasoning upon which discussions are based, applying cases to hypothetical facts, distinguishing one case from another and seeing the development of doctrine in particular areas of the law unfold. The weakness of the method is that it is an inefficient way of teaching students the set of rules which make up a particular area of law. A student exposed to the case method will find it essential to follow the syllabus in a more traditional narrative textbook and perhaps to make his own notes or synopses of each area covered. Where the case method is used, the class can easily become dominated by a small number of eager students. As always the student is urged to make strenuous efforts at participation and avoid any temptation to linger in the background.

In American law schools the method is used in teaching very large groups of students sometimes in excess of 200. Also in American law schools, there are very often no seminars or other small group classes, so presumably the method can be used to good effect. My own experience is that it is very hard to prevent the emergence within a class of a group of 'strenuous non-participators'. If you find yourself in a class which is exposed to the case method then if you are not a naturally extrovert speaker, the vital effort must be made right at the beginning before there is any danger of your falling into the overlooked group.

It is equally important, since you will have no systematic exposition of the subject from your lecturer, to follow the course in a clearly written textbook. You cannot, if the course ends in an unseen written examination, rely on notes taken from case method classes to provide the back-bone of your revision. You will need to make your own full notes and to do this right from the beginning of the course. You will probably derive most benefit from case-method teaching if you are able to anticipate the lecturer by a substantial margin and read before each lecture not only the case material set, but also further textbook and journal material and prepare your notes on that part of the syllabus before the classroom discussion. Do not despair if at the beginning a part of the course taught by this method appears unproductive and confusing. It is undoubtedly a very much slower method of covering the syllabus than the traditional method of lectures and seminars, and you will need to persist in your programme of preliminary reading and vigorous participation in class in order to achieve rewards.

Clinical legal education

Many law teachers have thought that legal education would be improved by the involvement of students in some form or other of legal practice. After all, this is a principal method of educating doctors, the argument runs, so why should it not have its place in educating lawyers?

In the development of legal education this century in England and Wales, there has probably been an undesirably large gap between those involved in the academic side of legal education and the practitioners. Neither has there been the tradition of senior members of the practising profession holding academic posts which is so important a feature of the medical profession. Nevertheless, in various ways, clinical legal education of one kind or another has become a feature, albeit a small one, of the overall scene.

One model which clinical teaching takes is the involvement of students in live cases. Several colleges have set up law clinics or law centres which clients are encouraged to attend in order to receive advice and possibly other legal assistance. Occasionally the performance of student advisers at such a clinic becomes an assessed part of their course.

In other courses, some form of stimulation of 'real' legal problems may be used — varying from the examination of some legal document to the re-creation of extensive examples involving lengthy sets of materials and complex scenarios.

There are dangers involved in an enthusiastic espousal of clinical legal education. Cases that arrive willy-nilly at a law clinic have no particular ordered relationship to the fields of legal doctrine with which a degree student must become familiar. There is also the very prevalent risk of students becoming swept whole-heartedly into this work because it is such an exciting challenge. It is easy then to lose sight of the all-round academic goals which legal education must pursue. A final danger and a much more controversial one is the difficulty that can be caused by the desire of students or staff to use the law clinic experience to put the world to rights. Conflicts of interest can be generated between students and their colleges; issues such as student grants, immigration and housing can become items of impassioned debate and the focus moves from the legal into the political arena.

In their professional work, lawyers are constrained by professional rules — a code of ethics. There is a strict discipline dealing with confidentiality, duties to their clients and conflicts of interest. This is not necessarily present in students' law clinic work — though it seems to this writer, at least, much more satisfactory that it should be. It is equally important for students to accept other forms of professional discipline. Proper files should be kept, telephone calls and interviews properly noted, appointments made and kept and the adviser's duties to his client fully recognised.

If the work takes place in this kind of background, then, within limits, it can be valuable. The student cannot in a 'live' clinic learn much law — the collection of cases is so haphazard and the range of legal issues addressed in a law degree so great. He can, though, learn a great deal about the relationship between legal rules and their practical context. He can gain valuable, supervised experience of the discovery of legal issues in a client's jumbled case history, and of the skills involved in giving clear and helpful legal advice. Hopefully, the student will also become aware of the responsibilities involved in putting oneself in the position of another's legal adviser.

It may be seen from this that it is the writer's feeling that experience of clinical work is a valuable complement to a student's proper academic work rather than a substitute. It is one of the many experiences that can be used to enrich the academic stage of a lawyer's education and make the essential learning that takes place in the library and lecture room more valuable and memorable.

Whether the clinical programme you are offered includes live cases or sets of simulated case studies in the form of documents and so on, you will find it much harder and much more time-consuming than instruction through the familiar pattern of lectures and tutorials. If we consider one area where the simulated case-study method might be used you will see the added dimension.

When you learn basic property law, you will find the topic of registered land, and the topic of co-ownership of land both quite hard to grasp in the classroom. The problem areas which you are dealing with can be recreated using registered land documents, conveyances and other documents. Recreating the academic problems involved through documents such as these requires the production of quite complicated material. In order to understand it, the student has to make some considerable effort but, having done so, instead of learning a set of legal rules in the abstract, he has seen how they operate in the practical setting in which they appear to lawyers. He is able to use the rules working in their real context instead of a set of abstract referenceless rules. For the student, the drawback of this method is that another set of material has to be mastered. The reward is eventually a more all-round understanding of the subject in question.

In the 'live-case' law clinic, it is even harder to see any relation between the learning experience offered and the traditional course of lectures and seminars. Real life refuses to follow the orderly pattern of a textbook or lecture course. Cases involve unexpected or confused legal issues or issues purely of fact or credibility. Consequently, this kind of experience is better seen as a complement to the academic programme. It will increase a student's awareness of how his/her knowledge may be later developed and provide an introduction to the acquisition of professional skills but it will not actually form a large part in completing the academic foundations of a legal education.

If you are envisaging embarking on 'live' clinic work in your course or as a voluntary extra, try to see this as preparation for practice in a real sense. Law clinics at colleges in the past have run into difficulties where students (and teachers) have had no sensible idea of professional practice and seen the clinic as a campaigning vehicle. Campaigning for social and political change is something in which you may very well become involved — the lawyer has much to contribute in this area. It is, though, a different thing from representing and advising individual clients and should be kept apart.

You will require an ethical framework in which to work. You will not yet be in a profession so you will not be bound by its traditions and rules. Your teachers or supervisors probably will and can be expected to give you careful guidance. You might like to read *A Guide to the Professional Conduct of Solicitors* published by the Law Society (1993). It should give you much to reflect on when you consider individual ethical problems in your clinical work. Perhaps your law clinic will have clear rules and cover issues such as the following.

(a) Can you deal with cases in which you have a potential conflict of interest, eg where 'the other party' is your college or university?
(b) With whom is it permissible for you to discuss a client's affairs? How wide is the circle of confidentiality? Does it extend to fellow students or only some of them, law faculty staff or only some of them? Who has access to an individual client's files?
(c) How should you conduct yourself if you have correspondence with other professional advisers? Have you any duties of truthfulness or fair dealing to them or does 'anything go'?

You also need something in the way of office procedures. Files must be maintained and kept properly secure. You must have some means of making yourself available to your client. It is probably much better if you cover some of these practical matters by written guide-lines. This may be especially important in a student law clinic where the same person does not deal with an entire file from beginning to end and it is essential that your work so far be comprehensible to others.

You may find in your own college that there is no existing law clinic run on an official basis. There may be one run by students or you may feel students should fill a gap and commence one. This will, indeed, be a potentially valuable experience — there is no substitute for real experience, although the lessons it gives may be hard-earned. If you are involved in a student-run clinic, I think the above strictures as to ethical standards and having an established office routine are even more important. It is my strong belief that you will learn most of value if professionally qualified and experienced staff are willing to be involved.

Mooting, mock trials and role playing

These exercises have a marked similarity to clinical legal education but can be discussed separately as having a separate tradition and identity.

Mooting

A moot is an oral argument on some contentious point of law. A moot is set as if it were in a court of law. Some person, usually a member of the teaching staff or a visiting lawyer, takes on the role of a judge either of the Court of

Appeal, or the House of Lords. Those appearing in the moot are divided into two teams of two — Leading and Junior Counsel for the Appellant and Leading and Junior Counsel for the Respondent. The moot problem prepared by one of the lecturers will be carefully constructed so that there are two interlocking points — one to be taken by Leading Counsel and one to be taken by Junior Counsel. It is conventional for both counsel for the appellant to address the court, followed by both counsel for the respondent. The presiding judge is at liberty to vary this convention. When the time comes for you to participate in a moot, your lecturers will doubtless provide detailed guidance on what is expected from you. The following may be of some assistance, nonetheless.

(i)   Do not present a welter of authorities. Students frequently feel impelled to show the judge that they are aware of every last case on a subject. In the brief time allowed in a moot to each participant, usually no more than fifteen minutes, this will not impress. As you will know from attending lectures, following complex oral arguments is quite difficult. The number of cases should be kept small. What is demanded is clarity of argument, the demonstration of analytical powers, and the ability to make oneself understood. The good moot speech is surprisingly simple and uncluttered.

(ii) Do not write out the whole of your speech to the court even in order to rehearse it. It is a convention that counsel must not read their argument to the court. It is in any event extremely tedious for a judge to be subjected to somebody's written prose read out verbatim.

(iii) An important test of the good mooter is the ability to deal with interjections from the judge. These will sometimes be extremely penetrating and demand a considered reply. Consequently you will be expected to pause briefly before replying. If, indeed, it is more convenient for you to deal with the point at some later stage then say so. On no account then omit to answer the question at the appropriate point. If possible deal with the question as it arrives — try to meet it with pertinent authority and reasoned argument, not mere rebuttal. From time to time you will moot in front of a judge — perhaps a visiting lawyer — who has slightly misunderstood the facts or the legal points you are making. It will have been a long day in court, the sherry beforehand was plentiful and the room is warm — his concentration has lapsed or he has, as the writer once witnessed, irredeemably confused your case with your opponent's. As counsel, you must firmly but politely correct the judge and put him on the path of magisterial rectitude. Bluntness in this situation is not recommended — but no lawyer worth his salt will judge your arguments the less favourably because you have rightly stood ground and he is found to have erred.

(iv) It has been the custom in the past for dress in moots to be formal, at least to the extent of dark suits for mooters of either sex. You will certainly be told in your college if that is required. Even if there is no explicit instruction, you should be prepared to dress in a way appropriate to the setting. An appeal court demands some sobriety both of dress and demeanour. In the same way the audience, if any, should try to approximate their behaviour to that which may be expected by the visiting public in a court of law.

(v) In citing authorities it is expected that you will be able to refer the court to the exact reference. You should be able in the middle of your speech to turn to the correct volume of the law reports, cite the exact reference and read the relevant brief passage from the law report itself. In citing from books and learned articles the convention has been that authors are treated as authorities only after their death. This led to the curious custom that if the author were alive, counsel would adopt his or her words as part of counsel's argument. The custom is no longer rigidly followed; but it is still wise to use references to such material sparingly, and especially to avoid reference to textbooks to support trivial propositions.

(vi) You will still be expected to address fellow counsel and the court formally — fellow counsel as 'my learned friend Miss Smith' the judge as 'My Lord' or 'Your Lordship'. The first counsel to address the court will go through the ritual known as 'making one's appearances'. An example of this would run as follows:

> My Lord, in this case I appear for the Appellant, Sugden, together with my learned friend Miss Smith, and my learned friends, Miss Jones and Mr Hyde, appear for the Respondent, Challis.

Students are quite often reluctant to participate in mooting. Making a sound argument in a moot involves a great deal of time and effort. It *is* worthwhile. The experience of research is valuable. The experience of oral presentation of complex legal argument is invaluable training. The experience of being put to the question by an incisive presiding judge, trying though it is at the time, will stand you in good stead for later more searing encounters. It is unwise to turn your back on a challenge. Generations of students have enjoyed the experience of mooting and gained greatly from it.

Mock trials

These are more cumbersome than moots. Students take the roles of all the participants in a jury trial including witnesses, defendant and jury. The part of the judge is very often taken by a more senior person. Nevertheless, the mock trial is essentially a more light-hearted event. Characters frequently dress the part, assume quaint accents or amusing mannerisms. Sometimes this all degenerates into knockabout comedy. While not too serious a part of the education experience, there is no doubt that participating in such an entertainment can be good fun and may point the odd valuable lesson as to courtroom procedure, forensic skill or rule of evidence.

Role playing

Other less structured forms of role playing may be encountered, especially in seminars. Participants may take the role of a pressure-group arguing for reform of the law, of proponents of a particular legal philosophy or even of the plaintiff or defendant in litigation. For example, the seminar might be on the issue of whether the criminal law should be based on an equation between punishment and responsibility, or between deviance from normal behaviour and the need for treatment. Students could then adopt the position respectively of a proponent of the traditional view of punishment as retribution and an advocate of treatment of offenders in place of punishment. Exercises such as this in the form of game-playing undoubtedly enliven proceedings. It is, moreover, not unlike the real-life role of a lawyer, to have to argue a given brief, not the one in which you happen to have faith.

Developments in skills teaching

Legal education has historically been quite rigidly divided into academic legal education and vocational education. The former concentrates on a systematic and critical understanding of the main areas of law. The latter concentrates on things more directly concerned with practice. In both stages of legal education concentration has been much greater on learning law than on learning lawyer's skills. However, in recent years there has been a heated and productive debate about the proper role of skills teaching in legal education. More will be said about this in Chapters 10 and 11 which deal with the schemes of training for barristers and solicitors. Some discussion of the place of skills training at the law degree stage is also desirable.

It is helpful to ask the question — what lawyerly skills should be developed in the academic stage of a lawyer's education? The answer first and foremost is skills of legal research. By this I do not mean esoteric historical analysis. I mean the ability to find, use and apply legal source material; the ability to read cases and statutes and apply them to new or complex situations. This set of skills is developed throughout the course by students who read widely and learn to use properly the materials available in their law library. The bare pass student who relies almost entirely on lecture notes and introductory textbooks will fail to develop these very important abilities. As you will see when you begin the formal study of law, change in the laws and in the legal system is now an endemic process. The good lawyer is one who can comprehend these changes and make use of them in practice. There is now more need than ever to develop basic research skills while reading for one's law degree.

There are also other skills which should be developed by lawyers and it may be of interest to list these and examine their relevance to law degree studies.

- Skill in presenting legal argument in writing
- Skill in presenting legal argument orally
- Advocacy
- Counselling
- Interviewing
- Drafting of legal documents
- Negotiating
- Business skills
- Computer literacy

The first two items in this list are matters which should be at the core of your legal education. They are closely related to the research skills I have already discussed. Your law degree should provide ample opportunity for developing your muscles in these areas.

The remaining 'skills' on my lists are more controversial. There are many academics who believe that their development belongs more properly to the vocational stage of a lawyer's education. I believe, however, that using legal materials to perform 'tasks' in these 'skills' areas is something that will not only produce better ('more skilled') lawyers but will also improve the quality of the academic experience as such.

There is room on a good law degree programme for students to have experience of lawyers' activities such as drafting, negotiating and counselling. There should also be opportunity for students to examine related business areas and appreciate the relevance of computers and modern business information technology. None of this should in any way diminish the importance of the systematic analysis and criticism of the law. On the contrary, it will assist understanding — because practical use and application must do so. It will improve appreciation of the real role of law in society by bringing the classroom experience nearer to the real world. Many law schools are now embracing whole-heartedly the importance of 'skills' in legal education. In choosing a law school for your studies I would suggest that this is a relevant factor. The world in which the future lawyer will operate will be an even more challenging one. A high level of skills will be at a premium. Developing these will in future come to be a continuing process throughout a lawyer's education.

One example of the kind of exercise that you should expect to perform will show how drafting documents could become an important part of your education. You will learn in looking at property the important difference between a licence and a lease. A licence can be a permission to occupy another person's property. A lease is a similar arrangement but in English law has the status of being an interest in land. The difference between such a licence and a lease may be of great practical importance. The tenant may have his continued occupation guaranteed by an Act of Parliament. The licensee may not. A typical drafting exercise could be — 'A client wishes to grant a licence of a shop on Oxford High Street for the next year to the Liberal Party as its campaign headquarters. Draft a suitable document.' This exercise requires the bringing together of substantial knowledge of case and statute law before a successful — albeit simple — draft document can be produced.

Such an exercise can then be taken a stage further by introducing other important skills. For example, a student can be asked to draft a letter to a client explaining, in terms the client will understand, the nature of the legal arrangement. The same exercise can be transformed into a negotiating session. One side is briefed to represent the 'tenant' and as to the desired outcome from that point of view, and the other briefed to represent the 'landlord' clearly with a different desired outcome as to the terms and effect of the agreed document. This form of negotiation requires a sound understanding of the difficult legal issues coupled with the ability to deploy this knowledge to good effect. It is an excellent way of reinforcing the understanding of legal rules.

Interviewing and negotiation

The introduction of exercises of interviewing and negotiation into an academic law course is quite controversial. Many law courses are coming to involve such tasks. As you will see later in this book the professional courses for solicitors and barristers involve assessment of such skills. I am very dubious myself as to whether there is much place for the formal teaching of these skills. Practice at interviewing and negotiation has a small but useful place to play in a lawyer's education — the rest is learned in the rough and tumble of practice.

However, as with other skills simulations useful settings can be devised in which to puzzle out legal problems, to analyse and apply legal concepts.

The most important lesson such exercises should instill is that the foundation of all practical lawyering is sound research, understanding and knowledge of law. If thoroughly based on this foundation then practice of negotiating and interviewing is of value. If it is an exercise in negotiating or interviewing divorced from research and deployment of legal information then it is little more than an amusing game.

Computers in the classroom

It will not have escaped the student of any discipline that computers have
intruded into many and often quite surprising areas of human activity. The
part which computers will play in legal education in the future is at present
rather hard to see — though there is no doubt that it will be significant and
long-lasting. It can be expected that virtually all new students of law will
have had some experience of computers. Certainly as the next few years
pass, it will become unheard off for a person to leave school without some
hands-on experience of computers, some insight into how they function,
and some idea as to the nature and structure of a computer program. The
question is what specific part computers can play in the study of law.

Information retrieval

It is likely that your college will subscribe to LEXIS — the very large
commercial computer database. These very large databases consist of a store
of legal primary source material, case law and statute law, in computer
readable form. A subscriber to one of these services is able to use a computer
terminal in his office or college to interrogate the database and discover if
it has any information relevant to his problem. An example will assist. The
student wishes to know if there are any decided cases on liability of farmers
to hikers who are trampled by rampaging bulls. The first step is to formulate
a search request.

Searches into these two computer databases are made by typing into the
terminal a request for the computer to search its records and produce any
containing stated words. If we take the example in the last paragraph, you
would formulate a request using the words 'Farmer/Hikers/Bull'. The
computer will then test this search against its files of cases and the display
unit will inform you if there are any cases containing all three of these words.
If you carry out this search on the Lexis database, you will find there are no
cases on file containing these three words. The search reformulated with
the words 'Walker or Hiker and Field or Footpath' produces 383 cases. If
the words 'And Injury and Animal' are added we end up with four cases.
But these concern injury by a hunting horse, a guard dog, a case involving
calves and a cyclist, and another involving pheasants. An alternative search
using the words 'Bull and Personal Injury' produces 37 cases. If the words
'And Hiker or Walker' are added the result is that there are no applicable
cases. When you study this area of tort law you might find it amusing to
return to this example. Are there really no cases involving bulls and hikers?
How would you formulate a request to discover analogous cases?

This example gives something of the feel of the new databases — at
present they may be more interesting than useful. They can be used to good
advantage in statute law to check the present form of Acts which have been

much amended. Undoubtedly in the future such databases or their analogue will play an important role in the office. You will find when you leave college that computers are already much used in the office in word-processing and in accounting. Keyboard familiarity and an understanding of the uses and limitations of computers are skills to be coveted. It is silly to adopt a dismissive attitude to innovation simply because in its early stages it has clumsy limitations or because expectations have been raised too high by the over-loud claims of its apostles.

Word processing

Lawyers now depend very heavily on word processing. It gives legal offices the ability to rearrange and amend a long document and reproduce it quickly in a professional format. Lawyers do not expect to spend much, if any, of their own time operating such machines. For the law student, though, the basic word processing and keyboard skills are of great value. I would recommend every student in any subject to take the trouble to acquire such familiarity. Many pieces of written work have to be produced during a law course. The growing emphasis on skills training will, in addition, mean that they must be produced in the form of legal documents, letters of advice. A student who has mastered the fairly straightforward applications of word processing will find such tasks very much lightened. I am certain, also, that tutors are so pleased to see neatly typed, professional quality work that this is reflected in the grade awarded.

Teaching through computers

You may also expect to be exposed to computer-assisted learning. A lecturer will have written a problem or series of problems in such a way that it can be used as a teaching exercise through your college computer or a micro-computer. The computer, or a tutorial sheet, will reveal the problem. The visual display on your computer will then ask a series of questions. You will provide answers or, more probably, in the present state of technology, choose from a menu of possible answers. The computer will provide comment on your answers and lead you on to further questions. This kind of computer-tutorial is quite difficult and time-consuming for the lecturer to prepare. As yet computers seem to be able to deal only with 'yes' or 'no' answers, so their use in higher education is limited. Nevertheless, such an exercise has two functions. It can be a useful stimulus to student interest in difficult areas and assist in the clarification of a complete set of rules. It also provides an introduction in the form of 'hands-on' experience to the use of computers. That is something which is to be welcomed by any contemporary student.

Alternatives to lecturing

It would not be right to leave the subject of innovation in law teaching without a glance at the possibility of dispensing with lecturers and employing more student-based course structures. At its simplest this may mean a small group meeting more or less regularly for seminar-type discussions on the subject in question. At a more organised level, students may be provided with 'custom-built' learning packages or materials and be expected to pace their own progress through a part of the course studying the material in prescribed sections and meeting singly or in groups to review progress and discuss difficult topics. This approach is dignified by the name 'self-paced learning'. Law schools have adhered fairly strongly to the traditional methods of instruction and you are more likely to find this kind of 'lecture-less' approach, if at all, on the final stages of a degree course. Very commonly when used it is associated with some form of continuous assessment. Whether this is so or not the absence of the routine discipline of a steady lecture programme throws a much greater onus for self-discipline on the student. It requires a much more conscious effort from students to map out their work programme and organise their own time. The process of self-discovery of the subject is doubtless an invigorating alternative for the student to the more passive role often encouraged by the lecture/seminar programme. Like other forms of radical innovation it is much to be welcomed — in strict moderation.

Distance learning and part-time degrees

Some universities have for many years provided evening degree courses in law. The University of London has a long-standing external degree for which tuition is available in some centres. Recently universities began to look at the possibility of providing 'distance learning' modes for courses. In respect of each of these possibilities the sensible advice has to be that it is harder to complete a degree in any of these ways than by the 'traditional' full-time routes. A part-time law degree might involve attendance on two evenings for tuition from, say, 6 pm to 9 pm. On top of this the student will have to find very many hours for private study and should be able to make some time available every week for study in the law library. Our own experience is that many students fail in the early years of a part-time degree course because they simply have not calculated the huge commitment of time and energy involved. The whole degree will take, on average, four to five years and the impact of this will be considerable on any successful student's life. Every year from a long-standing part-time law degree course such as ours, students graduate with great credit and a number progress to their professional examinations. At the other end of the scale, a large number always fall by the wayside because the demands of part-time study are so great and in the end beyond them.

The present picture is now very diverse and the Appendix of available courses will demonstrate this. There are many universities offering distance learning programmes and many offering part-time evening courses. For nearly all students a course with the opportunity for some attendance and ready contact with other students and lecturers is the preferred choice.

5 The law library

The law student will spend a great deal of his time in the law library. Even the most rugged of practising lawyers will have regular recourse to his library — if he is carrying out his work at all properly. It is common these days on law courses to ensure that students receive a systematic introduction to the law library and its use. Even so, you will find that ability to use the library efficiently and enjoyably is a facility that develops slowly. The variety of materials in the law library is large and you will take some months to become familiar with their different uses. Law books tend to be written in a somewhat forbidding style — perhaps an inevitable by-product of their complex subject-matter. You will need to persevere when you are frustrated and confused — you will need to read sometimes without being at all sure of what is the useful product of your reading. If you persist until the style and format become familiar you will develop, unconsciously, skills of reading legal material that will provide both pleasure and profit throughout your professional life.

Material in the law library is contained in four main sections: the law reports and statutes containing the primary sources of law; the academic journals and periodicals; the textbooks and monographs; and finally, the bibliographic works and encyclopaedias. The geography of each library is obviously different and the first stage of learning law for any serious student is to become thoroughly familiar with that in his own college. In your first week or so at college, you will as mentioned have some guidance from your lecturers in this — usually coupled with a 'library tour' and some carefully structured 'library exercises' to introduce you to various species of legal text. Enter into this part of the programme whole-heartedly. Even if the 'search exercises' in the library do not excite your imagination, remember that they help to lay the foundation for the whole of your legal studies.

The amount of detailed information given to you on an introductory library tour is usually such that it cannot all be remembered, let alone fully digested. It will take you some months to feel at home in the library; to know where to turn for a particular reference, and so on. The use of a library is a skill that is learned not taught. You will obviously listen carefully to your own college's talks on the subject; read thoroughly the material they give you and perform these 'library' exercises. At the end of this you will probably still not feel entirely at home in the library.

In the following weeks you will find yourself deluged with references on reading lists, in lectures and in seminar material. It is at this stage of following up and reading references that your training as a law library user starts in earnest. The process is frustrating. Each reference takes a while to locate. Some seem unobtainable. Where on earth will I find (1789) 3 TR 148 or 72 SALJ 246? When you do unravel the reference and locate the series, a more resourceful student has arrived there first — and you must mark time or proceed to the next reference, until the volume becomes available.

The weak student will withdraw from this process only too easily, taking comfort in his lecture notes and the textbook or some condensed version thereof. The good student will soldier on until his familiarity with the lay-out and the abbreviations grows, and retrieving the correct report from its place becomes second nature — a matter of only a few seconds. Nothing can be written to replace this trial and error process of growing acclimatisation to the library and if it is shirked in the early days of your legal study, it can be replaced only with the greatest difficulty. The temptation to leave things until later or to cut corners at this stage will very much reduce the quality of your later studies and prevent you acquiring the 'feel' for case-law material which is the hallmark of a well-trained lawyer.

Finding and using law reports

It is not the purpose of this book to provide a bland catalogue of the variety of law reports. Those available in your library will be listed in some prominent place in the body of the library. You will quickly locate this list and use it to acquaint yourself with the series available in your library.

There is now an extremely useful text containing detailed guidance on how to use the contents of a law library. This is *How to Use a Law Library* by Dane and Thomas. You will find this book a valuable companion to your studies — it probably cannot be usefully read as a whole — but more fruitfully kept by you for occasional reference and explanation.

The law reports described

The series of reports which are used most by students are the Law Reports, the All England Law Reports and the Weekly Law Reports.

The *Law Reports* or, as they are properly called, the Law Reports of the Incorporated Council of Law Reporting are as near to an official series of law reports as exists in England and Wales. These contain the overwhelming preponderance of important cases decided since their first publication in 1865. The Law Reports are presently published in four series, each of one or more volumes a year. They are: Appeal Cases (AC) consisting of cases decided in the House of Lords or the Privy Council; Chancery Division (Ch); Queen's Bench Division (QB) and Family Division (Fam). The series of Law Reports published have varied from time to time, reflecting changes in the division of work in the High Court. A table of these changes is found in Dane and Thomas (p 20).

Earlier law reports

Before 1865 when the Incorporated Council of Law Reporting commenced its work, the system of publishing decided cases was quite chaotic.

From the reign of Edward II to Henry VIII there were published series of reports of cases known as Year Books. Probably these originated in longhand notes of cases taken by trainee lawyers. The language used is not modern English and, as they are of extremely limited value to the student of contemporary law, you are most unlikely to be called upon to read them. Various volumes have been published by the Selden Society. If your law library is housed in a general library, this part of the collection will probably be in the history section of the general library.

The law reports to 1865

Until the reforms of the court system in the second half of the nineteenth century, both the court system and law reporting were something of a jumble. Law reports were published privately and in individual series which lasted sometimes only a year or two and sometimes many years. It was common for each series to be called after the name of the law reporter who collected the cases. These reports are accordingly known as the 'nominate' reports, and your library will probably have some volumes of reports published by a variety of these named reporters. They are in fact little used today because almost all the important series of private reporters are collected in one or two series — the *English Reports* or the *Revised Reports*. Any case to which you are referred before 1865 will be reported in one of these two series or, if it is not, your lecturer will explain whether or not he expects you to discover the case in your college's library.

Although you will find the nomenclature of individual nominate reports confusing, it is simplicity itself to look up a case in the English Reports. The final two volumes (177-178) consist of an alphabetical list of the cases found in the remaining volumes.

There are still very many cases referred to in basic law subjects which are reported in the English Reports. This is especially so in contract law. Nevertheless, as general advice, you will find your time more profitably spent reading the leading cases of the last twenty years in common law subjects than ferreting around among the faded relics of another century's ideas. Cases in the old reports are frequently badly reported, the judgments confusingly expressed and I think on the whole not so fully reasoned as in the contemporary period. Our present judges are, taken as a whole, a better educated group than at any previous period.

When you are given references in these reports you should not shirk the undoubted effort involved in making sense both of the reference and the eventually discovered report. The occasional foray into the English Reports is a part of the good student's all-round training.

Other contemporary law reports

The two series in your library that you will find most useful in your day-to-day study of law are the *Weekly Law Reports* and the *All England Reports*. The former is published by the Incorporated Council of Law Reporting and the latter by Butterworths.

The *Weekly Law Reports*. This series is published in three annual volumes. The first volume contains those cases which are not intended to be included in the Law Reports. In the national hierarchy of law reporting this series stands next below the Law Reports. It aims to provide a comprehensive coverage of all the Supreme Court, House of Lords and Privy Council cases worthy of reporting. (The 'Supreme Court' includes the various divisions of the High Court and the Court of Appeal.)

The *All England Reports*. This is the most important contemporary private series of reports and in terms of its acceptability for citation in court is accorded considerable status scarcely inferior to the Weekly Law Reports. Again the series aims at comprehensive general coverage and is now published in four annual volumes, the volumes being published in consecutive weekly parts. All serious students of law will wish at some early stage in their career to take out a subscription to one of the weekly series of reports. Whether to choose the Weekly Law Reports or the All England Law Reports is a matter of personal taste. The weekly issue of each will contain cases relevant to your course and other cases of political or social significance. Looking at random at the last three issues of the All England Reports on my desk, there is a case on the effect of a husband mortgaging the family home without his wife's consent, on liability of a doctor for an ineffective vasectomy and against Mr A Scargill, Leader of the NUM, involving breach of duty as a trustee of the miners' pension fund. (See [1984] 2 All ER 585, 513 and 750 respectively.) The cases reported reflect on important issues of the day; should damages be paid to parents for the birth of an unwanted but healthy child?* Is it proper that trust law should prevent trustees of a pension fund exercising their investment duties for political purposes?** If you subscribe regularly to this series, and make a point of leafing through each weekly issue and reading through important or interesting cases, you will do a great deal to make yourself a better informed lawyer and to understand the role seemingly dry legal doctrines play in the social and political ebb and flow of the country.

You will also find during each year of the course that new leading cases reported during the year are hard to obtain in the library and the ownership of your own set will be very useful. Lecturers are prone to set questions on striking current developments in case law.

Other series of law reports

There are many other series of law reports from English and other jurisdictions which you will find in your library. Mysterious references to law reports and journals can be checked in a number of volumes (notably: *Where to Look for Your Law*, *Sweet & Maxwell's Guide to Law Reports and Statutes*; the front page of any volume of Current Law Yearbook; the front pages of any issue of the Index to Legal Periodicals). Some of these which might otherwise be overlooked are worth mentioning.

Estates Gazette. The *Estates Gazette* is a magazine which students of law will not customarily read. It is published for surveyors and estate agents. Yet it contains almost all the important cases on real property law, landlord and tenant and other matters of interest to the landed professions. The judgments are printed in full and the reports quite often cited in court and very often in learned articles. You will often find in this magazine reports of cases of current interest in the property area which you do not find easily or at all elsewhere.

In addition to the law reports the magazine often carries notes of interest to students of law — often written especially for students. These can be read with value by law students especially if they concern some complex area of law which the student finds for the first time explained clearly in this 'layman's' magazine.

Property and Compensation Reports. This is a valuable series of reports published privately. It contains reports of property law cases that you will not find or not find readily elsewhere.

Abbreviated Law Reports. The weekly journals (see later) — the *New Law Journal*, the *Solicitors' Journal* and the *Law Society's Gazette* — each

---

*   *Thake v Maurice* [1984] 2 All ER 513.
** *Cowan v Scargill* [1984] 2 All ER 750.

contains brief reports of recently decided cases. These are the first reports you will come across of some important newly decided case. The regular reading of one of these magazines, including its case reports, will be an important part of your metamorphosis into a fully fledged lawyer.

There is a plethora of other reports (English and overseas) which you will find in your library. Not all are really useful: there is a strong element of commercial opportunism in some recent ventures into this area. You will gradually as your use of the library develops become fully aware of the range of material on offer and its varying value. The important watchword is not to shrink from the little effort involved in chasing up puzzling references — there may not be gold at the end of every trail but if you do not set out on the search there will be none at all.

Computers in the law library

The potential usefulness of computers as an aid to the retrieval of legal source material has already been noted in the previous chapter. Very probably the terminals themselves will be located in your library and viewed as part of the library resources. You should take any opportunity afforded to become familiar with the way in which case or statute material can be searched in this way. If you have no hands–on experience with computers you may find the experience a trifle daunting but nevertheless it is one you should certainly grasp.

Textbooks in the law library

These are arranged in the same way as other non-fiction books in a general library, ie according to a conventional subject classification. You will quickly enough be able to sort out which subject groups appear where in the collection of texts. There will usually be a separate 'set text' collection of textbooks which are loaned to students only for short periods for use in the library — the books in this collection being those, generally, which it is hoped students will acquire for themselves.

A law library is not really a lending library — most of the textbooks, even, will have their use restricted to 'reference only'. It would probably be a good thing if borrowing from the library was proscribed altogether and students encouraged to read the necessary text then and there. You should especially avoid the modern danger of photocopying part of a book or article, filing your copy and then letting it slide from your mind — in the belief that reproduction is as good as perusal.

Journals and periodicals

Particular attention to the use that can be made of these is given in the following chapter. Within the library, bound law journals and periodicals will be collected together on the shelves in alphabetical order according to the title of the journal.

Usually there will be found on a separate display rack the current issue or recent issues of each journal subscribed to by the library. You will probably develop the habit of glancing at new issues from time to time as you enter the library so that you can read those pertinent to your present studies. Some regular features in journals will have great current interest — you will find, for example, the weekly editorial in the *Solicitors' Journal* has a valuable commentary on current legal topics. Similar columns — more conservative in the *Law Society's Gazette*, more radical in the *New Law Journal* — will also come to attract your regular attention. This is a specialised branch of journalism. At first much of the debate in these columns will perplex you — but persist, and you will come to be a well-informed lawyer. The legal profession is under stronger pressure for change at present than perhaps at any time since the Judicature Acts of the 1870s. Much of the debate is found in the regular correspondence and columns of the weekly journals. If you browse through these throughout your time as a student, you will all the sooner be able to play an active part yourself in the great discussions which are shaping the future provision of legal services.

Bibliographic sources and similar works

A very important series of books in the law library will be found gathered together at some convenient place usually near the entrance to the library. These are the encyclopaedic works of reference or bibliography which play such an important part in legal research — particularly so far as the busy practitioner is concerned.

At the beginning of your career as a law student you will not find these works of enormous value. You will rely mainly (and quite sensibly) on references provided in your lectures and in your main textbooks. Later on you will need to prepare lengthier essays or other pieces of work or perhaps participate in some clinical legal programme. You will then need to be able to discover for yourself references in a particular area of law.

Quick reference works

One of the simplest levels of reference is the Law Dictionary. *Jowitt's Dictionary of English Law* in two volumes is quite detailed and because of its articles on long forgotten legal persons, incidents and maxims an amusing read in itself. Given that this will certainly be on your reference shelves, there seems little point in a more concise dictionary — though students sometimes buy and find a valuable use for *Osborn's Concise Law Dictionary*. (On the subject of dictionaries all students should possess a good English dictionary. *Chamber's Twentieth Century Dictionary* or the *Concise Oxford* are good enough. The *Shorter Oxford* is well worth the extra investment and can often be purchased at discount through book clubs.) Also in the quick reference category are the manuals of legal reference referred to above.

The encyclopaedic works

These particular works are much used in the lawyer's office but worthy of some description especially as it is felt that the law student too often passes them by unused.

Halsbury's Laws of England. It is hard to describe the flavour of this work which sets out to gather under subject heads an encyclopaedic account of every contemporary legal subject. Rather curiously Dane and Thomas (in *How to Use a Law Library*) refer to it as 'a most important source of information and you will need to refer to it throughout your course of study'. Neither of these statements is entirely true. You will certainly not refer to it whether at college or after, more than occasionally. Its most useful function is not as a source of law but as a source of reference.

However, *Halsbury* is encyclopaedic in its coverage. It contains the vast bulk of the references on any area of law with which you are likely to be concerned. It is from time to time cited in court and some sections contain detailed and authoritative accounts of the law. Material in the encyclopaedia is contained under alphabetical subject headings and the headings within each volume are printed on the spine. There are two general index volumes and although the size of the work is formidable, its use presents no difficulty.

A work which is similar in scope to *Halsbury* is *The English and Empire Digest*. This is arranged in similar fashion — by volumes alphabetically according to subject matter. The work is probably not nearly so widely used nowadays as *Halsbury* and it consists of summaries of decided cases and not of authoritative statements of law. It does quite often contain references to further reports of particular cases or references to cases not cited in *Halsbury*, and for that reason should not be overlooked.

Two specialist practitioners' encyclopaedias may also be mentioned. *The Encyclopaedia of Forms and Precedents* is an invaluable work for practising solicitors. It is published in volumes arranged under alphabetical headings. Law teaching at undergraduate level has for many years been rather divorced from the different requirements of legal practice. Opinions differ as to the validity of what remains a clear distinction between the 'academic' stage and the 'vocational' stage of training lawyers. For one reason or another, law degree teaching has refrained from the use in any systematic or widespread way of materials such as contracts, court pleadings, or deeds culled directly from legal practice. So, you will not during your undergraduate legal career have much direct recourse to the strictly practitioner texts.

But *The Encyclopaedia of Forms and Precedents* is by far the best example of a 'precedent book' published in our jurisdiction. It aims for comprehensiveness and on the whole succeeds, except in the areas where the pace of change is quickest. You will find it useful to look at specimen documents and the notes thereon in very many areas — the introductory material is often very helpful indeed in assisting the reader to grasp difficult areas of law or procedure. This encyclopaedia is undoubtedly the work most used by practising solicitors and its occasional perusal will assist your growing understanding of the relationship between the law you are being taught and the work of a practitioner.

Atkin's Court Forms is an encyclopaedia of court forms, pleadings and related documents. It is the bible of the practising barrister. This publication is also arranged in volumes under alphabetically ordered headings. It can provide stimulating background material to even the most tedious part of a course, eg in constitutional law — how would you obtain a writ of Habeas Corpus — what steps would you take, and what will the court order you obtain actually say? Despite the simplification of many areas of legal practice the drafting of pleadings, ie the formal documents in a law suit setting out a party's claim, defence, counterclaim, defence to a counterclaim and so on, remains an important part of the lawyer's art and you will derive much instructive amusement from this work.

Current Law. This is a unique work. The full publication consists of the following.

(i) A monthly issue throughout the year which has brief references to decided cases, learned articles and the progress of legislation. The subject matter is arranged under alphabetically ordered headings. This claims to contain 'all the law from all the sources'. It does not — there are inevitable omissions and occasional indexical slips. But, for the serious researcher it is an essential tool. When you are preparing a long essay or project, you will find its use mandatory if you are to ensure that you deal with all the latest references.

(ii) *Annual Yearbook.* The material in the monthly issues is collected each year into one volume and this is again a most useful source of further references in any area.

(iii) *Current Law Statutes.* New legislation is issued throughout the year and collected in annual volumes. The important Acts of Parliament are annotated by practitioners or academics. These annotations are often a valuable source of insight into the effect of a statutory provision which has not yet been dissected in the textbooks.

(iv) *Current Law Week.* This is a recent addition consisting of a weekly newsheet of cases together with a focus on a particular area by an expert contributor.

There are now also many other specialist 'subject' encyclopaedias which you will find useful. These, however, will be found in the textbook section of the library.

Using the library for research

A real test of your familiarity with the law library will come when you have to prepare an original piece of course work, project or dissertation. It is true, sadly, that once this challenge arrives later rather than sooner in a student's course many are found wanting in the basic research skills.

Suppose you are asked to write an essay on whether a publican might be liable to a drunken customer if he fails to warn him that one apparent road from the pub leads to a 200-foot drop into a quarry, or if he in fact misdirects him onto this fatal road. The first problem as with all new legal tasks is one of classification. The lawyer who can rephrase the question to point him towards the right legal sources will be half-way home. In this problem there are three possible areas to search. The first is contract. Contract law is concerned with enforceable promises between persons. The customer is a paying customer and clearly he has a contract with 'mine host' — does this entitle him to correct directions?

The second area is tort law — this is the area of the common law which imposes upon one person a duty to another. Does it impose upon a landlord of a public house an obligation to take care of drunken customers or at least not to misdirect a customer? The third area that may be relevant is statute law. It is well known that licensed premises are very much controlled by Acts of Parliament. Is there any Act which is relevant to the landlord/customer problems?

A search for an answer will begin in a relevant textbook. Will a straightforward search enable you to tell that contract law and the licensing statutes can be discounted? Is the problem in a tort textbook to be found under drunkenness, landlords, misdirection, personal injury, or where? Suppose you decide that the correct questions are:

- Does the landlord owe a duty to volunteer instructions — that is, not to omit to see to the safety of his drunken customer?
- Does the landlord owe a duty not to give inaccurate instructions?
- Does the drunkenness of the customer — which may contribute to his downfall — provide any kind of defence to the landlord?

Examining these three questions in a tort textbook such as *Winfield and Jolowicz on Tort* will lead you towards the relevant case law. Some of these cases will require reading. You will then wish — having determined which are the relevant cases — to check that no further case law not mentioned in the textbook since Professor Rogers last updated the text is relevant to your problem. To do this you may use LEXIS (discussed in the previous chapter) or Current Law Yearbook discussed above. Whichever updating source you use you will here again have to be sure that you are classifying the question correctly. The end result of your search will involve clear statements from textbooks, examination of leading cases, and reference to any further cases not mentioned in the textbooks. In the course of your research you may also be directed to relevant articles which may illuminate the subject and provide interesting routes of enquiry.

In the course of your research you would eventually discover the interesting case of *Munro v Porth Kerry Holiday Estates* (1984) 81 LSG 2450. In this case a father sued the occupiers of a leisure centre on behalf of his deceased son's estate. The leisure centre was on a cliff-top. The son, after having consumed some alcohol, climbed over a fence and fell down the cliff and died. Should the court hold the licensee liable and, in coming to its decision, what test should it apply? Is discovering this case with very similar facts the end of your quest or does it leave questions unanswered?

6   The sources of legal study

The study of law is the preserve of the literate. It requires a good command of the English language and the successful study of law will prove difficult for students who do not enjoy reading and writing or who find these activities burdensome. The practical problem for a law student is one of selection — which materials should be read and which, for omission is inevitable, should be left unread; what should be written down in the form of detailed notes, which material should be browsed, read carefully, or systematically annotated? From the time a student commences a law course, these questions will very often present themselves to his or her mind and too often a clear answer, producing a clear pattern of work, will never emerge, but the student will muddle through, picking up some references, missing others, noting some trivial or inconsequential areas in enormous detail and omitting others. How is the problem of the disorganised, amorphous and massive nature of the legal literature available to the student to be surmounted?

We have already seen that the subject matter of each law course stated explicitly in the syllabus contains an implicit assumption that the taught and examined syllabus will be different and smaller, ie the 'hidden' curriculum. Accordingly, the scope of the course as defined by the syllabus that is in fact taught will provide the first and crucial source of guidance to the student on what and how to study.

But even when you have elucidated from the lecturer in lectures the subject matter to which he or she is giving some or particular attention, there remains a major problem of selection. Lecture notes often appear like sections from a stream of consciousness novel but with a heavy legal bias. There is case name after case name, references to numerous books, still more numerous articles bound closely together with the lecturer's own comments on the topic under review. Which of all these references will be read and how?

Should the student read the law itself or things about the law? There are primary sources — the reported cases and Acts of Parliament and there are even more numerous accounts of the primary sources — practitioner's tomes, textbooks, nutshells, articles, annotations, case notes and monographs. What will be suggested here is that it is essential to use primary and secondary sources together for different purposes and as a complement to each other. Primary and secondary sources will be considered in turn to see how best each can be used to satisfy the various aims of legal study.

Primary sources

Reading law reports

It has already been noted that there are two effective sources of law in England and Wales — the reported decisions of the higher courts and Acts of Parliament. To this must of course be added the mountains of law generated by the institutions of the European Community. The study of law, particularly in the early years of a degree course, is still overwhelmingly concerned with the first of these — the arrangement and analysis of case law. Students invariably have problems coming to grips with case law. How many cases should they read? Should the whole of the case be read, or some particular identifiable part of it?

The nature of the problem

A law case commences as a 'matter' on 'file' in a solicitor's office when a client, Mr Brown, calls on his solicitor for advice. The solicitor records this interview and the record is an 'attendance note'. Soon the potential defendant, Mr Black, will see his own solicitor. A correspondence, often protracted over many months, will follow. A writ will be issued; a defence filed; further and better particulars of the claim requested; and details given. In the course of time there will be a trial; witnesses will give evidence for many days; there is a difficult point of law; the learned judge reserves judgment; and the parties return to court some days later to hear the court pronounce judgment. The plaintiff loses and his lawyers feel he has a grievance. They appeal to the Court of Appeal. Opinion of learned counsel is sought and given, conferences and interviews follow. The parties assemble at the Court of Appeal in The Strand. There is a two day argument and the court reserves judgment. They return, and the three members of the court give a unanimous decision in favour of the plaintiff (or appellant as he has become) through the voice of Lord Justice Wright. The point of law is interesting, and the case is now reported as *Brown v Black* in the law reports.

The law report, however, contains only a fraction of all the papers, documents, notes and speeches that have culminated in Mr Brown's triumphant victory.

In order to examine this, it will be useful to look at one case between a number of parties and see how it was reported.

Hardwick v Johnson [1978] 1 WLR 683

This is a case you will look at both in contract law and in an introductory land law course, because it raises fundamental issues in both areas. Mrs Hardwick had a son called Robert. He was divorced. When her son decided to remarry for a second time — a girl called Janet — Mrs Hardwick decided to buy a house for them to live in. She paid £12,000 for the house — in 1972 this was quite a substantial price. The couple agreed to pay her £7 per week. Only £88 was paid and that in the first year of their occupation. They had moved in during 1973 and by 1975, although Janet was pregnant, the marriage had broken down. Robert deserted her. Mrs Hardwick brought an action in the County Court to regain possession of her house. In the County Court, Mrs Hardwick lost, and she appealed to the Court of Appeal. The hearing was on 5 and 6 December 1977 and the Court was able to pronounce judgment the same day. The mother lost again. Janet and her child could stay in the home indefinitely. When you read this case you will see that Lord Denning MR says, 'The correspondence and the pleadings show that the parties canvassed all sorts of legal relationships.' They are not, however, reproduced. You will have to read between the lines to see how the protracted legal struggle developed. The law report begins with the title of the case. This is followed by a series of jottings called the 'catchwords' which are of little value — though perhaps useful in catching the eye of a lawyer in a hurry. There follows a potted account of the facts and findings, the cases referred to and the history of the case. This is called the 'headnote' — for the beginner in law especially, this is worth reading as a prelude to reading the opinions of the judges. It is quite hard often to pick up 'the story' from a judgment and the headnote writer has already performed the task of doing so and making a précis of the most important aspects of the case. Having rushed through the headnote — for there is no point in dwelling on it — you come to the judgment of the court. In this particular case, all three judges gave a judgment, that of Lord Denning being the principal one, and containing a very full statement of the facts of the case as seen by him. In all there are five pages of judgment.

Reading the judgment

It is not important to settle in your mind exactly how much of each of these judgments to read. What is important is to settle the purpose for which you have read what you read. No one can have a good intellectual understanding of English law and the way it works until they have read a large number of cases in full. You can certainly become a lawyer without doing so. You can learn a lot of law, probably all that a working lawyer needs to know, from commentaries, guides, workbooks and textbooks. But I assume that you wish for something more. You want to be able to understand the way the judicial mind works, to see how new rules creep into the great body of case law and form some *critical* appreciation of the areas of law you are studying. In order to do this, you need to take cases in 'growing areas' of the law like the case under discussion and read them thoroughly and thoughtfully. However, you will also have, in looking at a case such as *Hardwick v Johnson*, a more direct objective — preparation for an examination in which the area covered by the case will be a part. These two purposes each demand a different approach to the material.

Reading for education

In order to develop the widest possible understanding of the common law and to develop your analytical ability as a lawyer, it is essential to read cases as fully and carefully as possible. You will find that the form in which judgments are written (or spoken) will become familiar and reading them less of a challenge. The first judgment in *Hardwick v Johnson*, that of Lord Denning, displays a familiar pattern. His opening paragraph gives a very helpful and typically clear summary of the problems that arise in the case. The following page consists of a review of the facts and previous history of the case — if you have read the headnotes, or been given a fullish lecture on the case, you will be able to skim through this although to do so means depriving oneself of the pleasure of reading Lord Denning's distinctive narrative style. Then Lord Denning turns to the relevant case law: 'So we have to consider once more the law about family arrangements ...' (p 688A). He proceeds to apply the law as he sees it to the facts, and comes to a conclusion about the nature of the relationship between the parties (p 688C). Having come to this legal conclusion — that the son and daughter-in-law have a licence — this is a legal term essentially meaning *a personal permission* — to occupy the house in return for £7 a week — he now examines the nature of that type of relationship to see if it permits the mother to have the result she desires — the eviction of her 'tenant'. When you proceed to the concurring judgment of Roskill LJ, you will see that it is briefer but different in emphasis. He says 'It is ... plain in my judgment, that there was here a licence' (p 690F) and he then deals briefly with whether the licence could be brought to an end by Mrs Hardwick. Browne LJ comes to the same decision and agrees with Roskill LJ as to the species of licence which the daughter-in-law and son had been granted. Having read this case, consider: what does it tell you about the enforceability of family arrangements? How does the court 'fill in' the terms of an agreement when the parties have left them unspecified? How did the judges decide that this arrangement was a licence and not a tenancy or a trust or a gift? Having considered these questions, are you able to write in a sentence or two: 'the reasons given by the Court of Appeal for its judgment are …' ? Can you use your statement of the reasons given in this case to predict how the court would decide a similar case? Does it add anything to your understanding of what kind of 'thing' a licence is? When you study the case you will find the judges differ as to the type of licence concerned — two say it is a 'contractual licence' and one says it is an 'equitable licence' (see pp 688H, 690F, 691G) — the nature of this distinction, and how the judges arrive at making it, you will find rather troublesome — is the distinction significant?

An example in full

Appendix 8 sets out a law report in full as an example for you to read. It is a report of the Court of Appeal in *Mullin v Richards* [1998] 1 All ER 920. The case involves facts with which every reader will be familiar. Two persons at school are fighting with plastic rulers and one of them is blinded accidentally in their right eye. The case concerns the law of negligence – were either the school or the other child, Heidi Richards, liable to Teresa Jane Mullin for her loss of sight? The case is a good example of judges making new law. When you read it you may be puzzled that such a common event as one school child injuring another accidentally should give rise in 1998 to new law. For there to be liability in negligence the court must find that there has actually been actionable failure to take proper care. What made the court decide there was no liability in this case? In what circumstances would the school have been liable? Are there any circumstances in which Heidi would have been liable for the accident? You need to be able to answer these questions to use this case in order to advise whether legal proceedings should be taken in similar cases.

Reading cases for examination purposes

It may have occurred to you as you read the above account of *Hardwick v Johnson* that it would be impossible to remember such a lengthy account of every case read, and even if it were possible it would not be usable in the examination in that form. In discussing lectures and lecture notes (see Chapter 2) the point was made at length that accumulating in digestible form the body of material that you will attempt to learn and, having learned, utilise in examinations is an important and ever-present goal of study. How can a reflective academic perusal of a case such as *Hardwick v Johnson* be absorbed into the *corpus* of your notes and brought forth to do battle in the examination hall?

An examination is an unusual form of exercise and like any other requires special preparation. Law students at the start of their career must find the relationship between the hours and weeks in the library and seminar room and the hasty scribble in the examination hall particularly difficult to comprehend. Law examinations and how to answer them are discussed in full detail in Chapter 8 but here a specific issue is addressed — how is the wealth of case material more or less digested during the year to be used in such exercises?

It is important to develop some feeling for the types and pattern of examination question that are likely to occur in the areas you are studying. Armed with this insight you will be better able to visualise how to utilise material from the case law you are reading. Let us take a particular example — in what kind of areas might *Hardwick v Johnson* occur? If the relevant course is contract law, there is only one area, that of intention to create legal relationships. Experience of studying past examination papers will inform the student that there is a relatively small range of questions in which this appears.

If the relevant course is an introductory land law or introduction to property course, there is a wider range of potential questions. There will be both essays and problems which raise pertinent questions concerning the nature of licences, the distinction between licences and tenancies and the questionable existence of some interest known as an 'equitable licence'.

An answer by a good student to a law examination question in the typical unseen written format of a three-hour paper with four questions will not exceed 800 words. The average of all pass papers (although this is only a 'guesstimate') is probably no more than 500 words per question. It will not escape your attention that there are a large number of cases on 'intention to create legal relations' and cases considering the 'nature of a licence' are prolific. In either area, reference will have to be made to a number of cases and a number of viewpoints. A question which might occur where *Hardwick v Johnson* is much in point would be 'Does the developing law of licences provide an example of "an interest which can cross the chasm which lies between contract and property"?' (Professor H W R Wade). The question calls for a searching review of case law in this area and for a particular look at the question of terminability of licences (where *Hardwick v Johnson* is vague in the extreme) and whether licences can bind third parties (where *Hardwick* is irrelevant). In such an essay, you will begin with a statement of the traditional view of the nature of a licence — you might couple this with an examination of how the court in *National Provincial Bank Ltd v Hastings Car Mart Ltd* [1965] AC 1175 — a case you will inevitably read thoroughly — defined, or at least grappled with, the distinction between rights which are 'property' and rights which are not. Then the central part of your essay will be taken up with an examination of some of the plethora of recent cases of which Hardwick is one. In this essay you may dispose of that case in a passage such as:

> *Hardwick v Johnson* was a case where the Court of Appeal had to consider the nature of an agreement whereby a mother allowed her newly-married son and daughter-in-law to occupy, for a weekly sum, a house she had purchased for their connubial bliss. When she sought possession against the deserted

wife the Court of Appeal had to analyse this agreement. Denning MR thought it was 'in the nature of an equitable licence'. The other judges both thought it to be a 'contractual licence'. All three judges agreed the mother could not terminate the licence but agreed it could be terminable in unspecified circumstances. They did not think, or at least articulate their judgments, in terms of property law theory — of rights 'in rem' or 'in personam' — but gave a pragmatic answer to the particular case at issue.

You will see that time will not allow more on this case — perhaps a briefer treatment might be preferred but even this use of the case utilises only a brief statement of the facts, a snippet from Lord Denning's judgment and a reference to the views of his two fellow judges. To have annotated the case at greater length in your own notes and attempted to memorise for the examination a far bulkier account of it would be to provide your memory with a needless and unprofitable encumbrance.

Thus, cases are to be read widely and mulled over thoroughly but annotated concisely.

The use of statute material

A statute is an Act of Parliament. In many areas of law now, Acts of Parliament are paramount. Early on in your studies you will learn the importance of the '1925 Legislation'.* Early on in contract law, you will see the very profound inroads that have been made by Parliament into traditional areas of judge–made law. Students find statute material very hard going. In latter stages of the course where huge areas of study are very largely statute-based (family law, company law, tax law, welfare law, industrial law, etc) the need for a sound technique for dealing with Acts of Parliament becomes even greater.

In the author's opinion, the problem of student difficulties in tackling the statute-based areas of law has a simple solution and, I feel, one that is told to students by all their lecturers. It is essential to become familiar with the words themselves of those Acts of Parliament which form the backbone of any particular part of your course. It is not sufficient to follow somebody else's paraphrase or synopsis of the important sections. You must master them yourself.

It is, thus, vital to equip yourself with your own copies of the relevant statutes. Many groups of statutes have been collected by publishers in sets of material intended primarily for student use. We can take one example. On your foundation course in property law, you will be referred time and time again too the 'LPA' (Law of Property Act 1925). Many of the provisions of this Act have to be known very well if you are to have any real competence as a property lawyer. On the same course you will be referred to many other

---

*   The Settled Land Act, Trustee Act, Law of Property Act, Land Registration Act, Administration of Estates Act.

'property statutes'. There are a number of very good collections of this material, including *Sweet and Maxwell's Property Statutes* and *Butterworths Property Law Handbook*.

When you commence your study of property law, you will need to buy one of these collections of statutory material. You will need to take the volume you purchase to tutorials and to consult it frequently. In a property law examination, and in the practice of property law, you need to be familiar with and understand the precise words of important sections of the legislation. This is not achieved by last-minute memorising of some condensed version of the relevant rules. It is best achieved by using the Act itself as you pursue the course; using it to prepare your essays and seminar questions and referring to it during the discussions that take place in your seminars.

Statutory language is forbidding. It will take you much intellectual effort to become at ease with the important Acts of Parliament in each subject. The task will be both eased and made more rewarding if approached not as one of comprehension and memorising but in a wider critical framework. Take the simplest of examples:

37 Rights of husband and wife
A husband and wife shall, for all purposes of acquisition of any interest in property, under a disposition made or coming into operation after the commencement of this Act, be treated as two persons. [Law of Property Act 1925, s 37.]

This has behind its simple and in the 1990s rather unremarkable pronouncement an enormous wealth of social history, a long struggle for the individual property rights of women and also a place in the highly technical doctrines of English land law. More than fifty years later, we find another Act passed concerned with the protection of one spouse's right to live in the matrimonial home owned by the other spouse.* In the years between 1925 and 1983, the matrimonial home has been the scene of enormous and exciting legal developments reflecting periods of the profoundest change. The effect of these social forces is found in the case law and more importantly in the cold words of intricately wrought Acts of Parliament.

As issues like those touched on above come to feature in your course you will become involved in much more than the mere comprehension of difficult draftsman's phraseology. You will try to understand how Acts were used to amend technical areas of doctrine inextricably muddled by the judges; how Acts are used to implement desired social changes and how these reforming measures are formulated and moulded by the forces of different individuals and groupings. (On the subject of the passage and use

---

* Now found in the Family Law Act 1996. If your interest is stimulated in this area you will find much of value in *The Family Home*, Murphy & Clark (1983) and a radical approach in *The Ties that Bind*, Carol Smart (1984).

of legislative material you will find *Legislation* by Miers and Page (1990) an extremely instructive book.)

In using statute material, the first great difficulty is in mastering the language and format. This skill is learned slowly, painstakingly, by thought and application. A real pleasure will be derived eventually from the ability to handle these strange forms for communicating the written word. It should not be forgotten, however, that the analysis of the printed word of an Act of Parliament is not in itself sufficient. Each small part of an Act is designed to carry out some important effect upon society — to remedy or prevent some undesired state of affairs, to confer or reduce the exercise of power, to punish or protect. The movements in society that produce legislative change and the effect which new measures produce will always be in your mind as you pore over some otherwise unexciting product of the parliamentary draftsman's skill.

Dealing with new statutes

The modern law is concerned as much with statutes as with cases. Under the increasing pressure of work Acts of Parliament seem to have become less clearly drafted than in the past. They are not 'a good read'. But, for the accomplished lawyer, a confident ability in the reading of a new Act is an essential skill.

How is this to be acquired?

We can look briefly at two examples — the Law of Property (Miscellaneous Provisions) Act 1989 and the Football Spectators Act 1989.

The first of these has only six sections, but before you become a qualified lawyer you will come to know part of it verbatim. Let us take a small part:

> **Section 2(1)** A contract for the sale or other disposition of an interest in land can only be made in writing and only by incorporating all the terms which the parties have expressly agreed in one document or, where contracts are exchanged, in each.

This sub-section is now one of the most important in English law. To read it you first need to read the remainder of the Act to ensure that you have understood any *definitions* or *qualifications* elsewhere in the Act which will affect your reading of these words. You will see that 'disposition' and 'interest in land' are both explained further in section 2(6). Section 5 tells you when the part with which we are concerned actually came into force.

Now suppose you are faced with the very interesting question as to whether words held on one computer terminal and transmitted over the public network can satisfy the requirement of being a *document* in *writing*. You will readily discover that these two expressions are not defined within the Act. A useful next step with a law reform Act such as this is to look at the Law Commission papers, its working papers and reports which lead to the Act being introduced. The Law Commission is a body set up to keep statute law under review and introduce law reform and codification. Before any reform is made it will have published consultation or working papers and reports. These are all kept in every college law library. They are invaluable for the student of statute law. They frequently contain refreshingly clear re-statements of the law as it was before the intended reform and of the intended effect.

A second further source of enlightenment may be commentaries written on the Act by academics. These are, with important Acts, often written in some detail and a number will be available. For Acts such as these there will be an annotation in Current Law, articles in the journals such as the Law Society's Gazette and New Law Journal. Commentaries written at the time an Act is passed can often provide the vital clue you need. For example, I have a collection of commentaries written on the hugely important 1925 property legislation during the period of the legislation — these I turn to very frequently. Nearly every important Act you look at as a student will have attracted the attention of academic writers at the time of its passing and these can often be used to good effect many years later.

As to the particular problem of what is 'writing' under the Law of Property (Miscellaneous Provisions) Act 1989 you may need to look much further to find an answer. In fact, on this precise point you would find there is no clear answer and you are left with no alternative except to argue by 'analogy' — to look at other cases where the law has been concerned with 'what is writing' and see if those areas will help you come to an answer.

Let us look briefly at the other statute — the Football Spectators Act 1989. In many ways this Act is typical of the way legislation may have to be dealt with by a solicitor. Suppose a Premier League football club was an important client of yours. You might be asked to brief the directors on the important consequences of this Act. This is very similar to the kind of work that is often attempted as a student project — giving it a suitable academic title such as 'The importance of the Football Spectators Act 1989 in the control of public disorder'.

Not surprisingly, the lawyer and the would-be lawyer might approach this task in very similar fashion. The first step is to read the Act for that is the law. You will, I know, find as I do that often in reading an Act much still remains opaque. The Act (section 8) creates a new corporate body — nearly every modern Act seems to create such bodies. This body is the Football Licensing Authority. What will it do? How will it operate?

Unlike a law reform statute such as the Law of Property (Miscellaneous Provisions) Act 1989 there may be little in the legal academic press about such an Act as the Football Spectators Act. But, both to impress an important client and to record a first-class mark on our statute project some further groundwork must be undertaken. Much of interest about the background of Acts of Parliament can be found from Parliamentary Debates.

The Bill is discussed in general in the Second Reading Debate. It is discussed clause by clause in the Committee Stage. These are the two parts of the procedure that are likely to provide interesting reading and penetrating insight into the way the thing will work. The Bill will also be preceded by reports or enquiries — in this case the enquiries into football disasters — these may not provide the nice legal analysis of the Law Commission Report but will provide important background facts.

Finally, with areas such as these there is often no substitute for personal enquiry. If you were a student doing such a project you would gain much from discussing the issues with your city's club and from direct contact with the relevant police force and, of course, the Football Licensing Committee. It is a good idea to let your enthusiasm carry you away. This will show in the finished piece of work or advice to your client.

Secondary sources

Textbooks

In your first and every other year of legal study you will gather at least one and possibly two or more textbooks for each course of study. The names will be repeated by lecturer and student alike as hallowed talismans — *Cheshire and Fifoot on Contract*; *Winfield on Tort*; *Smith and Hogan on Criminal Law*; *Megarry on Land Law*. The purchase of these textbooks represents a significant investment for the law student — what return is to be expected?

The first advice to give all eager purchasers of legal textbooks, is that they cannot be read as other books are read. A legal textbook takes an area of law and describes it from end to end with frequent excursions and prevarications and an indigestible wealth of detail and footnotes on the way. The book is not meant to be and cannot usefully be read from cover to cover. It may profitably be used as follows.

It is to be expected that the lecturer in each part of the syllabus will plan his programme so that you are aware of what is coming next. It may help to look over the relevant few pages in the textbook for a day or two before a forthcoming lecture. Detailed reading or intensive preparatory study are not worthwhile. You may delve deeply into things that your lecturer ignores, you may waste hours unravelling perceived mysteries which he disposes of with cogent simplicity. A light reading to grasp the framework and essential drift of a topic *may*, however, make lectures a more profitable experience.

Once your study of a particular topic is under way the textbook will be used to help in comprehension of difficult points and perhaps to amplify your lecturer's notes. Further than that it will be an important source of reference to supplementary reading of both cases and articles. In all these ways the textbook should be used as a signpost not as a prop. It is like an anthology of poems but with all the poems described briefly or tersely summarised — it would be a curious approach to literature to try to understand or acquire a feel for it by relying on such a work.

Case books

Before leaving the subject of student books, the other forms in which material is presented peculiarly for the use of law students may be mentioned. The first of these is case books.

Case books are collections of extracts from cases. They now exist in many areas of law. The idea that law may be studied almost exclusively through a programmed set of case reports or extracts from cases is discussed in Chapter 4. If your lecturer is adopting such a course of instruction, then you will be coerced into the use of a case book. Otherwise, it is suggested that the case book be approached with caution. Generally they will have space for only the cases of central importance. Many of these you should in any event make the effort to read in full. Case books do have uses which make it sensible, while not relying on one for your knowledge of case reports, to possess one for each area of the course, where available. You will find it valuable to read the selected extracts from cases you are, regrettably, too occupied to read in the library. In many — look for example at *Smith and Thomas on Contract* and *Weir on Tort* — you will find probing questions, suggestions and illustrations, some amusing in the extreme. Indeed these are frequently the most valuable part of a case book. Lastly, you will find it an aid to have the case book by you to refresh your recollection of cases long since read and fast becoming a blurred memory.

Study aids

Students will quite early in their career come across fellow students supplementing (or replacing) the traditional sources of legal study with a variety of handbooks, nutshells, companions and so on. It is customary for law teachers (who presumably write these) to be dismissive of their value. It can certainly be said that they are no substitute for a full study of the range of materials available in the law library.

However, there is equally no doubt that many students can benefit greatly, not only in time-saving, from making use of the careful guides by which other pilgrims have described the stony path to legal understanding. If you substitute these 'potted versions' for a comprehensive study you will inevitably not perform in the first or perhaps even the second flight of law students. In areas you find difficult, however, it is no confession of weakness to take advantage of the distillation of another's efforts and build on that.

One final word of caution. Obviously many areas of law are difficult to understand. It is possible that the confines of a brief commentary may make comprehension even harder — very often it will aid understanding to read a more detailed rather than a less detailed account.

Legal journals

For the purpose of discussion, an arbitrary division may be made between academic journals, professional journals, journalistic publications and student publications — the distinction is made purely for the purpose of illustrating the type of reading matter available and articles of the various types will be found in one and the same journal. It is the writer's experience that students do not *browse* widely enough in journals of all kinds — even the lighter-hearted range of articles about historical quirks, humorous incidents in practice and so on can be very valuable in bringing the legal world into a sharper focus and adding to the law student's perception of the place of his profession in the world outside.

But the starting point in looking at journals will be the academic journal, because it is to these that lecturers will most commonly refer the student. Amongst these the *Law Quarterly Review (LQR)*, the *Modern Law Review (MLR)*, the *Cambridge Law Journal (CLJ)* and the *Oxford Journal of Legal Studies* are the main generalist academic journals accepting articles and other pieces on the whole spectrum of legal study. There are also specialist journals such as the *Criminal Law Review, Conveyancer and Property Lawyer* and *Industrial Law Journal*, whose scope is usually self-evident. It may be of assistance to examine the typical format of such an academic journal to see what the student can expect.

Editorial notes/case notes

Each of these journals will begin with or end with or both begin and end with small pieces sometimes written mainly by the editor, sometimes unsigned commentary on developments and especially recent cases of particular interest. In this section the part most valuable to the student will be the *case notes* ranging from a paragraph or two to a short 'article' on a number of the most important recent cases. The usefulness of these case notes is often missed by students. They usually unravel the facts of cases clearly and explain the salient legal arguments which the judges have deployed. This exposition is then followed by comments explaining how the case fits in with existing case law, whether it is a desirable development, what awful consequences follow if the case should ever be applied and so on. Especially when dealing with controversial and 'key' cases the student will find a number of these notes. It should not be overlooked that cases the student finds difficult can be explained by reference to the case note in an ancient volume of one of these journals, and the case notes very often no longer cited in textbooks can be found simply by reference to the index to the volume for the year in question — think also what a pleasant surprise for your lecturer to find in the examination a reference to a case note which neither he in his lecture, nor the textbook in its footnotes has referred to.

The academic article

Articles are the staple of academic journals. For the student, they are of very varying and often limited value. Each published article aims in itself to be an original contribution to legal scholarship and it will not be surprising if the student still laying the foundation of his legal understanding has difficulties of comprehension. Particular uses which a student will find for such articles are as follows:

(a) Some will contain vital arguments pursued by his lecturer or tutor and such articles specifically emphasised in lecture or seminar must be read. Such references afford very useful indications to the student as to the drift of the lecture course and final examination.

(b) Many articles contain useful reviews of areas which have an abundance of case law and are ill dealt with, perhaps in existing editions of textbooks.

Where an area of the course is causing a special headache, this type of review article should be sought. At first in reading such a piece a student will very often feel that the business of its perpetrator has been to obfuscate rather than clarify. This is perhaps due to the inevitable tendency of academic writers to concentrate on 'the difficult bits'. A high degree of perseverance is obviously necessary if a student is to derive a positive gain from such reading. Perseverance in reading tortuous intellectual arguments is not in itself enough. What is needed is purposeful reading. You should have clearly in mind the gains you expect in reading an article — will it fill in gaps in my knowledge? Will it assist my understanding of this or that point? Will it give coherence or shape to a difficult area of case law? Will it provide a telling quotation which I can note for use in the coming examinations?

Another important use of the academic article is to comment on significant changes in the law. The student will obviously find it essential to read commentaries on reforms contemporaneous with his studies. What is easily overlooked is that in considering previous legislation that is no longer a novelty to the lecturer but of course is to the student, the commentaries written at the time of its passage may often be of value in allowing the student to see what the Act was attempting and how its effect was perceived before it was glossed by layers of case law.

The weeklies and professional journals

Reading one or other of the weekly journals or professional magazines is a very good way for the student to develop a general understanding of the modern legal world and a feel for the law. As an indication of how journals such as these may be used there follows a description of a few of these. The *New Law Journal* is a commercial publication primarily intended for practising lawyers but very widely read (and contributed to) by academics. The *Solicitors' Journal* is a commercial publication of very long standing intended evidently for the solicitor but widely read and contributed to by academics. The *Law Society's Gazette* is published by the Law Society and together with its companion, the *Guardian Gazette* (which is the name for the last issue of each month) is easily the most widely read legal periodical. In his or her student career the student should ensure that opportunity is taken to read these journals from time to time. They will convey a great deal about the legal world of which the student is becoming a part. The *New Law Journal* is frequently critical and probing into the legal establishment and carries articles of a fairly polemical character. The *Solicitors' Journal* is again often critical of aspects of the solicitor's role and professional organisation but the nuances of its commentary are more finely tuned and being written by practising lawyers for practising lawyers may be less meaningful to the student.

The *Law Society's Gazette* is essential reading for any would-be solicitor. The *Guardian Gazette* contains material directed also towards the barrister's profession and is essential reading for aspirant barristers. As do the other periodicals, the *Gazette* carries signed pieces by independent contributors. It also carries the official statements of the Law Society — about examinations, training regulations, conferences and so on. It has a regular column written by trainee solicitors for trainee solicitors. Once you are enrolled as a student member of the Law Society you will look forward to weekly sight of the *Gazette*. Read it regularly, since the regular columns and the debates carried on through the letter columns are not only informative and occasionally amusing but will gradually give you a very good insight into the preoccupations of solicitors and the nature of the profession and may help you considerably in deciding whether and in what type of firm you wish to practise. The *Gazette* will arrive weekly in its cellophane wrapper — if you find you are leaving these to pile up unopened or unread, ask yourself seriously whether you are enrolled as a student member of the right profession!

All students will find it of inestimable value to read one of these three weeklies punctiliously. Each makes a point of providing a comprehensive up-dating service which will keep you informed of the new cases, progress of Bills, other developments. Not all the articles will be worthwhile reading for students. Each has many very specialist articles — the Gazette particularly on property, taxation and professional practice. But where there are practically-orientated articles which relate to your course you should make the effort to read them and gradually acquire some comprehension of the manifold links between the world of study and the world of practice.

It will not take the student long to realise that there are too many journals published for it to be possible to become familiar with them all. It is admittedly invidious to pick out a small number of these for comment but it is probably helpful to select a further handful that might otherwise be overlooked and explain the use to which they might be put.

Legal Action. This is the monthly publication of the Legal Action Group, a society whose aim is the improvement of legal services. It is essential reading for the thoughtful lawyer. Its views are trenchant, sometimes intemperate, but it has gradually become the journal of a respected and influential radical movement. It asks serious questions which concern all aspirant lawyers — is the legal profession racist? Are equal opportunities provided for women lawyers? Is the Law Society putting its best foot forward in implementing the legal aid scheme?

Law Notes. This is a regularly up-dated monthly publication for law students. It is quite comprehensive in its coverage but perhaps fails to distinguish between the trivial and the important. Its notes are very brief but may provide a useful aide-memoire for the student who finds the time that can be allocated to academic life very curtailed.

Before leaving this wide subject of general reading, a word should be said about newspapers. Lawyers and law students require to be well informed about current affairs. The newspapers are full of interesting topics of a 'legal nature' — from questions of international law in the perennial danger zones of the world to the detail of murder trials painstakingly reported in the press. The sophisticated student of today will be aware of the political persuasions of the major newspapers and perhaps be discouraged by that. Whatever other reason might, however, direct a choice of newspaper the serious law student will read *The Times*. It was for many years the only newspaper with a proper law report. Now law reports are to be found in the *Independent, Guardian* and *Financial Times*. This daily law report service is much overrated by academic lawyers. It concentrates too much on the trivial and the sensational. It is, however, a vital way of noting contemporary developments in areas of law being studied. The *Financial Times* has been recommended as having regular stimulating articles on legal topics. *The Times* and the *Guardian* even more so have from time to time valuable and usually critical articles on aspects of the legal professions, the law in action and the judicial system. An interest and even excitement in these areas will develop as regular reading provides a knowledge of the issues, characters and dramas involved. Does the backbencher make an effective contribution to legislation? Should lawyers have a monopoly of particular areas of legal work? Are our judiciary able to respond to the exponential rate of social change? Is it divorced husbands or divorced wives who are dealt with harshly by our family law? In the classroom even such issues as these can seem dry — if you develop a sense of the forces at work in society that give rise to the need to answer such questions, you will also begin to develop an appreciation of the value to yourselves, and the future of the legal profession and the society in which it works, that will derive from the critical study of law.

The Internet as a source

Very rapidly the Internet has become a useful source of information about the law. There are now sites which contain in whole text from some of the information which law students should be reading. Organisations of interest which can be contacted on the Internet are:

http://www.lawsociety.org.uk/
http://www.online-law.co.uk/bar/index.html

These two sites give access to the Law Society and the Bar Council home pages.

The main law publishers have sites where useful information can be gathered. These are, eg:

http://www.butterworths.co.uk/

for Butterworths law Publishers.

Importantly for the student are sites which have valuable legal texts. For example Parliament is accessible at:

http://www.parliament.uk/

Through the site access can be had to daily Hansard, Bills in the course of passage from Parliament and a wealth of other valuable information about Parliament. The whole text of House of Lords' decisions is available on this site on the day that they are handed down:

http://www.parliament.the-stationery-office.co.uk/pa/ld199697/
    ldjudgmt/ldjudgmt.htm

Another court which has the full text of its judgments available on the Internet is the European Court of Human Rights. The address of this is:

http://www.dhcour.coe.fr/

Eventually, all the judgments of the European Court of Human Rights since it was established will be available on this site. Looking further into our European future the home page for the European Community is:

http://europa.eu.int/

This contains policy statements, speeches and official information in a colourful variety of European languages.

Information in specialist areas can be found in many places, of which good examples are:

http://www.companies-house.gov.uk/

Companies House deals with registration of companies and among the information available is an excellent series of notes explanatory of various aspects of company law.

http://www.open.gov.uk/land reg/home.htm

This is the home page of the Land Registry which deals with the bulk of property in England and Wales.

http://www.charity-commission.gov.uk

The Charity Commission is the registration and regulatory body for charities.

http://www.gtnet.gov.uk/lawcomm/homepage.htm

This is one of the very best sources of information for students. The Law Commission is the government body responsible for introducing law reform proposals to Parliament. It publishes a range of working papers, proposals and draft legislation. These papers often contain very clear accounts of areas of law in need of reform and are, thus, of obvious value to students.

The Internet is a constantly changing source and the above gives a taste of some of its present contents. The vigilant student will discover a growing wealth of resources which are multiplying rapidly.

General approach

I hope I have said enough to encourage the student to adopt an eclectic, wide-ranging approach to reading law. If you read, as few students now ever will, the preface to Coke's Littleton (a property law textbook revised in the seventeenth century) you will find the great judge saying:

> Our hope, is that the young student, who heretobefore meeting at the first, and wrestling with as difficult terms and matter, as in many years after, was at the first discouraged as many have been, may, by reading these Institutes, have the difficulty and darkness both of the matter, and of the terms and words of art in the beginning of his study, facilitated and explained unto him, to the end he proceed in his study cheerfully and with delight.

And how did Coke propose that this cheerful understanding be achieved?

> Mine advice to the student is, that before he read any part of our commentaries upon any Section, that first he read again and again our author himself in that section, and do his best endeavours, first of himself, and then

by conference with others, (which is the life of study) to understand it, and then to read our commentary thereupon, and no more at any one time then he is able with a delight to bear away, and after to meditate thereon, which is the life of reading.

I hope you have gathered enough to know that Coke's approach is very wrong in part. He is quite right that discussion with others must be of great help with understanding. He is wrong to adopt the 'textbook-hugging' approach. Too many students mull over the same words in the same textbook or in the lecture notes over and over again. This concentration on one digested source of law dulls the mind and the understanding and is the antitheses of good practice in studying law. The syndrome of concentration on a single textbook has long been an unwelcome feature in legal education. Contrasting views, different perspectives and different sources are the necessary ingredients for producing the well-informed lawyer who has a sound grasp of the common-lawyer. The advantages of reading in a variety of sources is emphasised in these brief sentences from Edward de Bono (*The Use of Lateral Thinking* 1967):

> It is not easy to get outside a particular way of looking at things in order to find a new way. Very often all the basic ingredients of a new idea are already to hand and all that is required is a particular way of assembling them ... This encourages much greater flexibility of mind, for the pupil is actively encouraged to consider a problem from many different points of view, and to appreciate there may be several ways of reaching a correct conclusion.

7 Preparing written work

Preparing essays and projects

Writing legal opinions and advice, complex letters and documents is a large part of the lawyer's business. Curiously legal education has more recently seemed to place little direct emphasis upon the teaching of these skills. From an early age we are educated in an atmosphere of scribbled lecture notes and even more hastily scribbled examination papers. Later on in the lawyer's office we find that modern lawyers do not in fact write but instead dictate into machines. This practice, fed by the deplorable standards of English now prevalent, has done a great deal to increase the sloppiness and unintelligibility of lawyers' written communications. Letters which seem to have no structure of sentences and paragraphs are commonplace. The public seems to think that the main skill of the lawyer lies in the unintelligibility of his written products!

It is to be assumed that the law student possesses a healthy competence in both spoken and written English. Sadly this is not always the case. It is only too apparent that schools these days place little emphasis upon spelling (perhaps not so very important!) or syntax and sentence construction (essentials of clear direct communication). Much of your experience on a law course will not be conducive to improving written English — it is very difficult in law lectures to make notes in any but the most rudimentary English. Where problem-classes take the form of a discussion it is easy to rely simply on hastily written notes and in unseen written examinations, speed of delivery seems more of the essence than the well-rounded phrase and skilfully constructed sentence. Nevertheless, you will, hopefully, be given plenty of opportunity to prepare written work for correction whether in the form of short essays or more ambitious pieces of work entitled thesis, project, long essay or whatever. Where essays do not 'count' towards examination assessment there is an obvious human tendency to treat them with less regard. They are, despite this, invaluable. Marshalling your

85

thoughts and the muddled information from textbooks, articles and lectures into an ordered coherent essay is in itself worthwhile training for a lawyer. Given the nature of legal source material, its prolixity and inherent ambiguity, it is a skill which comes naturally to no person. I have no doubt that time spent in preparing essays will be reflected in improved examination performance. Essay writing will have clarified your understanding of difficult areas and over a reasonable period improve your qualities of expression. Equally important is the feedback derived from having your written work corrected.

Feedback from written work

There can be little doubt that the attention paid to learning and teaching in law schools has improved in recent years. The arrival of the polytechnics and colleges of higher education as major providers of legal education has had a great deal to do with this. Of importance also is the acceptance by students of a role as active consumers of legal education instead of one as passive recipients.

The law teacher likes nothing less than a class of students who receive his words of undoubted wisdom with mute acquiescence. Law schools derive their *raison d'etre* and law teachers their salaried position from the presence of law students pursuing legal education. Consequently there is no need for students to be at all reluctant in coming forward to their lecturers to ask for advice or elucidation. This is especially important in respect of deriving benefit from written work.

It is all too easy for the law lecturer to write on student scripts remarks such as '!', 'how', 'why', 'what on earth do you mean by this', and so on. It goes without saying that written work will be marked promptly and returned to students but, even so, very often the mark and the comments will require careful explanation. Do not be reluctant in asking for this. The lecturers are engaged by the college full-time in order to teach you and will be only too glad to go over the parts of your essay on which you are still confused or about which you are unhappy. Your lecturer will probably be willing to explain how he would have structured an answer to the particular question, which cases he would have included and which articles referred to. This provision of a 'model' answer is valuable and something for which it is well worth your while to press.

Preparing written work

There is no value in hurrying through a set task merely for the sake of completion. In preparing, particularly in law, for any piece of scholarship the first task is researching the relevant material. It is of no profit to you whatsoever simply to repeat in your own more polished and elegant words the profound insights of your lecturer. In terms of developing skill as a lawyer, it is of little more value to cull your ideas secondhand from a textbook and rearrange them into the routine paragraphs of your essay.

Preparation for writing an essay in law begins in the library. The task must be kept in reasonable proportions. Each student essay cannot be a definitive work and the amount of time must be allocated carefully. Given that, you will not produce an interesting piece of work, saying something moderately novel about the subject on which you are asked to comment unless you read the relevant source material and make an effort to find in it that which is especially relevant for or against the theme of your argument.

Let us take a simple essay title that could be set as a first essay in a first year tort* course: '"In reality the existence of a duty of care is a question of fact not law." Discuss.' A tediously straightforward answer to this can be cobbled together straight out of the chapter on 'duty of care' in Winfield and Jolowicz and an even simpler essay derived from Chapter 11 of *Street on Torts* (9th edn 1993, Butterworths). The good student will already have read the great cases of the 1970s in which the House of Lords examined the approach of the courts to new categories of duty of care. He will find in these cases ideas and sometimes quotations to point or enliven passages in his essay. He will proceed from the textbook to read some of the many instructive journal articles to which case law in this area has given rise. He will find articles almost lost to sight but often extremely stimulating in this area such as J G Fleming 'Remoteness and Duty: The Control Devices in Liability for Negligence' [1953] 31 Can BR 471. An interesting but straightforward examination of some cases is given by C R Symmons 'The Duty of Care in Negligence' [1971] MLR 394–528. Before setting pen to paper in earnest, the diligent student will have read a much greater range of material than he can hope to digest in his essay. The watchword in legal research is to read widely but note only briefly. To understand a topic like that under review, many cases must be read and conflicting, perhaps ill-structured, judicial views pondered. Legal journal articles equally are often prolix and rarely wholly digestible at first sitting. When you read a lot you will begin to understand the shapes and patterns of rules and concepts which form a developing area of law. But, it is not profitable to make lengthy notes of this wide-ranging reading. Little can ever be reproduced in examinations or essays of the tortuous facts. You will not have occasion to refer to the multitude of almost analogous cases dredged up and cited in argument nor to recreate the winding thought processes of each learned judge. Keep your notes succinct so that you have on paper that which you can later find of practical use. The next and more difficult stage is rendering this chaos of information into your own semblance of order.

---

* You will find it easier to return to this example when you begin your tort course if you have not already.

Presentation of essays

Written English

Lawyers do not set a very good example to law students. Whether the reader is tackling the law reports or law books he will be oppressed by the amount of unexplained jargon and the unnecessary complexity of language and sentence structure. At the risk of quite untypical pomposity, I shall endeavour to provide a list of simple clues to good clear essay writing.

(a) *Write in simple sentences.* Clear English consists of short sentences made up of short words. In legal writing, complex thoughts have sometimes to be arranged in lengthy sentences with dependent and sub-dependent clauses, colons, semi-colons and parentheses. This should not be done unless it adds to the meaning of the pertinent passage. Avoid the temptation of drifting into complex sentence structure as an affectation of scholarship.

(b) *Use simple words.* This may seem odd advice to a lawyer. It makes, though, for much clearer English if you can save your use of long technical words for occasions when they are precisely relevant. Especially, eschew the use of words the meaning of which is not absolutely clear to you. Comprehensible English uses sentences and words which are as simple as the context permits. The Plain English Campaign has trenchantly argued for this viewpoint. It may amuse you to use their Gobbledygook Test (reproduced from the Plain English Teaching Kit in Appendix 4) to test the comprehensibility of your own English style. Inevitably, a worthwhile passage of legal prose will be more complex in structure than an editorial in the *Sun* but it need not be entirely incomprehensible.

(c) In preparing short essays you do not need to use the same style for references and footnotes as for a longer piece of work. The following instructions may assist:

(i) *Case names.* Usually these should be given in full. If a party has an unusually lengthy name, the abbreviation commonly used in the textbooks should be followed. In short essays there is no need or purpose in giving references to the law reports. If the date of decision is important to your argument it may be given in round brackets after the case title or simply in the narrative eg 'In *Entores Ltd v Miles Far East Corp* decided in 1955, the Court showed that it could adapt the rules of offer and acceptance to deal with new technology ...'. When referring to a case name in an essay it is conventional to underline the entire name. This reflects the practice in publishing of printing the names of cases in italics. It also makes the completed essay much easier to read and consequently to mark.

(ii) *Bibliography*. Students have often been encouraged at school to include at the end of an essay a bibliographical list showing the works they have read. In the case of a short law essay this is quite unnecessary. If you do refer to a case or published work with which you suspect your lecturer will be unfamiliar because of its exotic nature, then it will be helpful to give a full reference to this either in the text or by a *brief* footnote. Otherwise there is no need at all for references or bibliography.

(d) However brief the essay which you hand in it should have some structure. Students seem on arrival at law school to forget forthwith all they have been taught about the structure of essays. A piece of legal argument, like any other written work, benefits from having a discernible structure. At the very least it should have a beginning, a middle — divided into proper paragraphs — and an end. That much seems too mundane to require saying but the reader has not been subjected, as I have, to the reading of piles of essays which drift from a casual beginning to falter into an uncertain ending. Avoid a naïve ending, eg 'Therefore, I conclude that Frederick will win and win heavy damages.' Aim for an ending which leaves your reader with something to ponder, eg 'Thus, the political decision not to enforce anti-trade union legislation has created a power vacuum. Though endowed with seemingly enormous powers, the constitutional forces of law and order seem practically powerless. Does this herald some major realignment of constitutional forces in Britain?'*

On a practical note you will find it helpful towards your examination performance if your essay writing bears a reasonable relation to the piece of work you can be expected to produce in the written papers. Undergraduates' routine essays are usually much too long. They are not intended to be encyclopaedic in content or style. They are essentially limited exercises in legal analysis and expression. Given that the topic or problem on which you are writing will, almost certainly, be one on which you will be restricted to 40 minutes or so in the examination it seems sensible to restrict your written answer to an amount that can be written in that period of time. This will give you useful practice towards the exercise by which your whole undergraduate career will be formally assessed. Many students will find it a helpful practice to close their books, put away their notes and then allow themselves this more or less limited time to write out their essay.

---

* This, the reader will note, was written in 1984. How different these issues appear by 1994!

Preparing substantial pieces of work

Many law courses give students the opportunity to prepare a long essay or dissertation. Sometimes the desired length is as little as four or five thousand words; sometimes as great as ten or twelve thousand. Even for the second or third year student this can be a fairly daunting task and the chance is often missed of carrying out a work of both interest and quality.

The most important advice that can be given is to start early. Lawyers, perhaps all of us, have a culpable habit of leaving what must be done within a particular time right until the end of that available period. If you start early and work steadily towards a slightly early deadline you will enjoy the task more; you will suffer less from the temptation to 'get it over at all costs', and you will have time for the reflective thought and careful revision which will improve the finished quality of your work.

You will probably find, unless you have an unusual bent for legal writing, that beginning is the hardest part of all. The difficult step is clarifying in your own mind the content of your work. In some colleges you may be asked at the outset to find, or even be given, simply a title. Before you start work in earnest a little more detailed specification of your venture is required.

You will doubtless begin with the germ of an idea from something that has stimulated your interest in a lecture or seminar. It is a good idea at an early stage to talk this over with a knowledgeable member of staff, who will be able to direct you towards the most recent sources in that particular area and suggest valuable lines of enquiry. These preliminary readings and discussions should be directed towards producing, before too much time has elapsed, a precise title, a list of chapter headings and, if possible, a brief synopsis of what your essay will achieve.

You will probably experience some difficulty in arriving at the 'chapter headings and synopsis' stage. To my mind this is the most difficult part of the entire task. If, by this stage, you are developing a clear 'thesis' or 'plan' and meaningful chapter headings, the detailed research and writing should prove much more straightforward than expected. It is also my experience that students at this stage tend very often to aim for a work of too wide a scope. If your field of enquiry remains too broad and your consequent written work too general in approach, your final grade can suffer very badly. This is a most common shortcoming in student project-work and an area in which students are prone to disregard their lecturer's advice.

Presentation of the finished work

Each college will doubtless have its own rules or guidelines as to presentation of the finished work. It is churlish to ignore these, as some students will each year. To do so will inescapably lead to the marking examiner looking less favourably at your work. Some detailed points as to presentation may be of assistance.

(a) Even if it is not required by your college, a lengthy piece of work really needs to be typed — otherwise it is very tedious to read and a chance of making a favourable impression is lost. The most acceptable form of presentation to the reader is to type the material with generous margins, double-spaced on A4 size paper. Leave time to correct the typescript and have the corrections neatly included in the finished work. If you are not, as most of us are not, able to spot all the errors or infelicities in your own writing, persuade a colleague to read it for you (if this is permitted by your college rules!).

(b) Do not clutter up your work with pointless footnotes. It is, for example, common for students to cite students textbooks for very basic propositions. This can be irritating to the reader. Save footnotes for statements and opinions that are sufficiently distinctive or controversial to merit reference to some authority therefor.

(c) Footnotes are indicated in the text by a raised arabic numeral immediately following the pertinent word. The footnotes themselves are conventionally either printed at the foot of the page to which they belong or collected together at the end of the chapters or the entire work. For the reader there is no doubt as to the superiority of the first method cited. Special caution is needed in keeping the numbering of your footnotes synchronised with the footnotes themselves — where the text is revised or retyped this can very easily go astray and the numbering of footnotes should be carefully rechecked.

(d) Divide your work into clear chapters. Start each chapter on a fresh page. Within each chapter use a clear system of headings and sub-headings. An example of a suitable simply system of headings, taken from the publishers, Butterworths, is the style sheet reproduced in Appendix 3.

(e) In the citation of cases, statutes and other works it is important to keep to established conventions and to be consistent within your own work. American law students are greatly assisted by a small work published by the Harvard Law Review Association, *A Uniform System of Citation* (Gannett House, Cambridge, Massachusetts 02138, USA). This can be glanced at with profit by any would-be legal writer. There is no such work for English students. Some advice has been given in the relevant chapters of this book. A useful list of conventional abbreviations is found in the opening pages of any volume of *Current Law Yearbook*. (Because there is no standard list of abbreviations in England you may need to search in other sources and the following may be useful — *Osborn's Concise Law Dictionary* (the end); Dane and Thomas *How to Use of Law Library* (Appendix I); any volume of Halsbury's Laws of England (the beginning).)

(f)   Appendix 2 to this book contains a summary of the major conventions of legal citation. In using this remember that internal consistency is even more important than keeping to established conventions. Do not be tempted into a pompous or pedantic use of references. Not every single proposition needs to be justified by decided authority. In an examination it is wiser to err on the side of over-citation of authority. In a piece of written work, cite authority only for significant or problematical statements.

Above all aim for a style which is direct and uncluttered. Do not wander into obfuscation simply because you have not undertaken enough preliminary work to be able to deal with the topic clearly. There follow two examples of essay-writing style. Which will a marking-examiner prefer? How would you improve the other and still convey the same meaning?

The principle of waiver is simply this: *If one party, by his conduct, leads another to believe that the strict rights arising under the contract will not be insisted upon, intending that the other should act on that belief, and he does act on it, then the first party will not afterwards be allowed to insist on the strict legal rights when it would be inequitable for him to do so: see Plasticmoda Societa per Azioni v Davidsons (Manchester) Ltd* [1952] 1 Lloyd's Rep 527 at 539. There may be no consideration moving from him who benefits by the waiver. There may be no detriment to him by acting on it. There may be nothing in writing. Nevertheless, the one who waives his strict rights cannot afterwards insist on them. His strict rights are at any rate suspended so long as the waiver lasts. He may on occasion be able to revert to his strict legal rights for the future by giving reasonable notice in that behalf, or otherwise making it plain by his conduct that he will thereafter insist upon them: *Tool Metal Manufacturing Co Ltd v Tungsten Electric Co Ltd*. But there are cases where no withdrawal is possible. It may be too late to withdraw: or it cannot be done without injustice to the other party. In that event he is bound by his waiver. He will not then be allowed to revert to his strict legal rights. He can only enforce them subject to the waiver he has made. (Lord Denning in *W J Alan & Co Ltd v E L Nasr Export and Import Co* [1972] 2 QB 189 — discussing promissory estoppel, of which you will hear much in contract law.)

The second example is from a case brought against the Law Society by a solicitor trying to show that it had acted wrongly in imposing a compulsory insurance scheme upon its members, and then receiving a commission on each premium from the insurance brokers. Had the Law Society been in a position of trust for its members in so doing and thus rendered itself bound to account for the proceeds? Lord Diplock explains:

This left constructive trusteeship, and the Court of Appeal held that, although the Law Society did not act in the capacity of agent in entering into and maintaining the master policy, it nevertheless did so as trustee for the individual solicitors of the benefit of the promises by the insurers made in the master policy to insure those individual solicitors against professional liability. In this, for reasons given by Lord Brightman, I think they erred. This is one of those reasons which for my part I find conclusive in itself. The obligations imposed by the master policy and certificate of insurance on the insurers and each assured are mutual; they are not limited to promises by the insurers to indemnify the assured against professional liability conditional on the assured's acting in a particular way, as in a unilateral or 'if' contract. To an 'if' contract, since it involves no promise by the promisee to act in that way, it may be that the concept of constructive trusteeship of the benefit of a promise may properly be applied. But the master policy imposes on the assured as well positive obligations to the insurers, as in synallagamatic contracts. The concept of constructive trusteeship of promises which confer a benefit on a cestui que trust is not, in my view, capable in private law of extension to promises which impose a burden on a cestui que trust; an agent acting within his authority can create burdensome obligations on the part of his principal, a constructive trustee cannot. (*Swain v Law Society* [1982] 2 All ER 827, 833.)

You will come across this case when you study the duties of a trustee — to give Lord Diplock a fair trial you may need to glance at the case, which is not too lengthy!

The morals of this rather mischievous comparison are these: use simple words if simple words will do. Do not conceal your reasoning behind a conceptual smoke-cloud. Try to make each step in your reasoning clear and consecutive. If what you are saying involves a conclusion that may be open to doubt do not conceal that by a verbal sleight-of-hand. What you write is intended to be understood. It is not lacking in depth, necessarily, simply because it can be understood readily. You will find in Lord Denning a model of clear English if not in all ways a strictly model judge!

A note on plagiarism and copying

Nearly all degree courses now include an element of assessed course work. This course work has to be your own. Unfortunately, it is the experience of all universities that examples of plagiarism and copying occur from time to time. The result for an individual can be complete failure of the course and loss of the opportunity to become a lawyer. Work given for assessment cannot be copied or digested or reformulated from that of another student. If, as you must, you rely on other writers on the subject you must acknowledge their influence. If you quote directly from another author you must give an accurate reference for this quotation. Background reading in commonplace textbooks need not be referenced but the borrowing of original ideas and the use of all direct quotations must be. It is not sufficient to refer by name to a work in your bibliography if you have taken an idea or quotation from it – this use of someone else's original work must be properly noted. Thus, in an essay on contract you will obviously in preparation look at Anson, Treitel and Cheshire and Fifoot – this scarcely needs stating.

However, if an insight of Treitel informs your essay you should in a footnote to the relevant passage add an acknowledgment such as 'I am grateful to Treitel *Law of Contract* (Xth edn) p Y for the suggestion that ...'. If you use the words themselves used by Professor Treitel then those words **must** ne placed in quotations or parenthesis and a footnote reference **must** enable the reader to discover the origin of your extract. You may be tempted to use copyright (or apparently uncopyright) extracts downloaded from the Internet. There is no reason if they **add** to your thesis why you should not do this. However, the source must be identified as clearly as possible in the same way as any other resource on which you have relied.

Needless to say you should not lend your tape, disk, draft or copy of assessed course work to any other student until you both have had your separate work assessed. Most universities treat the lender and the borrower as equally guilty.

8 Undergraduate examinations

This chapter deals primarily with law examinations at degree level. The professional examinations in law present different challenges and are dealt with separately in Chapters 10 and 11. The material in this chapter will also be found useful by students studying law at a degree level on mixed degrees and non-law degrees such as accountancy and surveying. It will also help students who are attempting the Common Professional Examination for would-be solicitors and barristers.

It is a fact that all students embarking on law degree examinations and the other courses mentioned are already proven successful examinees. How curious, then, that the approach of law examinations is faced with such dreadful anticipation! Yet, the greatest difficulty for students is that law examinations still depend to an enormous extent upon memory and recall. Most undergraduate examinations and many of the professional examinations consist of unseen written examinations of two or three hours' duration.

This style of examining competence whether in academic ability or lawyerly skills does not commend itself to those able to contemplate the subject rationally. It does to a certain extent test knowledge and to a lesser extent skills of verbal expression and analysis. It is also a test of diligence — certainly a meritorious quality. The test takes place, though, in such artificial circumstances and under such an atypical form of stress as to leave one very dubious as to its overall suitability for the assessment of entrants to any profession. Nevertheless, it is time-honoured and it is undubitably there and the student must not shirk the challenges posed: there is no doubt that law examinations loom before law students as an all too terrifying prospect. Partly no doubt, this is due to the nature of the subject matter being examined. At first there is the unfamiliarity of the material being studied. There is also the rather odd style of law examination questions of which more below.

Assessment of law examinations

In a law degree performance is generally assessed roughly as follows:

70%+ = First Class
60%+ = Second Class (First Division)
50%+ = Second Class (Second Division)
45%+ = Third Class
40%+ = Pass

Typically this performance will be distributed in something like the following way. Out of any hundred students, one or at most a handful will obtain first class honours. A few will obtain a pass degree and a few more, perhaps more than 10%, will obtain a third-class honours degree. The remainder will obtain second class honours with the greater number of these falling in the lower division. It may be of interest to students to know that about 15% of those who embark upon law degrees as full-time students fail to obtain a degree.

The marking of examination scripts

This subject is worth some mention as some conclusions can be drawn which are helpful to the examinee. The process of arriving at student assessment is perhaps cloaked in more mystery than is necessary. Students have in the past found that the normal practice is that the raw marks obtained by them, at least in their final assessment, are not made known to them. The justification for this seems to have been to avoid arguments as to whether borderline decisions have been correctly made. Nowadays it is most common for students to be given access to their actual marks. Unfortunately students still generally have no access to their worked and marked examination papers. This is something of a pity as it would prove a salutary experience.

Law examiners tend to be somewhat grudging in the allocation of marks, particularly high marks. I recently checked the scripts of one college at which I examined and found that, in scripts with each question marked out of 20, the distribution of marks was as follows:

Marks per question	Percentage of total questions
15+	0.5%
12 to 14	5.5%
9 to 11	39%
7 to 8	37%
6 and below	18%

This little table is quite typical of the profile of marks in law marking. It illustrates the phenomenon that examiners call the *effective range* of marking. That is the fact that for each question the effective range of marks is between

6 and 14 with only exceptional cases falling above that range, and the overwhelming bulk of instances falling in the middle range. This tendency to mark so restrictively particularly at the top of a range is vividly captured in the French adage: '20 is given only to God, 19 to his saints, 18 to the professor's professor, 17 to the professor himself — so the student of French composition can't be expected to score more than 16'. (Quoted from Clignet 'Grades, Examinations and Other Checkpoints as Mechanisms of Social Control' in *Liberty and Equality in the Educational Process*, Chapter 10.)

These facts, the reluctance of law teachers, particularly, to use the full range of marks, the tendency in law examinations to use an aggregate sum as the main indicator of class achievement and the tendency of such a sum to produce a drift towards the norm have important simple implications for law students.

(a) Within any one examination paper, compensation for poor performance on or omission of a question is extremely difficult to come by. A student in a five-question paper managing 8, 8, 8 and deciding to go 'all out' on one further question is extremely unlikely to achieve the 16 necessary to pass. An excellent student managing 14, 14, 14 has little chance of achieving his aggregate of 70% by neglecting one question and going 'all out' for the others.

(b) Within any diet of examinations the same message applies as between performance in each paper. A student 'on a first' virtually has to achieve a standard of 'almost a first' in every paper to achieve something close enough to the aggregate to win his award.

(c) The clear message is thus that the full number of questions must be attempted and *equal time and effort* allocated to each.

It is important to remember, too, that the examination script you present is as likely to be looked at by examiners who do not know you well as examiners who do. It is the written words only on which you will be judged and only those which can be read by the examiner — perhaps someone rather impatient with the task — who will not pause to unravel the confused or obscure and cannot be expected to assume that the unintelligible or illegible was in truth correct or even profound.

The formal assessment process

In virtually all degree-giving institutions, the examination paper is set internally and moderated by an external examiner. Usually, before being sent to the external examiner, the paper is moderated internally in a committee drawn from those involved in teaching a particular course. This process of setting the examination paper and internal and external moderation will, for a June examination, normally be completed before March for the year in question.

The exact procedure of marking the examination scripts does not vary widely. In nearly every case of a degree examination, the scripts are marked internally and the marking standard and individual cases of difficulty are moderated by an external examiner. The progress of a student or award of a degree concomitant on the examination result is formally determined by an Examinations Board of some or all of those involved in teaching the course and the external examiners.

The procedure in internal marking — whether scripts are double-marked, marked blind and so on — in practice varies so considerably that it would be profitless to attempt to describe a common practice.

The class of your degree — does it matter?

There cannot be much disagreement that for the workaday lawyer, outstanding academic achievement does not have the same importance as professional and personal virtues such as integrity, reliability and diligence. This conclusion and the difference in kind between much of the achievement in law examinations and the later achievements in practice can too easily lead a student to settle for a modicum of effort and a performance lacking in distinction. Nevertheless, there are a number of sound reasons why each student is urged to look carefully to the quality of his or her performance in early study whether of the law or some other first discipline.

In some forms of employment, the quality of your academic performance will in itself be important, certainly if you wish to pursue a career in law teaching or a higher qualification in law. Also, more than ever in the past, law firms recruiting to their strength are explicitly concerned with the measured academic performance of applicants. This would particularly be true if you sought a career away from provincial private practice in a specialist city firm or in the increasingly attractive careers in the public service.

More important still than these considerations is the fact that your performance in your law studies is a direct measure of your knowledge, understanding and application of legal rules. Obviously, throughout your career you will wish to draw on this knowledge and on the training you have given yourself in the comprehension and analysis of legal principles.

In particular this foundation of understanding and knowledge if gained in the pursuit of a first degree in law will be of direct assistance in your professional examinations. It is a fact that the better you perform in your degree studies the better you equip yourself to perform in your professional studies. Analysis of the results in the Solicitor's Final examination has shown that there is a direct and very strong relationship between the class of a student's first degree and successful performance in the Solicitor's Final examination. This is not at all surprising since the degree is the academic foundation on which the somewhat more practical course for the professional examination is based and a sound understanding gained in the former is a prerequisite of success in the latter. It is worth knowing from an early stage in the law degree that obtaining a second class honours degree is the general requirement for entry to the bar vocational course for future barristers.

Different types of examination

Amongst their academic colleagues, law teachers have a reputation for conservatism in method and content. Very probably this reputation is deserved. Thus, it still remains true that in law school:

> The traditional three hour examination paper, combining problems and essay questions, remains the most widely used form of assessment. All the law schools responding to the enquiry relied upon such a paper for the major proportion of the overall marks awarded for a particular course. (Wilson and Marsh *A Second Survey of Legal Education in the United Kingdom*, Supplement No 1, p 23.)

The reason for this ascribed by Wilson and Marsh in the study, and quite properly so ascribed, is largely the influence which the legal profession has on law degrees, especially the need to obtain exemptions from the first stage of professional examinations (a point enlarged upon below).

Nevertheless, different types of law examinations are in use and some consideration is given to these and to the special problems associated with them.

Unseen open-book examinations

This is an examination paper not seen until the examination where the student is given the use of various materials ranging from Acts of Parliament through books of collected or annotated statutes to (very uncommon in England and Wales) the student's own prepared materials. The two special problems of this kind of examination, in the author's experience, might be given the watchwords *organisation* and *approach*.

Organisation

Suppose in a land law examination you are, as is now very common, given the use of *Sweet & Maxwell's Property Statutes* or in a criminal law examination, copies of the Theft Acts. It is noticeable how many students, although fully aware that this text will be available to them in the examination, and having taken the trouble to attend lectures and read textbooks and even reported cases, will not familiarise themselves thoroughly with the form, layout and content of the given material. This is particularly important if, like the property statutes, the text is bulky and its layout not instantly comprehensible. If you are not thoroughly familiar with the text and able to turn rapidly and confidently to different parts of it, then you will find in the examination that you can make little use of the text. The watchword is — learn the organisation of the work that will be supplied or the materials you are taking into the examination and be familiar with its content.

Approach

The reason lecturers are beginning to favour this type of examination is to decrease the need for the student to rely on sheer memory and by doing this to enable the examination to test better the candidate's analysis and handling and application and manipulation of legal rules rather than his mere reproduction of them. A good illustration from the author's experience is with one candidate's answer to the following question:

Q Explain the significance of the Law of Property (Joint Tenants) Act 1964.

(The reader may care to note that on the examination paper in question, this was half of a question in a paper in which five questions had to be answered in three hours and a model answer to this question is given at p 119)

This Act, as the reader may be aware, is a short Act of only four sections passed to deal with a rather complex lacuna in the 1925 property legislation.

The question was set in a second year degree examination and the examiner when marking the papers handed the script of one student to the author with the query, 'What do you make of this?'. The script was duly read and found to set out the three important sections of the Act with fair accuracy and passable clarity and the reply was — 'Nothing exciting but a fair pass in the 45% range'. But, it was then pointed out that the students had had, in this examination, a copy of the Act in *Sweet & Maxwell's Property Statutes*. In this case, reproducing the contents of ss 1–3 was worth virtually no credit at all. In any examination, whether open-book or not, a good answer to this question would explain the mischief the Act was passed to deal with; how the 1925 legislation tried to deal with this problem and why it failed; the incumbent practical difficulties, if possible; how this Act tried to deal with them and what the reasons were for the way it was drafted, including the exception thereto; and, if possible, point out outstanding problems in this area. In an examination where the text of the Act is given to the student, an answer which does not attack the question in that pattern or something approaching it can gain no credit — although in a completely closed-book examination, the mere reproduction of the contents of the relevant Act will suffice for a pass mark.

Seen examinations

Not greatly used in law, but not unknown, is the examination paper which the candidate is allowed to see some time before he is required to answer it. In some varieties, the examination paper is 'taken home' and the student given a period of days or even weeks to produce an answer, frequently of a specified length. In other varieties, the candidate has to reappear in due course in an examination hall and write an answer to the paper. In an examination of this kind, the general advice given on form and content of examination answer remains valid. The crucial change of emphasis is a heightening of the change illustrated in the last paragraph on open-book examinations. No credit is given for the kinds of skill involving memory and facsimile reproduction of texts but exclusively for the other types of performance which a law examination tests.

Multiple choice examinations

These are little used in law examinations in this country — although now quite widely used in medical schools. The author's experience of them has been limited to two law school aptitude tests used for university admissions (in law schools in England), and to some quite unsophisticated forms of this used in America. Because of their limited value in assessing the skills of value to lawyers it is unlikely that their use will be extended in the academic stage of legal education. Multiple choice tests are used as part of vocational courses for qualifying as a barrister — discussed in Chapter 11. They are used to assess memorised knowledge in topics such as civil litigation and criminal litigation.

Viva voce examinations

An oral examination, although universal in assessing higher degrees, is otherwise rarely used. There are two principal uses — to assess project work and to assess candidates who after the written examinations are found to be on the borderline between two classes or between pass and fail.

In these situations, specific preparation would probably be of little use and in any event the summons generally comes too late for this to be practicable. However, some general pointers may help to give confidence if the day does dawn.

First, it is particularly important to have your mind clear and alert. Do not stuff yourself in the ante-room with cribs and mnemonics, simply relax or go for a walk. Even the day before, do not cram ceaselessly at your worn-out notes but find some unlawyerly activity — tennis, squash, snooker, cinema or what you will — something to 'stretch yourself in the other direction' and leave your mind fresh and uncluttered.

Equally important is to have a positive attitude to the experience. The examiners want merely to find out what you do know and do understand — they are not concerned to badger and trip you. Invariably they will be on your side and see the viva as a way of letting you add to your written performance.

Finally, in the viva, do not rush or be rushed. Take as much time as you like. Listen carefully. By all means ask for a question to be repeated or rephrased. Think about your answer slowly and at length and do not be hesitant to divert the discussion into areas in which you are familiar and confident.

Continuous assessment

If by this is meant assessment by sporadic or phased tests of any of the above types then no separate treatment of the topic is necessary. However, the term more usually refers to assessment by reference to course work in the form of essays or projects undertaken during the course. Assessment of such work is dealt with in the preceding chapter dealing generally with the subjects of course essays and projects.

Very occasionally there is another form of continuous assessment based on the student's performance of other tasks of a lawyerly nature. Such assessment is associated with clinical legal education but incurs difficulties because of the subjective nature of the assessment.

Revision for examinations

Memory will play an important part in nearly all your law examinations. An able student can achieve a bare pass with moderate attention throughout the year and a modicum of revision. But even an able student pursuing this plan of campaign may miscalculate and fail.

It is important that you pace your effort throughout the year so as to avoid any temptation to overstretch yourself as the examinations approach. Ideally, you should have developed an even working week which will see you through the course and the examination period. When lectures and tutorials cease some weeks before the examination you should have ample time for revision without stepping up your working-hours at all, let alone to the absurd degree attempted by some students. A continuity of effort will prove more rewarding than periods of relative slackness followed by a fortnight's delirious cramming.

The mechanics of revision is not something on which it is valuable to be dogmatic. I would suggest that a clear timetable, not overdemanding in the hours allotted, is essential — but there is no doubt that some appear to profit from a more haphazard approach.

The essential advice on revision is that you must do as much as you can to render it unnecessary. There is a kind of student who will be very largely unprepared by Easter. He will have a scrappy set of lecture notes from some of his lectures. He will have a random and indecipherable clutter of jottings resulting from his tutorial or seminar work. He will have left unread many of the key cases and journal articles. Revision for this student will be a nightmare. Other students' notes will be photocopied to fill in gaps in his own. Cases will be read hurriedly and partially digested. As spring rushes on towards summer, his now frenetic work reaches a crescendo. He is up working till beyond midnight, meals are missed, panic grows. By the time of the examination he is exhausted, half-prepared and thoroughly frightened. All this can easily be avoided.

Take on the other hand the model student. His lecture notes contain a succinct record of each lecture — for he has attended them all — and are filed in order in ring folders. Each page is interleaved with the cases and supplementary material he has produced as a result of his own reading. There are brief accounts of the important cases, summaries of journal articles and, spicing the whole, useful quotations, further references and explanatory notes. When shortly after Easter the lecture course draws to its close, this student's preparatory work is complete. He has in one place already assembled all the material which he is going to utilise in the examination hall. All he has to do now is peruse this material sufficiently thoroughly for it to be at his finger-tips during the examination. His revision can proceed in an orderly fashion and in the confidence that he has laid a workmanlike foundation. If he keeps his head, he can achieve the ideal revision programme. That is one in which his hours do not increase during the weeks before the examination but if possible decrease. Remember there are more enjoyable things to do at college in the spring than repair the damage caused by previous ill-attention to your studies!

However carefully you prepare for the event, revision for examinations is a chore. The art of the successful examinee is to exercise foresight throughout the year and avoid the need for eleventh-hour excitement. The task can be made even easier by adding to your armoury of aide-memoires. It is a sad fact that much still depends upon memory. There will be large numbers of case names to commit to memory and a great deal of statutory material which many find even harder to recall in examinations. Although it is far from being a worthwhile academic venture, you will find a little effort put into practical organisation of this material very worthwhile. Cases can be arranged in suitable lists according to headings and other groupings. The same can be done with statutes in respect of which much memory work is required such as the sale of goods and unfair contract legislation and the enormously bulky property legislation. You will find that statutory material as presented by the draftsman is not a total jumble. Try to see how it is arranged in groups of sections according to subject matter, and how the arrangement has been arrived at. Try to produce an easily scanned 'revision scheme' of an Act which is likely to feature in the examination. It is likely that the work involved in this exercise will help to increase your understanding of the Act as well as assist in the drudgery of revision. It is too easy to study legislation piecemeal as a series of unrelated sections instead of building up an understanding of the whole.

Some of this advice may seem a far cry from the heady intellectual challenge anticipated by the beginner in legal studies. But, the examinations are there and have to be passed. The memory work is important and preparation for this trial a skill in itself. The comfort is that in order to make any worthwhile criticism of the law, it is necessary first to have both knowledge and understanding. The quantity of law is increasing at a rate that is sometimes alarming. The skills of digesting, organising and subsequently recalling a welter of detailed information will remain with you long after you graduate as will the solid acquaintanceship with law and legal reasoning which your methodical work has enabled you to acquire.

Specific revision preparation

One of the most difficult pieces of advice is to give general advice on revision. But, knowing that students must tailor this to their own needs, here is one approach. First, enough has been said to indicate that it is one's approach to the whole course which indicates success in examinations — the last week or so's revision must not be seen as of the greatest importance.

Assimilation of large amounts of material is important for any law examination. I think this is true even if the examination is totally open-book. My own experience at Columbia University twenty-five years or more ago was as follows. One examination was completely 'open-book'. Any material that we liked could be taken into the examination. Yet, my own experience was that there was no time during the entire examination period to look at any of this.

Assimilation should be seen as a part of each stage of the course from the beginning. Try to set aside a little time each week or fortnight for this purpose. Do not use this time simply to re-read your notes — action-packed and exciting though they doubtless will be. Try to digest the material into a pattern — perhaps as follows: topics; sub-headings; and under each sub-heading a listing of the relevant cases, statutes and perhaps articles or other material. You may wish after each case to add a few words reminding you of its importance. This skeleton of each stage of your course will be the backbone of your final revision. Its key words and ordered pattern of presentation will 'bring it all flooding back'. The recall you need in the examination must be effortless. For this, an orderly scheme on which your assimilation of material is based is very useful. Repetition in the learning process *throughout* the year is also a crucial part of laying the foundation for effortless recall of relevant material.

I believe, too, that this systematic structuring of subjects such as contract, tort and land law will lay the foundation for an understanding of the common law which will never leave you throughout your career.

I would predetermine your pattern of revision at the commencement of each year and keep to this. Work out in a revision chart when you will cover each subject for the first, second, third (etc) time. Try to keep to the same number of hours, approximately, devoted to study when lectures finish and the examination approaches. There is no need for the good student to 'step-up' the number of hours devoted to revision. The same methodical working week is what is required. In the summer term there is ample time for tennis, parties, country visits, weekends away and the countless more aimless forms of relaxation which are part of the richness of student life.

What to revise

Students constantly ask what they should revise — no lecturer can answer such specific questions. After all, the entire course of study is arranged as a whole. It is not arranged so that students can simply select enough to pass the examinations. Certainly students should participate in and benefit from the whole course. Nevertheless, as far as actual revision is concerned, it is possible to adopt a more ruthless approach. A typical examination will require four questions out of ten to be answered. Leaving out a simple discreet topic from final revision will simply reduce the choice to four out of nine. Such a small adjustment to the final stage of revision seems to me perfectly reasonable. Reducing by ten per cent overall, the material to be re-revised in the final few weeks can give a welcome feeling of 'space' and a much needed psychological boost. It is unwise to go significantly further in omitting material from revision.

Sitting the examination

The advice which follows is all obvious and all based upon common sense. You might at times feel it is wholly unnecessary. It is included because my experience has been that it is often ignored by students and always to their detriment. It seems probable that sitting examinations is one of those things that becomes a little harder with each fresh exposure to the experience. Consequently, simple steps must be taken to reduce the unnerving effect of examinations. What is said here is not novel. Try to let the novelty lie in the extent to which the advice given is noted and relied upon.

It is most important to remember that the examination tests your performance once and for all on the day of the examination. It is self-evidently detrimental to your performance to be physically and mentally tired. A student who has been a lackadaisical drifter throughout the year and who winds himself up to a Herculean effort of round-the-clock revision will do himself no good. You need to think in law examinations and to do that you need to be awake. It might be salutary to produce two quotations from a book largely about examinations:

> Over 80 per cent said they had been extremely tired from lack of sleep, either because they were unable to sleep or because they had curtailed their normal number of hours through working late into the night or getting up very early in the morning to revise.

> Fatigue effects particularly affected the exams coming near the end of the series. Those near the beginning were most likely to be affected by nervous tension.

The extracts quoted speak for themselves (both are from Miller and Parlett *Up to the Mark* (1974) p 90). Plan your whole period of revision and your work during the examination period so that you remain physically and mentally fit. Take plenty of time off for recreation. On no account shut yourself off in a ceaseless whirl of revision and ever more frenetic glances at your huge accumulation of notes.

The examination hall itself

The following is a simple checklist of preparation for the examination day.

(a) Ensure you are familiar with the whereabouts of the examination room. Check the examination timetable. Make sure you can arrive on time without being rushed and without having to spend too much time 'hanging about' with other candidates while the excitement mounts.
(b) Be armed with plenty of writing materials.
(c) If you are allowed materials in the examination, have this ready and in good order. Check to see that they conform with the examination rules. A silly oversight can lead to disaster.

When you are in the examination hall and told to begin — do not. Your first thoughts, particularly in the first examination, will be incoherent. Set yourself a simple procedure as to how you will read and re-read the examination paper and select your answers. When the examination begins, follow this careful procedure. It will still your spinning mind. Calmed by the routine of a familiar process the ability for rational thought will return. After selecting your questions begin to write slowly. The examination will be under way and you will not look back until the final whistle.

As a last word on the subject, it is worth repeating advice you will have been given a hundred times in your school career but which is still forgotten in the dread panic of an examination. Check and double check the instructions on each paper. Answer the correct number of questions and the correct number of parts of each question. In law examinations it is equally important to remember to follow the instructions for each question. If it instructs you to advise Fred, advise Fred, and not some other party or the parties generally. More attention is given to this topic in the following chapter — here it is sufficient to stress the importance of paying careful and deliberate attention to these matters.

9 Answering degree level examination questions

In this chapter a close look is given to the answering of law examination questions. This is not, of course, the *raison d'etre* of legal education. Passing examinations is still, however, the main criterion of successful completion of your education. In the bulk of law examinations the unseen written question-paper is the norm. This is likely to remain so for the foreseeable future, especially because the professional bodies — the Law Society and the Council of Legal Education — are insistent that this form of examination is a part of the essential test for would-be practitioners. Exams and examination technique must, therefore, be taken seriously. Much can be gained in the way both of enhanced performance and reduced anxiety by giving some rational and detailed thought as to how to approach the examinations.

Answering examination questions

Setting and marking questions for examinations is notoriously easier than answering them. If students had experience of being examiners they would be more successful in their role as examinees: the changes they need to make in style and content would be blindingly clear. It is necessary to return as a starting place to the question — what is special about the study of law? But, this time concentrating on a slightly different facet — what is special about answering law examination questions?

Types of questions

Law examination questions are readily divisible into two kinds: problem questions and essay questions. These two types of question will be dealt with separately and illustrations of how to produce a high quality answer and an analysis of the thought processes involved given. In reading these, it should be borne in mind that what is illustrated is how to answer examination questions during an examination *not* how to produce a complete account of each problem raised with no constraints as to time or space. Students who had the opportunity to scrutinise answers submitted by successful students would be surprised at their apparent simplicity and very often their brevity. There is no need either for a good answer to be packed with the names of countless cases. A good answer will reflect clarity of expression, clarity of analysis and a succinct and relevant use of cited authority.

There is not time in an examination, unless you know very little, for everything you know on a subject to be spelled out. For the knowledgeable student it is a paradox that a first class answer is as much a matter of omission or ellipsis as of inclusion. Equally it is an important truism that students most often fail not because they do not know enough to pass but because they are not able to deploy their hard-learned knowledge to good effect.

Problem questions

Students generally find problem questions more of a challenge than essay questions. But they should not be avoided — they provide plenty of opportunity for the well-prepared examinee to shine. Questions asked vary from the coyly brief (for example, the notorious question: 'A lets down B's bicycle tyres. Discuss.') to questions apparently styled on classical opera with many characters and a diffuse but strong story-line. In each kind of problem, the essential key is the identification of the actual legal issues at which the examiner is aiming — though this is harder in a three-hour examination if he has used a scatter-gun instead of a laser.

The punchline in problem questions

The punchline in problem questions is the rubric and it is frequently misunderstood or carelessly or cavalierly ignored. You will be asked to respond to the collection of strange events which make up a problem question in various ways. You may be asked to 'Advise Mr Smith' or 'Explain the defences available to D', or simply to 'Discuss', a command much like the instruction commonly added to Scottish problem questions: 'Quid Juris?' (meaning of course: 'What is the law applicable to these facts?').

It is important as mentioned in the previous chapter to follow this instruction to the letter. In cold print, this may seem rather trivial advice. In the examination hall it is all too often forgotten and the knowledgeable student comes to grief by answering the wrong question. It is especially easy if you are asked to advise multiple parties to overlook the different considerations which the examiner has skilfully made applicable to one or other of them. An addition to the rubric in the form of some slight twist to the facts is also often overlooked* and the proportion of the marks which the examiner has mentally reserved for this section of the answer jeopardised.

Structure of problem questions

The bulk of problem questions contain more than one issue and have other similarities in their structure which make it possible to describe a common method of approach. Having in mind a settled idea as to how you will attack the daunting set of facts presented to you is particularly important when you are faced with questions containing complex facts and many parties — a genre of question which seems to have become prevalent in recent years.

It is rare for a problem question to contain only one problem and it is important to remember that each problem raised must be dealt with. Where there are several problems, they will commonly require answering in a conditional sequence. This means that your answer to one stage of the question will depend on your answer to the next stage. It can usually be assumed that the 'answer' to any stage in this sequence is problematical, that is, it is a question of argument. This means that the following stage of the problem must be approached on the basis of more than one hypothetical answer to the first stage and so on. It is the success of the student in analysing a problem into this sequence and answering the problem systematically according to that pattern which is to a large extent the determinant fact in success. By and large, students will carry with them into the examination the same knowledge of very much the same case law and in answering problem questions it is this method of using and applying that knowledge that is most important. It will help to proceed to an analysis of a typical examination problem question.

Example One

Take as an example the following question which would be found in one guise or another on very many first year contract law papers. It concerns the problems of formation of contract and the legal approaches to one party's attempts to introduce a clause restricting his liability under the contract. (You will probably find it helpful to return to the detailed answers to the exam questions and reconsider them as you come to the pertinent subject in your course.)

'There is a notice in a launderette. It says "NO LIABILITY TO USERS FOR LOSS OR DAMAGE AT ALL". The notice is sellotaped to the inside of the door. A few yards from the door is a dry-cleaning machine; it requires two

---

*   For example, in the question last noted, 'Would it make any difference if A quite foolishly assumed the bicycle was his own?'

fifty-pence coins to operate it … Alfred enters the shop. He places two fifty-pence coins in the machine. He does not see the notice. He places his sleeping-bag in the machine. The cleaning-fluid is too strong and dissolves his sleeping-bag. When Alfred extricates the remnants of his sleeping-bag his fingers are badly burned by the cleaning-fluid. Advise Alfred on the application of contract law to his predicament. Would your advice differ if he had read the notice after inserting his coins and before pressing the "START OPERATION" button on the machine?'

First consider the answer given by the student who does just enough to merit a pass mark.

Answer A

The notice on the door is an exclusion clause. It must be part of the contract. In *Chapelton v Barry UDC* a man hired a deck-chair but it collapsed and he was injured. He had been given a ticket by the deck-chair attendant and the ticket had a notice on the back saying that the Council was not liable but the court said that this was not part of the contract and so he could recover. In *Olley v Marlborough Court* in a hotel case they were liable for loss of luggage where the notice was not seen until after the person went into his room in the hotel and in *Thornton v Shoe Lane Parking* the result was the same when a man was injured in a car-park — he could sue although there was a notice he did not see till he was in the car-park. The case is like the ticket-cases *Parker v SE Railway* and *Thompson v NWR* and the notice must be brought to the attention of the person before the contract is made. The position might be different if Alfred has been in the habit of using the launderette and had seen the notice before. Interesting cases on this point are *Hollier v Rambler Motors* and *McCutcheon v David MacBrayne*. This means that a course of dealings might have the effect of incorporating the exclusion clause in the contract so that the user could not sue. I would advise Alf that the clause is probably not part of the contract. The Unfair Contract Terms Act might also apply and since this is not a Sale of Goods Act case then whether the clause applied would depend on whether it is reasonable or not. This clause is not reasonable because there is no reason why Arthur should know that the cleaning-fluid is too strong.

If he had seen the exclusion clause it would have been part of the contract and anyway the clause was not reasonable so Alfred could still sue.

Alongside this, for comparison, consider the following answer which might be produced to this question by a first class student:

Answer B

It seems correct to assume in this case that the launderette is liable prima facie for breach of contract. This seems to be a clear breach of the implied term that the supplier of a service acting in the course of a business will use reasonable care and skill.

This problem is concerned with the effect of the exclusion clause on the launderette's liability to Alfred. The first problem is whether the exclusion notice becomes incorporated in the contract to clean Alfred's goods. If it does then the next problem is whether the exclusion covers the breach and finally if the exclusion clause does not become part of the contract and apply to this breach, whether its effect is vitiated by the Unfair Contract Terms Act 1977 in respect of either loss of the bag or personal injury. Finally, a different question of incorporation requiring an analysis of when the contract is formed is posed by the situation where Alfred does read the notice after inserting his coins.

A clause contained in a notice of this kind will be incorporated in the contract if reasonable steps have been taken to draw it to the attention of the other party — a principle established in *Parker v SE Railway*. Whether reasonable steps have been taken to bring the clause to the attention of Alfred is a question of fact — although the burden of showing this will be greater if, as here, the exclusion clause is not contained in a contractual document (cf *Chapelton v Barry UDC*). Also where the clause has a very serious effect such as excluding liability for personal injury, as may be the case here, then it may need to be more clearly drawn to the other party's attention (see eg *Thornton v Shoe Lane Parking Ltd* and cf dicta of Denning LJ in *Spurling v Bradshaw* [1965]).

Where Alfred has read the exclusion clause as is indicated in the rider to the question it will be incorporated only if the above rule is satisfied or if he read the exclusion clause before the contract was made — see *Olley v Marlborough Court* where the exclusion clause was read by a hotel guest in the room after booking into the hotel. An analysis of a similar situation to the problem in terms of offer and acceptance is given by the Court of Appeal in *Thornton v Shoe Lane Parking*. The ticket machine there (the laundry machine here) is seen as accepting the offer by issuing a ticket. The notice in this case was read after the offer was accepted.

In this case the laundry machine may be making a symbolic offer which Alfred accepted by putting in his money — in that case the notice was read too late to be incorporated. Alternatively, Alfred made an offer which the machine accepted (by switching on or flashing a 'Ready' light perhaps). On the facts as given it is difficult to see which in this case and whether the notice was read before the acceptance or not.

Even if the notice becomes a term of the contract, the laundry may not be able to escape liability in reliance on it. The courts construe such clauses 'contra proferentem' this is against the person relying thereon (see eg *Houghton v Trafalgar Insurance*). An example of this approach is in a situation where, as here, there might be strict liability (for breach of an implied term to clean the goods or even an express warranty written on the machine to that effect) and also liability for doing so carelessly (that is, negligence). In such a case a clause would be interpreted to apply only to the strict liability as in *Rutter v Palmer* unless the contrary was clearly intended as in *Archdale v Conservices*. Here the clause 'loss or damage at all' is like the 'all loss or damage whatsoever' in *Smith v SW Switchgear* — where the courts upheld the narrow rule of construction.

If there were no liability for such an express or implied term but only for negligent inflicting of the loss and injury in this case, then the clause would apply to such liability only if clearly intended to do so. A possible comparison is *Hollier v Rambler Motors*. A clause extending liability for fire damage in a garage did not exclude liability for such damage caused by the proprietor's negligence — the notice only gave a warning that they are not liable for such damage not caused by their negligence. Such a construction could well be placed on the clause in this case.

Finally the clause will be affected by the Unfair Contract Terms Act 1977. The launderette's liability is business liability within s 1. The effect of s 2 is that liability for the personal injury to Alfred is caused by the negligence of the launderette in using too strong a concentrate of cleaning-fluid and cannot be excluded at all. Similarly s 2 prevents exclusion for negligent damage to Alfred's sleeping-bag unless such clause is reasonable.

So far as strict liability for breach of an express or implied term of a contract is concerned, s 3 of the Act applies. Assuming as seems likely that Alfred is a consumer in this contract (s 12) as the launderette is in the business of cleaning and Alfred does not make the contract in the course of a business, then liability for breach of such a term can be excluded only if the exclusion is reasonable.

In each of these cases the test of reasonableness is contained in s 11 of the Act and is in terms of fairness and reasonableness given the circumstances in the hypothetical contemplation of the parties at the time the contract was made. Why should a user of a launderette be expected to contemplate that the owner will not only use a dangerously strong concentrate of fluid but also escape scot free — especially when this is a matter peculiarly within the owner's control?

Comparison of answers

A comparison of these two answers (A and B) is revealing as to what is required by a candidate in answering a problem question.

Introduction. The question of whether to write an introduction to an examination answer is a vexed one and regrettably one on which different examiners do differ rather markedly. The advice given here is if you are answering a problem question then a general introduction should be avoided.

For example, in answering this problem a student might write:

> This question is concerned with exclusion clauses. Such clauses have been the subject of much judicial and recently legislative concern. There has been a running battle between the interests of those who might be adversely affected by the operation of generously worded exclusion clauses and the interests of those seeking by skilful drafting of exclusion clauses to reduce the economic burden of liability for damage suffered by the users of their goods or services.

This is an attempt to set the problem against the background of the area of law involved.

There is no doubt that a discussion along these lines would be of great interest and even of value in understanding the forces at play. But, it is not an answer to the problem. It is not the job of work in hand — *advising Alfred.* Some examiners will not mind wading through such a prolix introduction but it can count for little or nothing as it does not answer the question — other examiners will be (perhaps only unconsciously) somewhat prejudiced by the gratuitous burden this placed upon their valuable time. In answering a problem question the candidate is consequently advised to address himself directly and at once to answering the problem in a brief manner. An introduction specific to the problem may, however, help the student to proceed to a systematic exposition of his or her answer.

The more specific introduction. Answer A contains no introduction and Answer B an introduction of a particular kind. The introduction given in Answer B is recommended for the following reasons: the task that very many students find really difficult in answering problem questions is to pose the problem which has to be answered. A problem question will commonly pose a number of questions which must be answered in some kind of pattern, and that pattern is a conditional sequence. The first step in seeing what this pattern is in respect of a particular problem question is to restate the problem, not in terms of the facts, *but in terms of the legal problems which they pose.*

The students faced with the egregious factual situations beloved of law examiners must first do the same — *state the problem.*

Added to this is the very difficult dimension for the average student that the question will contain a number of *dependent problems* which fall to be analysed in the 'conditional' sequence outlined above. If the student can state what these problems are and the order in which he or she will take them two very important things will be achieved. First, it will be demonstrated to the examiner that the student has correctly and clearly placed the factual problem in its legal context. Second, there will be set out a clear and concise plan of the answer which is to follow — one which covers broadly all the areas to be dealt with in the answer and in a manner which will give a shape and logic to that answer.

Before leaving the first note on the answers to this examination problem, it is worth examining another way of viewing the structure of the question in the form of an illustration which might make visualisation of this type of structure easier. That is in the form of a *decision tree* or *algorithm* (see p 115).

This type of flow chart or algorithm has also been suggested as a way of analysing complicated legal rules. A useful discussion of this is found in Miers and Twining *How to Do Things with Rules.*

Whether you choose to analyse the problem set in an algorithm or not, it is essential that one way or another you reach the stage of being able to analyse a lengthy problem question into a series of legal problems which your written answer will then dispose of. This can be achieved only by an exposure to a large number of such questions and practice at how to answer them. The crucial importance of this practice in the type of questions you are going to face in the examination cannot be overstated.

For the problem on p 110 a decision tree might appear as follows:

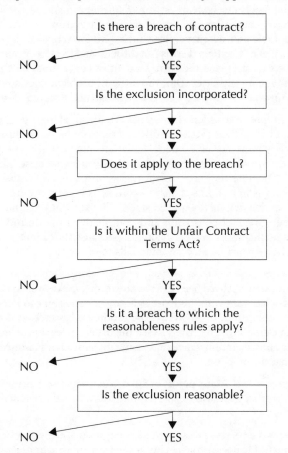

Content of answers

After this digression, it is now useful to turn again to the two model student answers provided above and compare the different performances of the two students.

The distinctive features of difference between Answer A and Answer B are as follows.

(a) *Coverage*. Answer A does not cover all the different problems posed by the question. It is not bad on the problem of whether the clause is incorporated in the contract but it deals with this as if it is the only issue of real importance and ignores the question of construction of the clause and hardly deals at all with the Unfair Contract Terms Act. In this last, the answer may reveal the working of a very dangerous psychological mechanism — *fear of difficulty leading to avoidance*. All students can follow the cases on incorporation — the facts are memorable and the principles simple. All lawyers find the structure of the Unfair Contract Terms Act difficult and its effect problematical. These two facts lead the weak student to concentrate on the former and to ignore the latter. But, the difficult problem does not go away. *Some areas of law are difficult to understand and hard to remember.*

That is a proposition which all students can grasp. Harder to grasp is the corollary. These difficult areas are difficult for everybody. Because they are difficult they must not be evaded — neither must the student expect to reduce them to a state of simplicity which simply does not exist. These areas are difficult because they are complicated — often this is because the case of statute law is in a confused state — often, as in, say, the area of illegal contracts, an inextricably confused state.* The student must not sidestep the difficult areas of confusion and complexity to be found. Equally important neither must she feel inadequate because she cannot produce the ordered clarity which the law so often fails to present.

(b) *Answering each part of the question.* The question, as is common, contains a rider: what if Alfred had read the notice, etc. In Answer A, the weaker student has dealt with this in a brief sentence and come to an extremely facile conclusion. In Answer B the candidate has tackled that part of the question fully, has tried to see the different legal problems raised in the altered circumstances and come up with a fair reasoned analysis of what this might be.

(c) *Source material.* Many points on how to introduce source material into an answer are dealt with separately (see below) — suffice it here to point out that:

Student A cites several cases on incorporation of exclusion clauses into contracts. He does not state clearly the principle illustrated by the case (see below). He cites facts that are irrelevant to the thrust of his argument, eg the thoroughly well-known story of the collapsing deck-chair. He also, and this is a particularly important point, becomes carried away on a crest of memory about the 'incorporation cases' and brings in the cases about habitual users (*Hollier v Rambler Motors*; *McCutcheon v David McBrayne*) that are not called for by the question. The student must produce authorities which are relevant to the facts

---

* A textbook writer tends to put this proposition more cautiously eg 'The law on this question is complex and not very satisfactory': G H Treitel *The Law of Contract* (5th edn) at p 361.

given, and not deal with a factual situation which he hypothesizes for himself. If the particular point as to habitual use of the launderette on incorporation is worth making on the question asked (which must be doubted) it must be made very succinctly, almost as an aside.

In contrast, student B categorises the legal problems succinctly by reference to the *principles* established in pertinent cases, eg he cites the well-known *Parker v SE Railway* case clearly as authority for a particular legal proposition which is briefly and accurately stated.

Also in contrast to student A, student B refers to the facts of the case only where necessary to make a clear comparison with the facts of the problem case and, thus, examine whether the principle in the decided case is applicable — a good example of this is the use of *Thornton v Shoe Lane Parking Ltd*, by using the facts of which student B is able to make a convincing attempt at legal analysis of the problem of incorporation in terms of the concepts of offer and acceptance and illustrate quite neatly how such reasoning might be used by the court.

A final useful comparison between Answer A and B is their different success in referring to statute sources. A is hopelessly vague and manages to refrain from penetrating the veils covering the Unfair Contract Terms Act in a way that leaves the examiner with considerable doubt not only as to whether he can apply the detailed and important distinctions within the Act skilfully but even whether he knows what they are. Student B, on the other hand, makes a good start of taking the reader (albeit quickly, as the question demands the covering of considerable ground) through the relevant distinctions showing clearly by reference to specific provisions that he understands the framework of the Act and can apply it in a situation such as this.

(d) *Statement of applicable principles.* It is noticeable that Answer B exhibits a much clearer disposition and analysis of legal principles than Answer A. The important difference here is that in Answer A the relevant principles are hinted at, eg in the opening reference to the exclusion clause, the candidate says: 'It must be part of the contract.' Candidate B tries to state the relevant rule as a legal principle, viz 'A clause contained in a notice of this kind will be incorporated in the contract if reasonable steps have been taken to draw it to the attention of the other party.' The rule itself is obviously familiar to all law students. The credit, however, is given to student B for a clear, lawyerly statement of the rule in its relevant context clearly illustrated by pertinent case law.

Essay questions

It is now helpful to perform a similar exercise of comparison, this time looking at answers to essay questions. Essay questions are often deceptive.

They appear easy but have hidden facets which deceive all but the very well prepared student. It is all too easy to produce a 'pat', straightforward answer which is simply a mundane account of the relevant area of law and can achieve only a mediocre grade. Often essay questions are seen by students as a 'soft' option to the more terrifying-seeming problem questions. On the other hand, it is probably harder to achieve a really good answer to an essay question. Much more is required of the student him/herself in creating an answer — the shape of the answer is not, as is the case in problem questions, dictated by a sequence of facts presented in the question itself. A great danger, therefore, is producing an answer which is simply so much regurgitated and formless material more or less connected with the problems at which the essay was specifically directed.

Example Two

This question occurred in a first year contract paper.

Q   The statement that the plaintiff is to be compensated for his loss is not, in itself, particularly helpful. For a breach of contract may cause many different kinds of loss and we have to ask for which of these kinds of loss compensation will be given. Discuss.

A very ordinary pass answer provided by one student read as follows.

A   Breach of contract has recently taken a most interesting turn into the area of injury to feelings and it is the latter aspect that brings a question over when particularly damages can and cannot be recovered. Initially one must show that one has suffered loss as a result of a breach.
     When a contract is broken the contract comes to an end and damages are recoverable for the loss sustained by the injured party. The damages received must be only the loss to the plaintiff and punitive damages over and above those suffered cannot be claimed. Although in some contracts eg the sale of land and contracts in which a trade secret is involved the plaintiff may finish with a profit being more than he could otherwise have made — *Maxim Nordenfeldt v Nordenfeldt.*
     Furthermore, the injured party must prove that a duty was owed to him by the defendant, that the duty was breached and that as a result of that he received damage, in short he must prove some form of damages either to his person, personality or property.
     The plaintiff is also able to claim for reliance loss, being the costs expended in expectancy of the contract being performed eg in *Anglia TV v Reed* the performer withdrew and they were able to recover this loss from him. Similarly loss of benefit of profits they could have made and restitution of damage caused is recoverable.
     The damage caused must not be too remote and it must be calculable. *Hadley v Baxendale* set out the principle of recovery in contract, the case involves a mill shaft which was (unknown to the carrier) essential to the manufacturing process. It was sent for repair and the carrier was

told to make the journey with all haste but he was not told why. The outcome was two rules. First, losses are claimable for losses which are a direct consequence of the act and secondly that losses were also recoverable if they were within the 'contemplation' of the parties. The test is thus different from tort. The basic ideas have remained as case law has developed. The *Victoria Laundries* case thus allowed a claim for losses of normal trade, but not an 'unexpected Government deal'. The *Heron II* allowed full recovery of cast sums because the ship carrying the sugar should reasonably have had it within its contemplation that the sugar was for the market at Basra and that it was unreasonable to extend the journey time from 12 to 29 days during which sugar prices slumped.

Parsons (Livestock) v Uttey Ingham tends to favour the tort principles and differs little from the similar tort case (the *Seale-Hayne* case). Nevertheless, it does point out that a difference exists. A similar case against a solicitor for incompetent conveyancing draws once more upon the *Hadley v Baxendale* principles.

The damages claimable must be calculated by the courts and the fact that it is a difficult task is no reason not to bother to sue eg *Chaplin v Hicks* in which a beauty contestant was awarded exemplary damages.

Finally the vexed question of whether or not a person can claim for loss to their happiness. Recent cases answer this question in the affirmative. *Bailey v Bullock* allowed a damage claim for a man whose mother-in-law had stopped with him, in *Cook v Spanish Holiday Tours* a honeymoon couple received damages for what is in effect loss of happiness. *Jackson v Horizon Holidays* and *Jarvis v Swan Tours* are similar and reflect the modern trend.

Example Three

An example of a first class answer to an essay question based entirely on statute law would be as follows:

Q   What is the significance of the Law of Property (Joint Tenants) Act 1964?

A   This Act was passed to remedy a defect in the 1925 LPA which has caused inconvenience in conveyancing practice. Where land had been conveyed to beneficial joint tenants, and one of them had died, it was the intention of the 1925 legislation that the surviving joint tenant should be able to deal with the land as beneficial owner and not have to appoint a second trustee to receive the purchase price as otherwise required by s 27 LPA. The problem was that a purchaser from the surviving joint tenant would not know if the beneficial joint tenancy had been severed so that the survivor was not able to sell as sole beneficial owner but should instead appoint a second trustee. For example, if a house was conveyed to Mr and Mrs Roberts and Mrs Roberts charged her share to the milkman and then unfortunately died, how could a purchaser from the widower know whether or not he was a beneficial owner?

The LPA Amendment Act 1926 had added to s 36(2) of the LPA a provision intended to make this position clear providing that nothing in the Act affected the right of a survivor of joint tenants who is solely and beneficially entitled to deal with the land as if there were no trust for sale. However, this did not enable the would-be purchaser to know whether the survivor was solely and beneficially entitled or not. So the 1964 Act was passed to remedy this situation. It provided that the survivor of joint tenants shall in favour of a purchaser of a legal estate be deemed to be solely and beneficially entitled to that estate. For this to apply, the survivor must convey as beneficial owner or the conveyance contain a statement that he is so entitled. In order to remedy any defects in titles for this reason between 1925 and the 1964 Act, s 2 declares that the Act is retrospective and is deemed to have come into force on 1 Jan 1926 and where applicable, conveyances executed before the Act was passed are deemed to contain the requisite declaration as to beneficial ownership.

It may be noted that the Act does not apply in three circumstances: Section 1(1)(a) provides that the act does not apply where a memorandum of severance signed by a joint tenant is endorsed on the conveyance to the joint tenants. Section 1(1)(b) provides that the Act does not apply where there is an entry in the bankruptcy register in the Land Charges Register against one of the joint tenants. In each of these two cases the purchaser will have noticed that the beneficial joint tenancy has been severed and that the survivor cannot convey as beneficial owner.

The third circumstance in which the Act does not apply is stated in s 3. That is in respect of any title registered under the Land Registration Acts. The reason for this is that under that system the trust interests are protected by appropriate entries (restrictions) on the register and the purchaser by seeing that such a restriction if present is complied with will be himself protected by obtaining registration.

Finally it may be noted that the Act itself is not without problems. One that has been often pointed out is the difficult position of a purchaser, say, from Mr Roberts in the above example who knows that Mrs Roberts mortgaged her share to the milkman. The Act literally seems to state that such a purchaser from Mr Roberts selling as beneficial owner will still take free of the trust interest. Thus, the statute will be used 'as a fraud' to defeat the milkman's claim! A more obscure drafting point is that s 1 applies only 'to the survivor of two or more joint tenants' — but, surely when, for example, Mrs Roberts has severed the joint tenancy, Mr Roberts ceases to be the survivor of two or more joint tenants and becomes the survivor of two tenants in common. The Act is clearly meant and is, of course, generally assumed to cover such a case. But equally clearly, its application to such cases will tend to increase the incidence of fraud!

Comparison of the two answers to the essay questions

Amongst law examiners, it is axiomatic that the good student will be as likely to tend to answer problem questions as the bad to answer essay questions.

It seems even a common creed amongst examiners that the essay questions are there to give the weak student a chance. Certainly it seems easy in practice to muddle through an essay without showing any distinction but hard to give an answer *demonstrating* real ability. There is no reason why this should be so, particularly since all law students have plenty of essay-writing experience in school examinations, and the advice given there as to form, directness and clarity is equally germane in answering law essays but it is rarely, in the heat of the moment, put into practice. Let us examine the pertinent points a little further.

Form. Virtually all the points on answering an essay question can be subsumed under this head. The second answer follows a clear logical pattern:

(a) The problem of the lacuna in the 1925 LPA is stated.
(b) An attempt to redress the problem and its failure is clearly stated.
(c) The operative part of the 1964 Act is set out.
(d) The exceptions to the Act are clearly explained.
(e) Problems remaining after the Act are explained or hinted at.

Set out like this it is the essence of simplicity, yet in the examination hall how very few students will set out their answer in such a way! Essay one is, in contract, typical of the average approach to answering this kind of question. The answer contains a fair amount of material but it pours onto the page straight from the student's turbulent brain. There is enough there to show the student has a fair smattering of knowledge about the topic under question but nothing to show that he can analyse, weigh the relative significance of different cases and provide a considered answer to the question asked.

When you are familiar with the topic covered by essay one you should try yourself to sketch out the form of answer that could be used to display your knowledge and understanding of the material. The following points should help you with this.

(i) How could you restate the question so as to provide an introduction which describes the legal problems you are going to discuss?
(ii) How would you state and illustrate the normal rules which apply in this area?
(iii) How would you state and illustrate the rules applying to more exceptional areas which illustrate deviation from the 'normal rules' which you have already outlined?
(iv) What particular areas of more recent development in the area would you single out for more lengthy treatment? How would you relate these to the theoretical background you have already set out?
(v) Try to round your essay off by opening up vistas of unsolved but important questions, or hinting at policy implications.

Other distinctions between essay one and essay two

1   Note how badly principles of law are set out in essay one. A good example is the basic principle in *Hadley v Baxendale*. You must practise both in writing and orally in seminars the basic skill of formulating succinct clear statements of legal rules.
2   The second essay provides a direct and straightforward answer to the question. The first avoids doing this and leaves the examiner to speculate from the amorphous pile of evidence supplied by the student as to whether he understands the question or not.
3   Note how the student in essay two provides in paragraph one a brief hypothetical illustration of the problem. He is then able to return to this illustration in the final paragraph to give a reasonable flourish to his conclusion.
4   Note the sloppiness of expression in essay one throughout and contrast this with the accurate lawyerly language used throughout essay two.
5   When you have examined these two questions carefully, and considered the form which the author of essay one might have used you might find it helpful to write out sections of his essay to see how easily he could have improved his woeful grade by taking notice of the above points.

Example Four

To conclude this section on answering questions, a further question will be taken and a method of producing an answer examined at greater length.

It will be helpful to work through one more problem question which is a salient example of a typical genre, that is, problem questions where there are a number of issues and parties to be sorted out. This would be a typical first year tort question:

Q   Adam, a surveyor, was sent by his company to inspect a ruined castle which it is thinking of buying. Ben owns the castle. Above the entrance gate was a sign 'No liability is accepted for any injury to any person entering this castle however caused'. Adam took his seven-year-old daughter, Catherine, with him to the castle because her mother was working. Adam fell into a dungeon through a rotten trapdoor and was trapped 50 feet below ground level. Catherine rushed off for help. She tripped over in the passage-way as she hurried towards the exit. Adam died as a result of this incident and Catherine was severely injured. Ethel, Adam's widow, seeks advice on any tortious claims she has against Ben on behalf either of herself, Adam's estate or Catherine. Advise her.

In dealing with questions which have numerous parties and facts your first tack is working out some kind of structure for your answer. From the beginning you need to note the claims you are asked to deal with — these are *Ethel v Ben*; *Ethel (on behalf of Adam's estate) v Ben*; *Ethel (on behalf of Catherine) v Ben*. In your answer you must deal separately with each of these three possible actions.

Secondly, you must proceed to analyse each 'action' into the 'points of law' involved and the result will be something similar to the following.

Ethel (on behalf of Adam's estate) v Ben

(a) Has she a right of action in respect of A's death?
(b) B's liability to Adam — is he a visitor? — standard of care owed?
(c) Exclusion notice — business use? — other defences? eg contributory negligence.

Ethel v Ben
Brief explanation of Fatal Accidents Act claim.

Ethel (on behalf of Catherine) v Ben

(a) Possible claim under Fatal Accidents Act (as above)
(b) Catherine a lawful visitor or a trespasser?
(c) If lawful visitor, standard of care owed.
(d) If trespasser, duty under Occupier's Liability Act 1984 — explain.
(e) Does B owe C a separate duty of care in her role as rescuer?
(f) Defences — possible contributory negligence? Causation.

You will see that even writing out the points to cover in note-form produces a lengthy answer. The difficulty in this kind of question is to give emphasis to the more difficult points, while still presenting your reasoning through the whole problem in a complete and coherent answer. The two difficult points are the exclusion of liability, dealing separately with the case of a lawful visitor and that of a trespasser, and the rather difficult conceptual problem of liability to a rescuer who is also a trespassing child.

When you have analysed sufficient examination questions purposefully, you will not find it necessary to write out notes on the question. You will be able to analyse the question into its parts without putting pen to paper. When you are able to achieve this it will save you much time in the examination. Some students find it more helpful to continue to write in note-form to the answer — and it may, indeed, assist as an aide-memoire while you write your full answer. My own conclusion, however, is that the need to write 'against the clock' still plays so large a part in law examinations that the counsel of perfection is to develop the facility of analysing questions mentally.

Having produced in your mind or on paper a scheme of your answer all that remains is to write your answer. To the present question, a first-class student's answer in examination conditions might be along the following lines.

Taking first Ethel's claim on behalf of herself or of Adam's estate: Ethel is enabled by the Law Reform (Miscellaneous Provisions) Act 1934 to bring an action against Ben providing she is Adam's personal representative. She can also bring an action under the Fatal Accidents Act 1976 on behalf of herself and Catherine. In the Law Reform action, Ethel recovers the damages due to Adam (but not in respect of loss of earnings after his death — see now Administration of Justice Act 1982, s 4) — and in the Fatal Accident claim, damages based on her and Catherine's financial dependency on Adam.

In each case, Ethel's claim depends first on establishing Ben's liability in negligence to Adam. It appears from the question most likely that Adam was a lawful visitor to Ben's castle. He was, thus, owed the common duty of care under s 2 of the Occupier's Liability Act 1957. There may be a breach of this duty in leaving an unrepaired and dangerous trap-door.

It is relevant, however, that this was patently a ruined castle and Adam a surveyor. Section 2(3)(b) of the 1957 Act provides that an occupier may expect that a person in the exercise of his calling will appreciate and guard against special risks incidental thereto. Would a surveyor of a ruined castle not take care to avoid any inherent danger? This line of argument also raised the possibility of Adam's contributory negligence or even the possibility (rather slight?) that he was *volenti* to the risk of visiting this castle.

Finally, if Ben's use of this castle was business use within s 1 of the Unfair Contract Terms Act 1977 (s 1(3)(a) or (b)) then his liability in negligence for injuring Adam is non-excludable (s 1(1)(c) and s 2(1)).

So far as liability to Catherine is concerned the Occupier's Liability Act 1984, s 1(3) must be considered. There is a duty of care if Ben is aware or has reasonable grounds to believe in the danger or the proximity of Catherine to the danger and the risk is one against which in all the circumstances Ben could reasonably be expected to offer protection. If there is a duty, it is a duty to take such care as is reasonable in the circumstances of the case.

So far as the exclusion notice is concerned, Winfield argues that the statutory minimum duty to a trespasser might be non-excludable. No authority is given and *Herrington* (now no longer a direct authority) suggests if anything the contrary (Lord Pearson adverts to exclusion notices in a way that seems to accept their efficacy). The exclusion notice may anyway be relevant in showing that Ben has discharged his duty by providing adequate warning — but is such a notice adequate precaution if he knows of the presence of children?

Catherine is probably also owed a separate duty of care in her capacity as a rescuer of Adam. *Videan's* case is authority that the rescuer is owed a separate duty of care. It seems not to matter in logic that the rescuer was first a trespasser. Some analogy is found in *Chadwick v BTC* where the plaintiff would have been a trespasser if he had not been a rescuer.

Liability here to Catherine will depend upon the reasonableness of her response to the peril Ben had created to Adam. Although her claim is not affected by Adam's contributory negligence (if any) it is affected by her own. Finally, of course, Ben might be able to show that the injury to her was caused not by his own breach of duty of care but by her carelessness.

Notes of completed answers

1   It is important to deal with issues on which the facts give no guidance one way or the other quite succinctly. Examples are: damages and the Law Reform and Fatal Accidents Acts; the possibility of a business user under the Unfair Contract Terms Act. On each of these points, the problem leaves you without the necessary facts to formulate a detailed answer. Consequently, do not make up a variety of hypothetical facts and produce a lengthy series of hypothetical answers to the problem. Simply state the alternative conclusion precisely and proceed with the next point.

2   The question covers too many issues for you to deal with any as fully as each might warrant in practice. The question is testing your skill at unravelling the legal framework where there are a number of parties, fairly complex facts and some difficult issues. In order to merit a good mark you must make a workmanlike attempt to answer the whole question in the form in which it is asked. You may feel that you can demolish Winfield's suggestion that the duty of care owed to a trespasser is non-excludable. If you produce a well-argued case on this point alone you will deserve credit — you may indeed succeed in devoting your whole time to this point or to the conceptually more interesting point concerning liability to a child trespasser who evolves into a rescuer. Such an approach may achieve a pass but it cannot merit much more, however extensive your answer, because it represents a contumacious refusal to tackle the question on which the examiner has decided that your lawyerly skills should be tested.

Further preparation for examinations

Let it be said in conclusion that law examinations at degree level no more have right and wrong answers than they do one correct way in which to set out the answer. But, there is a distinctive identifiable style to both questions and answers. Some time is usefully spent in actually running through questions and working out the pattern of answers. So, you will find it most useful to acquire a stock of past examination questions and give to them systematic attention along the lines indicated. Many students probably begin this exercise by acquiring past papers but fail to carry it through usefully. It is very easy to peruse lightly a past paper, identify the topics dealt with and put the paper down with a sigh of relief. In order to develop the vital skill of analysing questions until a clear pattern is discerned and then tailoring your knowledge to this pattern, more is needed.

In your previous education you will have been deluged with suggestions on how to produce good answers to examination questions. You will have received extremely useful 'tips'. For some reason or other students

uniformly discard all this accumulated wisdom on arrival at college —
assuming, perhaps, that undergraduate studies are so totally different that
it is now irrelevant. The simple advice you have already received on the
construction and contents of examination essays remains valid. It is
important to write in distinct paragraphs — yet, few students in exams seem
to. It is very worthwhile to learn telling quotations and sprinkle these
appropriately in your answer-book — yet an examiner may read a whole
batch of scripts and find none. It gives an answer extra polish and bite if it
contains carefully chosen reference to learned articles perhaps even with
suitable critical comment — but, such references are usually strikingly
absent from students' scripts ...

10   Becoming a solicitor

Becoming a solicitor is the object of a great majority of law degree students. Nowadays, students tend to proceed straight from their law degree on to the one-year Legal Practice course and from this into a two-year period as a trainee solicitor. Students who are graduates in other subjects than law take a one-year course in the core subjects of legal education* — this course is called the common professional examination, although there are other routes by which it is possible for the well qualified school leaver or for the experienced legal executive to qualify. The full rules are contained in the Training Regulations available from the Law Society.

At some time during your law degree course (or before embarking upon the common professional examination) you will, having decided to become a solicitor, enrol as a student member of the Law Society. You will then be sent by the Law Society further details of the training regulations for solicitors.

List of topics of which knowledge is essential before embarking on the new Legal Practice course: (see p 129)

Contract law

A good general understanding of contract law is essential for conveyancing, consumer protection and to a lesser extent employment and company law. Especially important in conveyancing is a good understanding of 'formation of contract'.

Tort law

A reasonable basic general knowledge of this subject may occasionally inform your answers in the heads mentioned above.

---

* Contract, tort, criminal law, trusts, constitutional law, land law. It is offered at the College of Law and universities listed in Appendix 1 and discussed further below.

Land law

Here a very thorough knowledge is required. The following topics may be especially noted:

Settled land.   A clear grasp of machinery for transferring title in settled property is needed. Beyond that only an outline is necessary.

Trusts for sale and co-ownership.   This is of central importance. A very good grounding is necessary. Especially important is transfer by a sole surviving co-owner.

Registration.   Registered conveyancing figures very largely. It is a help if the student starts with a good grasp of the Land Registration Scheme, types of titles, methods of protecting incumbrances and overriding interests.

Leases.   A thorough knowledge of general principles is required.

Covenants, easements, mortgages.   A good understanding of the basic principles in each of these topics is desirable.

Equity and trusts.   It is important both in conveyancing and succession to have a fair grasp of these topics. Especial attention may be given to administration of trusts and the appointment, retirement, removal and duties of trustees.

Given this preliminary understanding, the Legal Practice course will be found demanding but not especially intellectually demanding. There is a great deal to be learned, understood and digested and virtually all students find the weight of material and length of the course something of a trial. A sustained effort to work is required over quite a long period. Consequently some thought must be given to management of your time.

The writer's preference is for an even effort over the whole of the course, rather than for a crescendo of effort towards the summer. There is no choice in the examination papers. Attention must, accordingly, be given to each part of the course — nothing can safely be omitted altogether. The parts of the course studied in November need to be understood as well as those completed in May. So, steady and consistent application is called for. Classes must be attended diligently from the beginning of the course to the end. A fortnight's lapse may lead you to gain no marks on a question which takes up a third of one paper. Failure will then be inevitable.

All this poses different demands for the student from the more dilettante days of the undergraduate past. A very deliberate programme of recreation is needed to avoid becoming jaded and to ease the tension which the course produces. Obviously every student must find their own route to this particular salvation. But, I would advise regular, weekly days off — preferably the entire weekend. Equally large parts of the Christmas and Easter holidays should be kept *entirely* free of work. When the mind is absorbing vast sequences of material, periods of rest are vital otherwise you will feel murky and confined. Keep your nerve and take plenty of regular predetermined time off. Try to arrange a good long weekend break within your final revision period so that it eases off before the examination.

Qualifying as a solicitor — from September 1993

The new system — the Legal Practice Course

The Law Society at the end of the 1980s undertook a radical review of legal education. The broad pattern of these routes is set out in the following tables. But, it must be noted that within these different routes great flexibility of approach is possible and a welcome variety of courses will develop in the future. These should enable students to deal with the radically different pattern for financing higher education and training which has been emerging.

The philosophy of the new training system

Underlying the planning of the new solicitors' training system is an appreciation of the very fast changing world of legal practice. The Training Committee of the Law Society described the 'forces for change' as follows:

> The Training Committee considers that the two fundamental underlying forces for change to the training system are the continuing needs to improve the quality of entrants to the profession and to increase the system's ability to respond flexibly to changes in demand for solicitors' services. These two points are related. Even though it is widely accepted that the existing training system is greatly superior to that operating before 1979 the increasing volume of complaints against solicitors and the increased competition from other professions and 'paralegals' are increasing spurs to improve professional competence. The need for increased flexibility goes beyond the ability merely to increase overall numbers at a time of recruitment difficulty and then to reduce numbers when demand appears to be slackening. There must be an adequate supply of new practitioners in the right geographical location, prepared for areas of work increasingly in demand and with the ability to change direction should the nature of the demand for legal services change. The current system is inflexible in that it insists that most entrants to the profession go through a process of training designed to meet the needs of a young law graduate. Those stages under most control by the profession give insufficient scope for recognising the qualities and achievements offered by those wishing to come into the profession from other occupations and jurisdictions.

The underlying approach exemplified by this statement has led to the design of a system which allows flexibility and permits a significantly greater concentration upon skills training rather than placing a major emphasis on the learning of legal rules.

Different routes to qualifying

The different routes to qualification are given in Table 1 and Table 2 (below). Table 1 shows the different routes for persons who are taking a law degree. The first possibility is –

(a)   A law degree followed by the new legal practice course and then the two-year training contract in legal practice during which the trainee will attend a short professional skills course. Table 1(b) shows an alternative where the substance of the legal practice course is included within a four-year law degree programme. This is then followed in the same way by the two-year training contract including the professional skills course. Table 1(c) shows the possibility for a part of the training contract to be included in a sandwich version of a law degree. At the present time sandwich law degrees are few in number. In fact they are available at only Brunel University, Nottingham Trent University and Bournemouth University. It is possible that it will become a more attractive route if firms of solicitors are willing to take graduates of such degrees on the shorter eighteen-month training contract.

(b)   Table 2 shows the different routes for persons without a law degree. These follow into two groups. Table 2(a) is concerned with graduates in subjects other than law. These will take the graduate conversion course — known either as the Common Professional Examination or the Postgraduate Diploma in Law. This is then followed by the legal practice course, the two-year training contract and professional skills course. The other route is for non-graduates. Table 2(b) shows that they can obtain exemption from parts of the Common Professional Examination/Postgraduate Diploma in Law Stage by qualifying as Fellows of the Institute of Legal Executives. They will have to complete, then, the legal practice course and the professional skills course. They will, however, not have to undertake the training contract. Their practical experience as legal executives will have exempted them from this.

Content of the Legal Practice Course

The Legal Practice Course does not have an identical content in each institution which provides a course. The pattern will follow the following general format. There will be three 'core' subjects which will be present in each Legal Practice Course or in each exempting law degree. These subject areas will be:

- Litigation
- Conveyancing practice
- . Business law (that is, the solicitor and his business client)

Table 1
Qualifying as a solicitor by means of a law degree

(a) Qualifying law degree (ordinarily 3 years)
↓
Legal Practice Course (one academic year)
↓
Two-year training contract
↓
Professional skills course (during training contract)

(b) Exempting law degree (ordinarily 4 years)
↓
Two-year training contract
↓
Professional skills course (during training contract)

(c) Sandwich law degree (may be either a qualifying or an exempting law degree)   ↓

(Legal Practice Course — unless an exempting law degree)
↓
Training contract (at least 18 months up to six months of the normal two years being the 'sandwich element')
↓
Professional skills course (during training contract)

Table 2
Qualifying as a solicitor — persons without a law degree

(a) Non-law graduates

Degree — 3 years ordinarily
↓
CPE course — 1 year
↓

Legal Practice Course — 1 year
↓
Two-year training contract
↓
Professional skills course (during training contract)

(b) Non-graduates

Basic educational qualification eg 'O' levels/GCSE
↓
Qualify as a Fellow of Institute of Legal Executives
↓
Complete exemption from CPE
↓
Legal Practice Course
↓
Professional skills course (completed before admission)

In addition in each Legal Practice Course there will be two optional areas. These will be in large part at the discretion of each institution. It may require each student to choose one from a range of private client options and one from a range of commercial client options. Typical optional subjects will be family law practice, intellectual property, consumer law, commercial property transactions.

There are two subject areas which are important to all practising solicitors and will be required to permeate the course. These are revenue law and professional conduct and ethics. Considerations of European law will also be dealt with on each course. Where this topic is relevant the rules as to giving of financial and investment advice under the Financial Services At 1986 will also be covered. Sadly, in 1997 the law Society added compulsory examination in Solicitors' and Business Accounts to the legal practice course. This makes the assessment burden somewhat greater with little benefit to the overall value of the course.

A most important feature of the Legal Practice Course is its concentration on skills training. The course must provide essential skills training in:

* advocacy
* drafting
* legal research
* interviewing
* negotiation

As the course develops the proportion of time spent on skills training will increase proportionate to the amount of time spent teaching legal rules as such. Institutes will vary greatly in the extent to which this skills training is integrated with the subject teaching or is a more self-contained element of the course. Colleges providing an exempting law degree will be able to be flexible in the order of and approach to the material found in a 'stand alone' legal practice course. They will, though, have to include within the exempting degree all the elements of such a 'stand alone' legal practice course.

Assessment of the Legal Practice Course

Every course will contain an element of unseen written examinations. These will be set by the institution which is running the course and subject to external moderation on behalf of the Law Society in order to ensure that comparable standards are found at each institution. The examinations will normally be ones which permit students to use materials — such as notes and course materials — which they bring into the examination. The skills elements of the course will be assessed by students performing set exercises. For example videos of advocacy exercises may be used as part of the assessment of this very important part of the course.

Legal Practice Course — part-time

It is now possible to take the Legal Practice Course part-time. This can be done while in employment with a solicitor or not. The course will involve attendance at the university or college for a day or part of a day a week. Alternatively it may involve less frequent attendance but for several days or more at a time.

Part-time versions of the Legal Practice Course have two substantial advantages. They are in effect more financially manageable because of the possibility of combining the course with paid work. In terms of the education achieved there is also considerable possibility of benefit — if the course is combined with useful practical training in a solicitor's office then there is a very real possibility of the overall value of the Legal Practice Course being greater.

The negative side of part-time vocational education lies in two areas. Firstly, some of the larger solicitors' firms are very slow to see the advantage of this mode of education and may be reluctant to employ trainees on part-time training contracts. Secondly, combining work and study in this fashion may demand a greater overall commitment in both time and stamina. Speaking personally, as someone who did the former Law Society Part II examinations by part-time study, I can well see both its merits and demerits. In the end it comes down to either personal preference or economic necessity.

The part-time course may be taken over two or sometimes three years. The courses themselves differ very greatly in their arrangements although, of course, all have the same basic content as the full-time course. Appendix

1 tries to list those who are running a part-time course. An accurate list can be obtained directly from the Law Society.

Obtaining a training contract

Having completed the examination — successfully! — you will enter a training contract. In the new post-1993 scheme of education for solicitors the traditional name of 'articles' has been abandoned and called instead a 'training contract'.

The first hurdle you have to cross is to discover a solicitor who is willing to take you as his or her trainee. This is a very difficult subject on which to advise students. Entry into the training contract is not an organised or streamlined business. There is a fairly useful guide (the Roset Register of Solicitors Employing Trainees, published by AG-CAS) as to which firms take trainees and a minimum of detail about each firm. It will almost certainly be available in your college's library or law school. If not, it is available from the Law Society. There are also formal lists of vacancies maintained by the Law Society and by secretaries of local law societies. It seems that these are only rarely of help in directing students to vacancies.

The Law Society's Gazette does each week carry a few vacancies for trainees and also a smaller number of advertisements from persons advertising themselves as potential articled clerks. Given the large number of students placed every year this obviously caters for only a tiny fraction of the whole. It is possible, though, that a worthwhile offer may be found by responding to an advertisement. This has been particularly so in the autumn, when after the Finals' results were published a number of firms found that their expected trainees had failed to pass.

Local authorities regularly circularise law schools with vacancies and also advertise in the national and local press. The salaries paid are competitive, perhaps £2000 pa or more above salaries in provincial private practice. Until quite recently, it used to be widely said that local authority articles were not a good passport to private practice. I would doubt if this is still generally true. In a large local authority, you should encounter well-structured training, a high quality of supervision and an enticing variety of complex legal problems. Their vacancies are heavily over-subscribed. A good academic background — probably at least a better sort of second class honours — is needed to win a place and there will almost certainly be the need to perform well at a competitive interview.

The most common way of finding a training place remains the direct personal approach. The fortunate applicant will have the benefit of a personal introduction through a family friend or relative. Such has been the growth of the profession in recent decades that this avenue has been available only to a small minority. It is, however, possible for students to make their own contacts. Few students seem to attend the meetings of their local law students' societies. Solicitors are often met by prospective trainees in such surroundings as the Territorial Army or the Rugby or Cricket Club. Solicitors, rather unsurprisingly, like to take on as trainees those who have interests and backgrounds quite like their own.

I have known many students who have obtained satisfactory articles as a consequence of finding themselves vacation employment in a solicitor's office. Sometimes this can be found through a relative or friend. Very often students find such an opportunity by direct approach. You can expect to be paid little, perhaps nothing. The experience will, however, be invaluable. Firstly, you will discover for yourself what 'goes on' in a solicitor's office. This is a chance not to be passed over lightly when you are considering spending the best part of the next forty years in one. It also allows you to demonstrate to a potential principal that you will make a worthwhile trainee solicitor, are willing to work and can adapt yourself to the office set-up.

The larger firms in London and the provinces now have application forms for prospective trainees to complete. They expect high academic achievement and demonstrably high personal qualities. Success in debating, student politics, competence at foreign languages, significant achievement in sport and so on can all be important. Outside these larger firms, by far the greater number of students find their training place by a direct written approach to solicitors in a given locality. They write to all solicitors listed in that area in the telephone directory or in the *Solicitors' and Barristers' Directory and Diary* (published annually by Waterlow and containing a list under town names of all firms of solicitors with some small details of their practice). Whether you are making an approach in this way or in reply to an advertisement, it is wise to give much thought to your letter of application. I would favour a handwritten letter of application accompanied by a typewritten curriculum vitae. In your letter of application, which should be brief, try to indicate both your strong interest in working for the firm in question and something special about your background that makes you a desirable candidate. In your curriculum vitae include full biographical details, education, examinations passed and standard reached. Solicitors will also be interested in other areas — have you held office in societies and clubs, played representative sport, taken office in the Union at your college, etc? Try to demonstrate that you are a lively, sociable person who will be an asset to their firm. If there are features to your education that will assist, expand on them — have you represented your university in the National Mooting Competition, or written an extended essay on a complex aspect of commercial law?

Choosing a firm

It may not be given to many to select the firm in which to be trained but it is still worth some consideration. At the top of the tree in terms of earnings and important or prestigious clients are the very large London firms whose names are familiar household words. The major commercial cities have two or three or possibly slightly more similar firms. These firms have many partners — twenty or more. Their work is for large commercial concerns or institutions and to only a small extent for the private client. (Solicitors use the expression 'private client' work in contrast to work for clients who are commercial or industrial concerns or public bodies.) Some of these firms visit colleges on the 'milk run'. They all have very competitive entry. A very good academic background is required. Such firms will also delve deeply into an applicant's background. Is she fluent in any foreign language? Has she excelled in student politics or societies? Is he widely read and highly cultured? Will his background endear him to the firm's clientele? Has she the drive and motivation to equip her for a highly competitive working environment? In such firms, at least in London, salaries and working conditions are good. It is not the life, though, for any but the very ambitious. A period of competition with other trainees for a limited number of vacancies will be followed by a long period of competition with other assistant solicitors at various grades of status and salary before success is finally crowned with a full partnership.

Beyond these heady reaches are a wide range of respectable hard-working solicitor's firms. By and large they 'specialise' in private client work — conveyancing, probate, trust and tax work, crime, divorce and family disputes and a wide range of litigious matters. The size of partnerships ranges from the large number of sole practitioners to very large firms indeed of more than fifty partners, with the commonest being three to six partners. General advice on what to look for is extremely hard to give. On the whole it is best to avoid articles with a sole practitioner — he or she will probably be too busy to instruct you and there may well be little variety in the work. Beyond that, it is very much a matter of personal predilection. Some of the best and most independent-minded solicitors are found in small firms or as sole practitioners and may provide a wonderful introduction to a career in law. You must try to make a judgment in such a case as to whether the solicitor will set aside time for structured training.

If the type of work you desire and the locality in which you wish to practise is clear then choice may be straightforward. For the majority who are undecided here are a number of *flexible* pointers:

(a) The salary offered is little indication of the quality of your training contract. A good firm may well feel it can afford to pay little if its ex-trainees are prized employees. The good firm is one that gives emphasis to the training it gives the trainee rather than the measure of work it expects for the high salary it pays.

(b) Is there a clear scheme of training? Has there been a steady flow of articled clerks in the past? Have your conditions of work and supervision been carefully thought out by the firm or is it all 'hand to mouth'.

(c) You cannot obtain references about your potential employer, though it is vital for you that the firm should be reputable, honest and professionally in good standing. If you are lucky, friends or relatives will be able to advise. If not, you must rely on your own judgment based on very little evidence. Think carefully about the attitudes your prospective principal exhibits in the interview you have. What do they indicate about his values and standards? If you are looking for articles near your former college, your tutor should be able to warn you against the odd rogue firm which exists in any area.

Many firms, particularly where the college trains solicitors as well as undergraduates, make a direct approach to a particular law school. These enquiries very often come in the vacation when there are few students about.

What to expect from articles/training contract

The Trainee Solicitors' Group of The Law Society publishes a booklet — *The Trainee Solicitors' Handbook*. This is obtainable from The Law Society and gives advice and suggestions about your training contract.

The quality and style of training which you can expect is still very variable. Not a few trainees are 'thrown straight in the deep end' and allocated in their early days a considerable number of files to deal with and expected to muddle their way through with little or no supervision. In the past there have at the other extreme been solicitors who have given to their articled clerks little or nothing to do but left them simply to spend their time in idle conversation. This last is now rather unlikely as solicitors have to pay at least a minimum salary to their trainees and, in any event, financial efficiency has become very much the leitmotif of contemporary solicitors' practice.

Nowadays, these extreme examples are not so likely to occur with any frequency. The Law Society's regulations governing training are stricter than in the past. They now provide that trainees must receive experience in at least three basic topics. They must have the opportunity to learn principles of professional conduct and etiquette. They must also have the opportunity to practise the following basic skills: drafting, communication with clients and others, research, office routines (procedures, costs and legal routines). An obligation to provide this experience is contractually binding upon each principal.

In order to make the monitoring of the quality of experience provided more realistic, there are more detailed regulations. New trainees are given a letter of offer from their principal and this sets out certain basic information. The offer letter and the contract itself entered into between the firm and the trainee must both be sent to the Law Society — where they are scrutinised and, if appropriate, the contract approved and registered with the Law Society. In addition each trainee is required during articles to maintain a 'Training Record'. This specifies the tasks that have been undertaken and the risks employed. It will be in the form either of a diary or checklist covering areas of work undertaken.

The subject of trainees' salaries has for long been a matter of concern to the Trainee Solicitors' Group. There are still many practising solicitors who themselves received no payment in articles or only a token wage. There are even some who paid a premium. There is, accordingly, quite a strong built-in reluctance to paying a 'proper' salary. The Law Society has, however, stepped in to ensure that at least a minimum salary is paid. Each local law society will publish a guide to salary levels. A training contract will not be registered by the Law Society unless they are at the minimum figure specified in the relevant local law society's guide except when there are very exceptional circumstances. The minimum salary specified originally tended to be based on a university student's grant grossed up for a full year. Nowadays even the minimum salary levels are enough to live on in passable comfort. The bigger firms pay salaries significantly above the minimum level. They also frequently help to support applicants during the earlier years of training by paying course fees and bursaries. A student of strong academic attainment willing to accept training in a good commercial firm of the larger size has every chance of receiving substantial financial support during the legal practice course or common professional examination.

Despite the somewhat frequent attacks levelled by the press upon the solicitor's profession, a would-be solicitor can expect high standards of personal and professional behaviour from his or her colleagues. The levels of competence of the profession are rising under the new training and education regulations. An increasingly competitive edge has entered the working life of solicitors. In the future this will become even more marked. Nevertheless, I believe few who enter the profession will have cause to regret their choice. The work is both challenging and satisfying and also of great social value and there is still a great deal of personal control over one's professional life together with an ever-increasing diversity of career opportunities.

The financial side of qualifying

At present those who are well off have a distinct advantage in qualifying in either branch of the profession. During the initial degree, the financial position is the same as for other degree students. During the further year at college, or the further two years for non-law graduates, the position is more complicated.

It is possible that a local authority grant will be available for the Legal Practice Course or even for the extra common professional examination year. It is quite unlikely that a grant will be available for both. It is possible that you will obtain a grant for neither. The award of a grant is in the discretion of your local authority and policies and practices vary from authority to authority and from year to year.

Once you become a trainee solicitor you will be paid enough to live on — this topic is discussed above. But, there is still a period for many students — and for nearly all would-be barristers — when money has to be found from some source or other. The main banks may offer loan schemes on fairly generous terms for students qualifying in the professions. Loans for two or three years when no payments have to be made and interest accumulates below market rates are offered. The loan and the accumulated interest is then repaid in the early years of practice. In recent years, these loans have proved of value to numerous students.

The availability of training places

At the time of writing (1998) there are more would-be solicitors' trainees than there are places in training contracts. This illustrates very forcibly the way in which the profession is inexorably linked in its growth and prosperity to the financial state of the country as a whole. The 1980s were a time of unprecedented expansion and considerable financial success for solicitors in general. The 1990s commenced on a much more low key note. Some of the very large and successful firms were forced to make redundancies. The number of training places fell back. One effect of this has been to increase competition between students. Doing well on the degree and the vocational course is important. An element of vocation, even considerable willingness to accept relative hardship, may be necessary for someone struggling to enter the profession. I have no doubt myself that the profession is set on a long-term path of growth and prosperity. But, experience has shown that those who leave the profession quite often do not return. It is probable that for some years there will remain an excess of persons qualified for training places over the number of training contracts firms feel they can make available. This will obviously colour your approach to your studies.

11 Becoming a barrister

The Bar is a very small profession. There are approximately 9,000 practising barristers. The following table, taken from the *Law Society Gazette* (28 January 1998), p25, illustrates this:

	1996	Oct 1997
All independent barristers in England and Wales	8935	9369
Women barristers in England and Wales	2115	2272
Barristers in London	5883	6171
Women barristers in London	1403	1513
Barristers outside of London	3052	3198
Women barristers outside of London	712	759
Queen's Counsel in England and Wales	925	974
Women Queen's Counsel	60	63
Queen's Counsel in London	781	827
Women Queen's Counsel in London	53	57
Queen's Counsel outside of London	144	147
Women Queen's Counsel outside of London	7	6
Chambers in England and Wales		576
in London		302
outside London		274
Independent barristers in England and Wales practising as sole practitioners		156
Employed barristers in England and Wales		2450
Women employed barristers		938

Many more have qualified as barristers and taken up a career in the Civil Service, industry or commerce. The barrister's profession remains, to the general public, more glamorous than the solicitor's. The reality, particularly for the young barrister, may be rather different. For the newly qualified barrister unless he is very lucky life at the Bar is comparatively gruelling and for some years at least not overpaid.

Practising barristers work together in small groups called chambers. A set of barristers in chambers share an office and other administrative expenses. Their office and their business life is organised by their clerk with a number of clerical and secretarial assistants. Although the barristers share chambers, they do not work in partnership. Barristers work for themselves and must depend on themselves for work and income. This last is an essential distinction between life at the Bar and life in a solicitor's office. There is no holiday pay, no sick pay and no pension fund. Barristers are dependent from the beginning to the end of their careers — or until elevation to the bench — upon their own earning power and physical and mental resources.

The main clients a practising barrister has are solicitors. It is these he or she must impress if the practice is to become worthwhile. All contacts with solicitors in the way of arrangements of fees, collection of fees and the making of appointments and acceptance of briefs are conducted through the clerk — although the maintenance of punctilious ethics is no longer quite so absolute. The barrister's clerk is, thus, a pivotal part of the process by which a fledgling barrister will gain a reputation with potential client solicitors.

Because of its size, the Bar can be greatly affected by the incidental effect of legislative changes of procedural reform. In the late 1960s and early 1970s the Bar enjoyed a boom resulting from increases in legal aid work. From the mid-1970s on, the volume of work suffered considerably because of withdrawal of legal aid for various areas of divorce and other work.

The picture in recent years has been a large number of qualifying barristers pursuing an apparently non-increasing amount of work. There have been suggestions that the Bar is over-crowded and attempts made to restrict the number qualifying — of which more below. There has also been an increase in the number of new chambers established or split off from existing sets. Overall it is probably correct to say that a newly qualified barrister will find that these are not balmy days. But an advocate of outstanding quality, a person who is prompt and thorough in paperwork and in preparation will always make his or her mark. There is always work available for those with a demonstrable aptitude.

Qualifying as a barrister

Like the solicitor's profession, the barrister's scheme of education is divided into an academic and a vocational stage. Virtually all entrants will be graduates and most of these graduates with a law degree. Graduates in other subjects take the common professional examination (Chapter 10). Whether the student is a graduate in law or another subject, generally speaking a lower second class honours degree must have been achieved.

The regulations dealing with the acceptance of non-degree students and those without a second class honours degree are not considered here. They are to be found together with other information of assistance to would-be barristers in the Calendar of the Council of Legal Education (address in Appendix 5)

Bar vocational courses

The bar vocational course is available in the following places:

BPP – London
College of Law – London
Cardiff University and University of West of England (joint course)
Inns of Court School of Law – London
University of Northumbria at Newcastle
Manchester Metropolitan University

Entry to the course is though a clearing system called CACHE. The system is that applicants obtain a computer disk from the Bar Council. The necessary details of the application are added to the disk which is then returned to the Bar Council.

All the above have available a one-year full-time course. In addition there are the following:

(i)   the Inns of Court School of Law has a two-year part-time course;
(ii) the University of Northumbria has a four-year LLB which exempts its graduates from the Bar vocational course (see p 211).

All the Bar vocational courses are approved by the Bar Council and cover broadly the same law and skills areas. Applicants are allowed to list **three** choices in order of preference. Application to the four-year LLB at the University of Northumbria is through the usual UCAS system. Presently there are substantially more applicants than places on the course. This means that some care must be taken in filling in the application form.

The form gives the applicant the opportunity to demonstrate their suitability for the barrister's profession. Experience of activities such as mooting, mock trials, work experience in the legal profession are important. Experience of debating, activity in student societies are other things that may be valuable. There is no doubt, despite the relevance of these things, that the most weighty factor is academic experience – primarily the class of degree obtained – although A levels and GCSE O levels are important.

Routes to qualification

The different routes to qualification are described in the following paragraphs. It must be noted first that those intending to practise must

Table One

Routes to qualifications for barristers who intend to practise at the Bar of England and Wales.

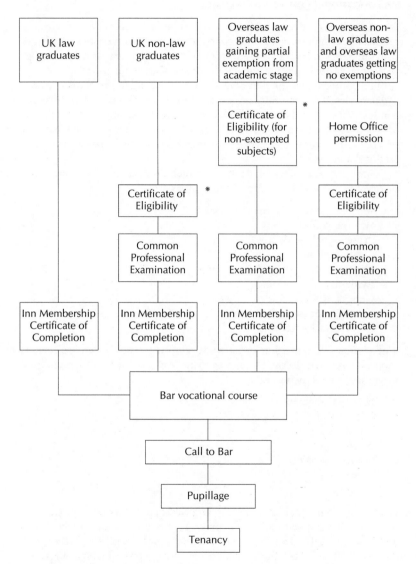

Certificates of Eligibility to sit the Common Professional Examination are issued by the CPE Board at the Council of Legal Education (address in Appendix 5).

follow one of the routes set out in Table One (prepared by the Council of Legal Education).

The vocational course for barristers

All persons intending to qualify to practise in England and Wales are required to attend the vocational course at one of the universities or colleges providing this course. The course runs for one academic year from October to the end of June and is arranged in three ten-week terms.

The course is designed to give practical training in the skills required by barristers. It concentrates on court procedure, evidence and professional conduct. In the third term students elect to specialise in one of three areas of practice. These are general practice, commercial practice and Chancery practice. The latter is concerned with areas such as real property, trusts and landlord and tenant.

There are nine areas of study for which there is specially published material from Blackstone Press. These areas are:

> Advocacy and inter-personal skills
> Written skills
> Professional conduct
> Civil litigation
> Criminal litigation and sentencing
> Evidence
> General practice
> Chancery practice
> Commercial practice

The course is designed in order to develop the skills which are seen as especially relevant to the life of a barrister and the course designers have identified the following skills:

> Fact management
> Legal research
> Interviewing
> Negotiating
> Opinion writing
> Drafting
> Advocacy

During the course, tuition is both by large lectures and small group tutorial work. There are specific areas of knowledge to be covered during the course and these are dealt with as follows. First, great emphasis is given to the topics of *adjectival* law. This is the law concerned with the procedure in court cases. This is largely taught in the first half of the case in three topics — Civil litigation, criminal litigation and evidence. Other material is covered by a series of short course modules and overview lectures at appropriate places during the course. A short-course module might last from, say, five to thirteen weeks and the following topics are covered:

> Basic accounts
> Business associations
> European Community law
> Sentencing
> Tax

Overview lectures are used to provide a background of awareness to important areas of law which may arise in practice.

The topics to be covered in these lectures may, for example, be:

> Conflict of laws
> Human rights
> Legal Aid
> Social security law
> Family law
> Sale of goods
> Landlord and tenant

In addition to these topics, teaching based upon the Bar's Code of Conduct is intended to permeate the course.

Assessment on the vocational course

Multiple choice tests are used to assess memorised knowledge in civil litigation, criminal litigation and evidence. The skills programme is assessed by in-course assessments during the year. These are based on practical case studies. The third term ends with the final assessment. This is described by the Inns of Court School of Law as follows:

> It consists of a videoed advocacy presentation by each student, and four written papers, one of them on the module work of the third term and the other three testing the application of the remaining six skills.

These final assessments are not a memorisation exercise. Candidates are entitled to use their course materials and expected to show a competent standard at the skills necessary for the early days of practice at the bar.

Entry to the vocational course

Formerly a person who was a member of an Inn of Court and intended to practise in any member state of the European Community and had the required standard of degree was entitled to entry onto the vocational course. The current position is that entry is competitive. An application must be obtained from the Bar Council. This must be submitted by October in the year before entry. Candidates will be required to take a critical reasoning test.

Joining an Inn of Court

All barristers belong to one or other of the four Inns of Court — Gray's Inn, Lincoln's Inn, Middle Temple and Inner Temple. Before you register on the vocational course, you must have joined, or be in the process of joining, an Inn. You will normally join an Inn as a student member before completing your degree. If you do so, as most students do, before the end of your law degree then you must satisfy certain rather complex requirements as to your GCE or equivalent examination passes. The requirement is spelt out in a complex fashion in the annual calendar of the Council of Legal Education (Schedule 1, Category 11(b)). It is broadly equivalent to grade C passes at 'A' level but each aspirant student should check his own qualifications against the regulations.

It is not very material which Inn you select. It used to be said: Lincoln's Inn for Chancery work, Gray's for the provinces and overseas students, Middle Temple for the poor and Inner Temple for the rich. There is no more than the faintest glimmer of truth in this aphorism. Personal, family or college contacts may direct you towards one Inn or another. Otherwise, it does not greatly matter which you elect to join. Barristers from different Inns can and do practise in chambers together. It is said that Gray's Inn has the best in alcoholic refreshment and the quaintest dining customs involving the dining barristers in a variety of verbal practical jokes and rituals. Such considerations may sway you one way or the other.

Pupillage

After passing your Bar examination you will enter into pupillage. Pupillage is a period of twelve months spent as an unpaid assistant to a fairly senior barrister. During this period you will be expected to learn sufficient about the ways of the legal system to be able thereafter to practise as a barrister without any direct supervision.

You will receive no salary during pupillage. However, some chambers do make quite substantial pupillage awards to their pupils. During the second six months of your pupillage you will be able to receive briefs. It is not very likely, however, that solicitors will rush to instruct you — although you may be lucky in being given work other members of your chambers are too busy to handle.

Training during pupillage

Here is a description of the pupillage system as it operated until quite recently:

The traditional arrangement for pupillage was that a newly-qualified barrister, in return for a fee of 100 guineas, became the pupil of an established junior barrister, the master. Payment of the fee entitled the pupil to have accommodation in the chambers of his master, sometimes in the same room, to see his paperwork and to accompany him to court, receiving advice and instruction on what was done. At a later stage of his progress, the pupil might hope to be found a little work of his own. If he was judged to have done this well, and fitted by age, ability and disposition into his master's set of chambers, he might hope to be offered a seat in chambers when pupillage was completed ... The system described above worked well in the first half of this century for those who had the connections and the money, and the recognised ability or good fortune, to enable them to find a conscientious pupil master in a good set of chambers. (*Royal Commission on Legal Services* 1979 p 643)

This extract still captures the essential flavour of pupillage. The training given is still largely unstructured. In the first six months a pupil is not allowed to receive instructions on his or her own account or appear in court. At the end of that first six months the pupil master will sign a certificate saying that the pupil has completed six month's satisfactory pupillage. From that time for the remainder of the pupillage the pupil is entitled to appear in court and accept instructions on his or her behalf. At the end of the year of pupillage a certificate is given by the pupil master that the year's pupillage is completed.

During pupillage there is little control over the content of training. Pupils are required to complete a formal check-list of the experience gained during pupillage. The check-list must be of a form approved by the Bar Council.

The financial side of pupillage

There is a book published by the Senate of the Inns of Court and the Bar giving details of awards to pupils offered by chambers in London and the provinces. This will be given to you when you register as a student on the vocational course. In addition, the various Inns each have their own booklets, giving details of the awards on offer to their students. In each case this is available directly from the Inn. There are scholarships awarded as a result of special examinations or other tests of scholastic merit, as a result of testimonial and interview or for success in the Bar examinations. If you are lucky, you may obtain enough for your subsistence from such a source.

You cannot count on earnings of any substance being received during the year you spend in pupillage. Neither is it wise to expect very much from part-time earnings. You will need to make a sound impression in your pupillage year and the period immediately following. Your earliest chances for work will come from briefs which your more established colleagues in chambers are too busy to take on. It is important to be available to pick up any similar opportunity. Equally, your reputation will be formed during these early months. You cannot afford to lose work because you are involved in some part-time activity.

Nevertheless, there are opportunities in legal journalism and quite a reasonable chance of finding some part-time law teaching work at one of the many colleges where law is taught. I would advise you to accept such a commitment only outside normal court hours otherwise, because of your prior commitment to honour your teaching obligation, you will have to forgo court work from time to time.

The Bar Council has, since 1988, recommended that sets of chambers make grants or payment to their pupils during the pupillage year. The more lucrative commercial sets of chambers are in a position to make substantial payments not dissimilar to the amount graduates can expect to earn in London. Other sets of chambers may find such payments realistically out of the question. A 'safety net' can be provided by chambers providing that pupils will have guaranteed earnings up to a certain amount.

The financial position of newly qualified barristers remains unsatisfactory for those who believe that professions should be open to all on a basis of fair competition rather than financial or social background. For the most able, there is the chance of attracting sufficient financial support and making a flying start at fee-earning. But it must be very few who qualify and continue into practice relying entirely upon their own resources. The topic of bank loans for students has been mentioned above in Chapter 10. A would-be solicitor feeling sure of future employment is perhaps safer relying on such a loan than a would-be barrister.

In an established chambers, the new barrister, rather than having to attract his own work, can cut his teeth on work which is sent to the chambers because of the standing of its other members or their long-standing harmonious relationship with instructing solicitors. Much of the work in a good chambers is in fact attracted to the chambers rather than the individual barrister. A well-inclined clerk, impressed by the start you have made, may well ensure that as a new entrant you receive a fair opportunity by being given a share of this work. You will have already realised that the quality of chambers in which you find yourself is a very important contribution to eventual success.

Obtaining pupillage and obtaining chambers

Places for pupils, as for articled clerks, are found only in a very haphazard fashion. It seems a fair summary to describe the process of finding pupillage in the way one barrister described it to the author — as a lottery.

There is no neat solution to the problem of obtaining pupillage. When you join an Inn as a student member you will be able to join the sponsorship scheme in which a senior member of the Bar becomes your sponsor. The sponsor may be able and willing to assist with pupillage. In each Inn now, there are chambers which make vacancies known to the pupillage committee of their Inn and interview would-be appointees with the intention of selecting those apparently most able.

It is still generally true that students have to rely on family, connections or pot-luck. It is an unlucky student who cannot find chambers in which to complete pupillage — but the real problem is that completion of a pupillage does not in itself enable you to commence in practice. In order to practise as a barrister it is essential to find a seat in chambers after your pupillage has finished. The chance of doing so is obviously greatly enhanced if the pupillage has with it some prospect of a permanent place in chambers. Even if this is the case, winning that place will depend largely on 'if your face fits'. School, family and college background are still much more important than one would expect in a career which in the public interest ought to be 'open to talents'. This is one of the many facts which lead a great number of informed commentators to propose that the legal profession should no longer have control over their own schemes of entry and training. It is fair, though, to say that the pupillage system has undergone in recent years a slight transformation towards a more rational system of placement and the immediate future is likely to see further efforts towards improvement.

Obtaining a pupillage in the provinces (ie outside London) is even more a matter of relying on existing connections or manufacturing your own. It used to be said a few years ago that the student finding pupillage outside London would have a good chance of obtaining a seat, subject to being approved by his or her fellow barristers. As to the present time, this does not seem to be so and the provincial pupil, also, might very well have 'no place to go' at the end of pupillage.

Barristers who have completed their pupillage do, especially in London, quite commonly hang on for a further period or periods of six months as 'squatters' or 'floaters' trying to eke out a living while they wait for something to turn up. Many give up the struggle and seek more secure employment in the Civil Service, in government posts in Europe, or in commerce, or industry. The qualification as a barrister remains perfectly marketable.

12 The postgraduate study of law

Research in law has very different meanings. Students may find it interesting to consider the varieties of research in which they find their own teachers are engaged and the importance of this to the development and improvement of the legal system. The range of law research undertaken at law schools has grown quite considerably over the past decade or so. It may, briefly, be described and divided into the following categories.

Empirical research

The last twenty years or so have seen a more or less general recognition that empirical (or socio-legal) research has a proper place in law schools. These two expressions refer to studying aspects of law in operation or aspects of the legal system using the methods developed by social science. This methodology involves, for example, survey research through questionnaires or interviews, the systematic analysis of official or other published statistics or the use of techniques as varying as participant observation and content analysis.

If you have an opportunity on your undergraduate course to study the methodology of social enquiry you will find the exercise very valuable. The past few years have seen a sometimes vitriolic debate as to the worth and objectivity of the social science method. The debate has entered the political arena. Much of the criticism has been ignorant or bigoted — unfortunately the debate has detracted in the public regard from the strength of the social sciences as the legal profession can all too easily learn to decry the profound insights which are to be gained from social scientific enquiry.

An example of the areas of disagreement may be of interest and illustrate also the difficulties involved in producing social-scientific research of objective and lasting value. Suppose you wished to examine the behaviour of our county courts in actions brought by landlords against tenants in which the landlord seeks to have the tenant evicted from the premises. These actions are known to lawyers as 'possession actions' since the landlord's aim is almost invariably the eviction of the tenant. You could readily examine the frequency of such cases and the success of defendants. You could relate this statistically to whether defendants had legal representation. These are objective matters and an indisputably objective survey can be undertaken. But, you will also wish to obtain more quantitative data. How do judges treat tenants? What is the quality of performance of lawyers assigned to these cases? Are they well-prepared in the complex law involved? Is the law properly applied in difficult cases? You will wish to obtain by your study of some county courts on certain days data that is of more universal validity.

Some of these questions are ones the investigator will have to use indirect measures to test. It might be relevant to consider the length of cases or the age or experience of the solicitors involved. It might be relevant to try to record what happens between the parties in the precincts of the court during periods of adjournment. What kind of bargains as to payment of arrears of rent are struck between the parties? What role does a tenant's legal adviser play in any such negotiation? Can an observer who might feel strongly as to the political and social issues involved produce a scientific record of what happens? Developing techniques to study such difficult areas of social behaviour is one of the most exciting areas of research. You will readily see how interesting involvement in such work could prove, and how vital it is to the improvement of our legal system. You will also see how easily evidence produced in such investigations can be the source of political controversy and how important it is that the analysis of accumulated data, or even its very collection, is not distorted by the researcher's own strongly felt beliefs. During your professional life and the education which precedes it, you will often be presented with arguments based on conclusions from research of a similar nature. In order to assess for yourself whether the evidence produced is reliable it will be essential to have some understanding of the nature and techniques of social science research.

Traditional legal scholarship

The bulk of academic lawyers, however, are involved in research of a very different nature. They engage in legal writing and the scholarship precedent to this, having as their aim the production of a book or an article in a journal. The variety of works to which they contribute are described at some length in Chapters 5 and 6 of this book.

There is no methodology of legal scholarship as there is of science and of social science. This sometimes leads research of this kind to be regarded in a different light from research that is more easily seen to be such.

Work of this kind is the province of the person who is interested in library work. It is not necessarily, though, work completed entirely on one's own and working in a team on a writing project can prove very satisfying indeed. The work can also prove very exciting. Changes in the law, whether case law or statute law, can obviously stimulate very great controversy. Commenting on the developments gives one a chance to contribute to or provoke constructive debate.

Other fields of research

Apart from traditional legal scholarship and the socio-legal field, there are other areas in which the law graduate may be able to pursue an interest in research. Mention has already been made in Chapters 4 and 5 of the growing role of computers in legal education. A few universities are undertaking research in this field and advertise occasionally for research students or research assistance. Lawyers interested in a research or teaching career could also consider taking a qualification in some related field and among the disciplines where there is research carried out with a strong legal flavour are: information (librarianship), economics, history and political science. A period of systematic exposure to ideas other than as presented by lawyers or academic lawyers is likely to benefit any aspiring researcher.

Becoming involved in legal research: taking a postgraduate degree in law

Further degrees in law will be by research, by further course work or by a combination of both. There is considerable variety of one-year postgraduate courses in law and some opportunity for further study.

A taught Master's course leading to LLM or equivalent qualification will not represent all that dramatic a change from your first degree course. It will consist of a variety of lectures and seminars and lead to examinations very similar to your previous law examinations.

What is to be gained by such a course? You may wish to study an area which you have studied previously only scantily or not at all. There are, for example, such programmes taught in Britain in sociology and law, criminology, comparative law, international law and welfare law.

Equally you may simply wish to study in a different or a particular college. There is much to be said for taking a postgraduate course in a different jurisdiction. It does seem sensible for anyone who can find the opportunity to do so to spend a year studying law in the United States of America. Both the legal system and the system of legal education experienced in another jurisdiction will prove good sources of constructive criticism of our own style of doing things.

Selecting a postgraduate course

A student embarking upon a postgraduate course should have good upper second class ability. It is not perhaps as necessary that you have actually achieved this standard on your degree as that you have the requisite ability and motivation. You will receive considerably less direct teaching and supervision on a postgraduate course. If you are not certain of your ability your tutor should readily provide a frank opinion.

You will at an early stage need to choose between a taught postgraduate course and one pursued primarily by research. Taught courses have been briefly described. An LLM by research will almost certainly take you more than one full-time year to complete, and although three years are allowed for a doctorate by research most students who complete do exceed this period.

Pursuing a degree by research will prove more taxing and ultimate completion of the degree is a good deal less certain. It is not a course to embark upon unless you have a good clear idea of the area in which you will carry out work. You will also need the backing and encouragement of a supervisor who is interested in your project and willing to devote a considerable slice of time to assisting you.

Law teachers have very different attitudes to the role to be adopted by a supervisor in a research project. Obviously the work must be that of the student and not of the supervisor. But attitudes to the proper amount of help and supervision to give vary very greatly. For the student, however, there can be no doubt that the greater the amount of assistance, advice and critical appraisal you receive, the more chance there is of achieving a successfully completed thesis.

For this reason, caution is advised before embarking upon a degree by research only. Seek to ensure that your supervisor has some real and abiding interest in the research you propose. Test his or her reactions carefully to ascertain that you are starting with reasonable horizons to your research. You cannot research into a subject as large and open-ended as 'the need for reform of property law' (though there may be a crying need!) nor can you pursue for a whole thesis the case law on frustration of a lease! You need from the beginning a specification of your project which is neither too ambitious nor too easily exhausted and you will almost certainly need the assistance of a committed supervisor in arriving at this specification.

The life of a research student or research assistant

If you pursue a further degree by a course of study and examination, then your working life will be very much the same as in your under-graduate days. If you enrol for a degree by research alone or obtain a post as a research assistant it will be different. As a research student or research worker you will be very much in control of your own pattern of work. There will be no, or virtually no, lectures or seminars for you to attend. Very often formal supervision is less than one session with your supervisor per week. You will require a capacity for independent work and the ability to organise yourself and meet deadlines which you have set yourself or, more satisfactorily, set in consultation with your supervisor. Many students who embark upon degrees by research fail to complete and obtain the desired qualification. The underlying cause is very often the failure to create a framework within which to stage completion of the various parts of their programme. There is a temptation to delay writing up any section of the final report. This is very risky. The longer you delay putting pen to paper, the more timorous you will become. The task will seem even greater. Your files of notes and boxes of findings will multiply around you. If you can, early on in your research, formulate a clear idea of the shape of your final report or thesis, this will help you greatly. You will be able to begin writing early chapters on previous research in the area, background, design of your research programme and so on. Once your writing is well under way the mountain you have to climb will shrink into perspective. Final completion will seem assured.

Part-time research

It is worth mentioning that even after you qualify as a lawyer or begin some different career there are still possibilities for research. A part-time further degree can be obtained either by a course of study or by research. Both routes are arduous. Obtaining a Master's degree by evening study will take two or three years of attendance at college. Obtaining a research degree by part-time study is likely to take at least three years. Neither is a course to be embarked upon unless you are strongly motivated and can be reasonably hopeful that the domestic and work situation will leave you ample time to devote to study.

Other than a further degree as such, there are interesting professional qualifications which can be obtained by part-time study. Three examples that might interest lawyers as their careers develop are in accountancy, arbitration and taxation. The Association of Certified Accountants* offers a Diploma in Accounting and Finance. This is available for non-accountants to gain a grasp of the subject and could be of great interest to lawyers operating in a commercial environment. The Institute of Taxation offers qualifications based on its own examinations which are fairly stringent. The Chartered Institute of Arbitrators also has its own examination scheme. Although membership of the institute is not required in order to practise as an arbitrator it would undoubtedly assist in obtaining entry to this field of work. You should note that the minimum age for full membership is 35.

* The addresses of the professional bodies mentioned here are given in Appendix 5.

Finance for a research degree

Grants are awarded in small numbers by the Research Council, the British Academy, or the Department of Education and Science. (For useful addresses see Appendix 6) Before making application for an award obtain careful advice from your tutor as to the appropriate body and procedure as this will depend on the particular course or programme which you have in mind. Competition is very great and a very good second class degree will normally be the minimum requirement.

In order to obtain a current list of law schools in the Commonwealth and the degrees they offer, write to T C Colchester at the Commonwealth Legal Education Association, c/o Legal Division, Commonwealth Secretariat, Marlborough House, Pall Mall, London SW1Y 5HY, and ask for the *Directory of Schools of Law in the Commonwealth*. Your law school will have a copy of this directory in any event. The further directories listed in Appendix 6 will assist you in discovering other sources of funding both in the Commonwealth and elsewhere.

If your interest lies in the United States of America, then there are suitable courses and funds available. The address from which to gain further current information on the awards and scholarships available is given in Appendix 6. Some persistence may be necessary in order to obtain financial support in the United States.

The prestigious Ivy League university law schools have post-graduate study programmes which are suitable or even tailormade for overseas students. Columbia University in New York, Harvard in Boston and Yale in Connecticut are the leading law schools. Others might well have a programme that would interest you and your enquiries will reveal to you the enormous number of institutions offering law degrees in the States. To obtain a place with financial support at one of the first flight American law schools, you will need an excellent academic record. You will probably need a first class honours degree or a reference from your tutor that you were near to that standard.

The value of further academic qualification?

Very few practising lawyers have higher degrees. It is also a perhaps surprising feature of law teaching that very many, perhaps the majority, of law teachers do not have higher degrees. What considerations, therefore, might propel you down this not overly well-trodden path?

It is certainly at present much harder to obtain a teaching post in law in higher education than it has been for several decades. If you wish to become a law teacher, a further qualification may be a help. It is another curious fact of life that very many law teachers have no professional qualification or experience of practice. Either further academic qualification or professional experience or both is to be desired.

It may be that a further degree of some kind may be a useful means of entry to specialised areas of practice. There are specialist commercial law degrees available and a performance of distinction on one of these may conceivably assist in finding a place in a large London firm. It has to be said, though, that the academic and practitioner's legal worlds remain undesirably far apart and the effect of dazzling academic qualifications upon the hardened and successful practitioner can well be less than startling.

In reality, it will interest in the thing itself which drives you on to further study in law and which will provide both the excuse and the justification. Even students not so motivated will find in the years ahead that they have to participate in compulsory continuing professional education. (At present this applies only to the majority of qualified solicitors.) So the spectre of the classroom will remain even for the least enthusiastic! The immediate past has seen quite an improvement in the training and education of lawyers, particularly solicitors. The future with its twin challenges of ever more complex and multivariate legislation and of an increasingly rugged climate of competition, makes it ever more important for lawyers to be fully equipped for their task. There will certainly be an ever-increasing need for specialists in many fields.

Lawyers now find themselves in an area of continuous and far-reaching law reform. Their working practices are being radically altered by new technology. Their professional codes are, quite rightly, under the continuous scrutiny of a much more consumerist society. You can have no doubt that even with all this background of change which will amount to a revolution in the lives of the legal professions lawyers will have an increasingly important role to play in our more complex society. The challenge which you have set yourself in embarking upon the study of law is, thus, as boundless as it is important.

Continuing professional education

The Law Society has recognised that solicitors' education will continue throughout their career. A scheme for compulsory continuing education for solicitors was first introduced in 1985. Initially the scheme applied only to those qualifying after that date but it is being extended to cover the preponderate number of practising solicitors. The scheme involves attending a small number of courses during each year and collecting the required number of continuing education points. Continuing education has, of course, as its prime purpose the updating of the solicitor's legal knowledge and skill. It is not intended to be an extension merely of academic study. However, it is possible for solicitors to continue their compulsory continuing education with the acquisition of valuable vocational qualifications. London Guildhall University, for example, has an MA in business law from which the commercial practitioner can gain much. Northumbria University has an LLM (Advanced Legal Practice). This includes topics such as marketing, financial management and personnel management. It also permits development of a particular area of specialist practice such as commercial property or professional negligence litigation. Specialisation within the profession is undoubtedly a major force for the future and courses such as these will be important in assisting in such development. The Bar has also taken the first steps toward a system of compulsory continuing education.

13 The use of legal study

It would not give a complete picture to the student to finish without giving some idea of the value of the study of law. It is not intended to give a guide to all the many careers which are open to law graduates. Instead the available possibilities will be considered in a more general and wide-ranging way and also consideration given to the more general benefits that may be derived from legal education.

The legal professions

Enough may have been said already to convince the reader that a complete and rounded legal education can be obtained only by pursuing, after the academic stage of legal education, a professional qualification. It may very well be desirable that all students and all teachers of law should be exposed to and at some time involved in legal practice to a greater or lesser degree. But, there are very many reasons why entering one of the legal professions does not suit each law student and there is, of course, very much of benefit to be gained from a study of law in the lecture and seminar room alone.

The content of legal study

The first gain from the study of law is that things are learned which are of use to any citizen. In other European countries it is quite usual to find that some study of law, the legal system and the process of government is a mandatory part of the school curriculum. This is not so in Britain and as a consequence our educational system is the poorer and our citizens less able to analyse for themselves many of the complex social phenomena found in twentieth-century life.

Equally valuable is the training in reasoning and dialectic which is derived from studying law. It is perhaps this above all facets of legal education which has resulted in lawyers being able to find attractive career prospects in many walks of life other than the two legal professions. At the end of the day, the degree to which legal education develops your powers of critical reasoning and skills of analysis is more important than the minute detail of individual legal rules. The facilities developed by grappling with the difficult and conflicting arguments and concepts gained in lectures, seminars and private study will be of inestimable value thereafter. There are many careers available to the qualified lawyer and many where a previous study of law will be directly relevant or at least of value. It is proposed to examine the widely varying career possibilities commencing first with the typical career patterns of a solicitor.

Career opportunities as a solicitor

Assuming you have completed your education as a solicitor and finished your term of articles — what careers are available?

The range of firms engaged in private practice has already been outlined in Chapter 10. If you take the decision, as the overwhelming bulk of solicitors do, to remain in private practice, then the first divide to cross is whether you wish to practise in a 'City' firm or in provincial private practice.

In provincial private practice you would expect, if of good practical ability and if willing to work whole-heartedly in your firm, to be rewarded with a partnership by your early thirties. There is no set career pattern. For some the offer of partnership will come earlier and for others not at all. The terms on which you are offered a partnership will vary greatly. An example will illustrate how your career might develop.

Suppose you join the firm of Austin, Peabody and Mitchell in Oldcastle. There are four existing partners and they take you on as one of their three assistant solicitors dealing variously with domestic conveyancing, commercial conveyancing and criminal litigation. You join them as a neophyte assistant solicitor and quickly find your feet as an advocate. You will have an office of your own and your own secretary. From the start you will deal with your own clients. Your days will be spent in interviewing clients, representing them in court, and in dictating correspondence and other documents. If you have very serious crimes on your plate, these clients may be represented by counsel and either you or, more probably, a clerk from your office will attend the court with the barrister.

After perhaps a few years as an assistant solicitor you will be offered a partnership. What will this mean? The four existing partners own a business together. They may as a partnership own premises and cars and will undoubtedly own furniture, office equipment and a library. They will expect payment for your share of this. In addition, the existing partners own a valuable business in the form of the firm's established goodwill and hence profitability. They will also expect some contribution from you towards this.

Your payment for the share of the firm which you will acquire on becoming a partner may come either from accepting a salaried partnership for a period of time, accepting a reduced share of the profits or from a direct capital contribution.

In contrast if you work in a large 'City' firm then you will be working as part of a much larger team. There is likely to be a more distinct hierarchical organisation. The process of becoming a full partner will be longer and more problematical. The work you undertake is likely to be more specialised or compartmentalised and to require a higher degree of legal skill. You will work for a much longer period of time under supervision. In the long run, the financial rewards may be very great indeed.

Types of solicitors' practice

It might be of assistance to persons contemplating a career in the legal profession to give a clearer idea of the types of practice available. Solicitors practise in firms varying in size from the 'one man band' to firms with over a hundred partners. What are they like?

The 'one man band' or sole practitioner may be a very unprofitable outfit carrying out a range of mixed private client work, mostly routine conveyancing and probate. It may be, on the other hand, a highly profitable enterprise run by a flamboyant practitioner with a flair for some particular area of work. Many sole practitioners make only a modest living in the region of £30,000 per annum; many make a very good living indeed dealing with a large volume of work handled by supervised clerks.

The typical provincial firm of solicitors might be the firm of Austin, Peabody and Mitchell already briefly described. It is this type of firm which has been regarded widely as the model for the profession. It has a spacious building in a Georgian terrace in the centre of Bath or York. The partners have quiet offices furnished with rows of scarcely disturbed calf-bound texts, heavy wooden furniture and gilt-framed prints. The bulk of the work is what is known as 'private client'. That is, handling the legal affairs of reasonably affluent persons. Important areas of work will be conveyancing of houses, dealing with the estates of deceased clients, unravelling the property disputes arising from matrimonial problems and probably some criminal work. The larger the firm the greater the emphasis on the commercial clients and the greater their size.

In the larger provincial towns and cities there will be firms that see themselves as primarily commercial. They may have between fifteen and forty partners. Clients will be development companies, local authorities, building societies, housing associations and bodies such as universities, hospitals and independent colleges. Here the work will be becoming more specialised although still in wide bands — the partners specialising in different kinds of property work, general company work, construction and development and so on. Partners in medium-size firms in smaller towns may expect to earn in the region of £50,000–£100,000 and in the larger commercial provincial firms sums in excess of £100,000 per annum are not uncommon.

The very largest firms are nearly all in London and these nearly all in or proximate to the City of London. A typical firm might be Margraves. Firmly esconced in EC1 it occupies twenty floors of a glittering glass tower within 200 metres of the Bank of England. There are 110 partners and just under 1,000 employees in total. The most senior partners earn sums in excess of £250,000 pa. But, there are several tiers of partners and the route to the top is lengthy. Clients include foreign states, government departments, one of the large clearing banks, a handful of the best known public companies, a fashionable London football club and so on. The work is highly specialised. Lawyers tend to work in teams which may be long-lasting or established for specific projects. Specialisations may be in dealing with large-scale City frauds, dealing with company flotations on the Stock Exchange, tax planning for large landed estates, handling environmental law problems for large industrial clients …

As well as these broad categorisations of work there are firms which have quite specialised practices. There are firms with trade union based practices, firms specialising in medical work, shipping law practices and some who specialise in criminal defence. In part your own political and social predilections will determine whether you will find your niche in this kind of specialist area.

Before leaving this rough typology of types of practice it is worth singling out the 'legal aid practice'. In every large city there are firms which have specialised in dealing with the legal problems of the poorer client. Since much of the fee income derives from the legal aid scheme they are, among lawyers, characterised frequently as 'legal aid practices'. Work in such firms centres around areas such as housing, landlord and tenant, immigration law, criminal work and matrimonial and other general 'family' work. Solicitors in such firms generally do not reap or seek such great financial rewards as in other areas. Many, however, have linked their legal practice with other career developments such as in local or national politics. Some firms from such a general base have grown to be very large firms with a much wider base than their origins might have suggested. The work in such firms can be every bit as complex and satisfying as in commercially orientated firms – and, of course, much satisfaction can be derived from the nature of the practice itself.

Solicitors in local government

Local authority legal departments are often very large and they deal with an enormous range of work — conveyancing, prosecutions, civil personal injury litigation and industrial law are major areas. In addition, the legal department provides legal advice to every other department of the local authority. This might vary from a query about the legality of closing a local authority crematorium and disposing of its contents, to questions arising when parents appeal against a decision as to which school their child should attend.

Working in a local authority legal department is likely to involve the exercise of a fair degree of legal expertise and some possibility for specialisation. However, as solicitors proceed upwards in the hierarchy they become less involved in law and much more involved in administration. You will aspire ultimately to the post of Chief Executive in a large authority — a man who will have very little at all to do with the prosecution of day-to-day legal business.

A post in local government provides the beginning for what might become a long-term progressive career. The work may lack at times the cut and thrust of private practice. It will also lack the feeling of independence which might come from being the proprietor (or part-proprietor) of your own firm. It will, by way of compensation, lack the financial uncertainty which some may feel is inherent in private practice. It will provide at least as stimulating a field for the development of your legal skills as private practice.

Careers in central government

Each government department employs lawyers. Specialist lawyers operate for example, in the Home Office, the Land Registry, the Lord Chancellor's Department and the Charity Commission. Entry into any Civil Service post is by open competition. Vacancies are advertised and applicants ultimately are chosen by a Civil Service selection board. As in local government, careers can progress over a lengthy period and the ultimate reward of income and status can be every bit as good as private practice generally if never quite so high as the incomes of senior partners in large city firms.

The work involved can vary enormously. A legal assistant in the Land Registry, now in fact an Executive Agency, will specialise in conveyancing practice and within that be called upon to deal with quite difficult and technical points. A lawyer employed in the Parliamentary Counsel's office is engaged in the highly specialised task of drafting legislation and assisting in its Parliamentary progress. On the other hand a legal assistant in the Lord Chancellor's office may be concerned with supervision of the legal aid system or some aspects of court administration.

A career in one of these departments will give very little scope for individualism or making 'your own mark' for many years. The ethos of the Civil Service insists on a lengthy period of 'breaking in' employees and the career offered is not for the incautious or flamboyant.

Opportunities are available for articles in the government legal service and this may prove to be a stimulus to recruitment. The government legal service has for some years been plagued by recruitment problems and has had difficulty in drawing in the very skilled legal talent which this work demands. It may also be that the trend toward decentralisation of government services will make this work attractive to a wider range of persons.

Crown Prosecution Service

The Prosecution of Offences Act 1985, s 1 established for the first time a national prosecuting service for England and Wales. The Director of Public Prosecutions is the overall head of the Crown Prosecution Service but its actual administration is decentralised into area offices. The lawyers who conduct the prosecutions are known as Crown Prosecutors and they may be either solicitors or barristers. The overwhelming bulk of prosecutions for criminal offences is now handled by the Crown Prosecution Service which has on the whole been a success. One of the greatest hurdles it has had to overcome has been the recruitment of sufficient numbers of able lawyers to handle the work. Salaries paid by the Service have not been high and this has been an obstacle to recruitment. The work, however, has its attractions for some. It may be a good way for the young advocate to develop the necessary skills for a successful career at the Bar.

More specialist fields

The number of specialist fields in which lawyers work has grown a great deal in the past decades. There are local authority prosecuting solicitors' departments whose work speaks for itself. Public corporations such as the Post Office who are large property owners employ specialist conveyancing solicitors. The media employ lawyers who specialise in relevant areas of law — contract, defamation and, presumably, labour relations. Lawyers play a prominent part in the work of a variety of statutory bodies, such as the Race Relations Commission and the Equal Opportunities Commission. Also, there are frequent opportunities for lawyers in the various European bodies — the work in these appearing to be very highly paid but requiring some knowledge of European languages other than English.

Work in law clinics and law centres

Many lawyers would like the opportunity to work in an environment which differs from the commercialist ethos of private practice and wish to use their skills in the assistance of the more disadvantaged parts of the community. All large industrial areas have some form of public service law clinic or law centre. Frequently an experienced lawyer is required to man such an office as supervision is not available. To obtain a very good idea of the range and style of work, you should read *Legal Action*, the journal of the Legal Action Group — a pressure group formed to improve the quality of legal services and whose zealous campaigning has on the whole been very beneficial. This journal contains features, articles and commentaries on events in the legal world of especial interest to those in the 'welfare rights' field. It also contains a classified advertisement section which will give a good picture of the employment opportunities available.

Law graduates or lawyers with an inclination towards the caring professions might investigate the possibility of work in areas such as social services, the probation service, or the prison service. The skills demanded and professional ethos vary too widely amongst these differing professions to be described here. It is self-evident that different perspectives on life will be found in the law graduate aspiring to be a police officer or prison governor and the graduate aspiring to be a child–welfare officer.

The wider field of industry and commerce

For law graduates and lawyers alike, there will be many suitable vacancies in all varieties of industry and commerce where legal training will be both of value and valued by the employer. There are frequent vacancies in law publishing. Lawyers can compete on an equal or better footing with any candidate for a 'management trainee' kind of post. Many very large firms have their own legal departments. In the world of finance, institutions such as building societies and banks have very specialist legal departments and lawyers might specialise in aspects of conveyancing or trust work. Other firms require lawyers who specialise in commercial contracting. In all these areas, it would always be my advice to students that there are advantages in being professionally qualified. It undoubtedly will add to your status in the organisation and it will give your career greater flexibility. You will not find that after you have grappled with a problem your employer still feels he has to turn to a 'lawyer' for an answer.

A career at the Bar

Enough has been said in Chapter 11 to indicate that at the present moment a career at the Bar is likely to be very difficult in its early days. In your pupillage you will not have received much formal training and will have earned little money. On completing your pupillage, you are metamorphosed into a complete barrister. But, solicitors are unlikely to come flocking to your door bearing briefs marked with enticingly high fees. What will your working life actually be like?

Let us assume you have taken a place in a well-founded set of chambers which has been established for many years. Assume also that you have no family or personal connection which will cause solicitors to send you work. You will probably share a room with two or more other fairly newly qualified barristers. You will attend chambers diligently during normal working hours but, unlike your counterpart, commencing work as an assistant solicitor, you will have no ready-made allocation of work.

At first you will be given some simple work which your chambers' colleagues are too busy to undertake or which the clerk diverts to you from work sent to the chambers generally. This may involve a plea in mitigation on behalf of a convicted criminal, a simple criminal matter in the magistrates' court or some small piece of civil litigation — perhaps an interlocutory matter in divorce proceedings dealing with maintenance or custody. You are also likely to be asked to draft paperwork (pleadings or other documents) for your busier colleagues.

Although the early tasks you are given will most certainly be mundane, you will be judged by their execution. The successful barristers in your chambers will not long suffer an idle or incompetent addition to their numbers. The solicitors who send work to your chambers will soon tell your clerk if they do not wish you to be employed in their client's affairs. You will accordingly prepare even the simplest matter or piece of paperwork with the utmost thoroughness.

As you are seen to be able and effective, so your personal practice will grow. After a few years you will become as financially self-sufficient as if you had become a solicitor. After some years more, you may become very well-off indeed. Your life will then be very arduous.

Your continuing practice will depend on your continuing efficiency and ability. You will be in court most days. You may have to travel frequently and for quite lengthy distances. You will have conferences with clients on your free days and in the early evenings of days when you have been in court. You will have to read your briefs, carry out your research and draft your paperwork in the evenings and, as your practice grows, at weekends too. At the height of a busy, even hectic, career as you near your fifties you can with reasonable optimism look forward to becoming a Queen's Counsel perhaps or to the prospects of appointment to one or other judicial office. The ratio of judicial posts to suitable appointees is high.

Alternatives to practice at the Bar

Of the Bar it may well be said that many are called but few are chosen. Many qualify and practise not at all and many practise for a short time and find they are not making sufficient headway. For these, many of the career avenues already outlined in local, central and European government, or in industry or commerce are available. The qualification as a barrister still has considerable cachet and marketability. This is some comfort when considering embarking upon a career at the Bar. These days it is no disgrace at all not to succeed in establishing a viable practice or to leave to pursue some other interesting career avenue. The experience at the Bar will undoubtedly prove valuable and interesting if not necessarily profitable.

Foreseeing the future

An outline has now been given which is sufficient to provide a clear indication of the enormous range of employment possibilities which you may pursue after your formal legal education is complete. You will also be interested in trying to formulate some view as to what the future holds in store for law graduates and if it promises to be more or less rosy than the past!

At the time of writing, the solicitor's profession is receiving considerable public attention. Its monopoly over residential conveyancing has been studied by the Farrand Committee and legislative change is taking place with the effect that non-solicitors will be permitted to provide a conveyancing service. This will involve the profession in the loss of some of the most lucrative part of its work. Other changes, too, are afoot. Solicitors are now permitted to advertise in the press and on the radio. They have relaxed their professional rules so as to allow solicitors to practise in association for instance with estate agents. These changes are indicative of a forthcoming widespread time of change in solicitors' practice.

Courts and Legal Services Act 1990

This very important Act received the Royal Assent in 1990. The purposes of the Act so far as the carrying out of legal work is concerned is stated as follows:

> **Section (17)(1)**   The general objective ... is the development of legal services in England and Wales (and in particular the advocacy, litigation, conveyancing and probate services) by making provision for new ways of providing such services and a wider choice of persons providing them.

The Act has as its goal the removing of what were seen to be undesirable restrictive practices upon the provision of legal services. In 1985 the Administration of Justice Act created the new profession of Licensed Conveyancers. These new legal professionals have as yet had little overall impact. The Courts and Legal Services Act is intended to take things very much further.

Its main effect on the legal profession appears to be in the area of conveyancing and probate. Broadly the Act will permit the work to be undertaken by banks, building societies, insurance companies and other approved bodies. It cannot be doubted that they will have in the relatively near future a significant effect on the overall shape of the profession. It is not at all likely that firms will be able to derive the bulk of their profit from house conveyancing and administration of deceased persons' estates. Some firms may find the change very hard to accommodate within established work practices and partnership structures.

The Courts and Legal Services Act presages changes in court work. It opens up the possibility of a wider range of advocacy work available for solicitors. This is, at the present time, an area of considerable uncertainty. It may be that both at the Bar and in the solicitor's profession the real future lies with the more specialist practitioner. There will also, without doubt, be a higher proportion of employed lawyers in the future.

From the profession's own point of view, employed lawyers have in the past been 'looked down on'. Both barristers and solicitors regarded private practice as the main stream of each profession. But, there has been a growth over the past decade in the number of solicitors and barristers employed in large organisations. Many see the future lying as much in this area as in private practice. This is very arguable but it is quite unarguable that there will never be a shortage of demand for persons with high quality legal skills.

I do not myself have any fears as to this period of change damaging the profession — quite the reverse. As you will find, when and if you qualify, the legal professions are composed overwhelmingly of diligent and honest professional persons striving to provide a valuable public service. Competition is not to be feared. Neither to be feared is the occasion, presented by this review of the solicitor's role in conveyancing, to consider how best to improve the quality of legal services in other areas. There are many areas where the service provided can be expanded and improved. The pre-trial preparation of criminal matters, and advice and representation in welfare, landlord and tenant and housing cases, are obvious examples. I think you can look forward to an increasing diversification and improvement of the range of services offered by solicitors.

The whole development of society tends towards a world where legal regulation and hence the need for sound legal advice and representation is to the fore. There will be a growing need for the involvement of solicitors in many areas. At present there are government proposals for a wider-scale professionally qualified prosecuting service — there are also other long-overdue proposals to strengthen and extend the range of the legal aid services. All in all, there is every reason to expect that the solicitor's profession will arrive in the twenty-first century invigorated by changes that have been and are taking place in its pattern of education and training and reinforced by a period of healthy competition.

In past years, the Bar has represented a much more volatile employment picture than the solicitor's profession. At present it appears, if anything, over-manned and a hard arena in which to succeed. As discussed in Chapter 11, the profession has taken quite drastic steps to reduce the influx of new barristers. Like the solicitor's profession, the Bar will benefit from the creation of a new prosecution service and the extension of legal aid services. Perhaps the future will see renewed moves for fusion between the two professions, although this does not appear especially likely just now. It is certain that the Law Society will campaign vigorously for a wider range of judicial posts to be offered to solicitors — although it seems unlikely that this will have any dramatic effect upon career opportunities at the Bar.

Both branches of the profession are likely to be very much affected by the revolution that is taking place in office and information technology. Mention has already been made in Chapters 4 and 5 of the new role computers are coming to have in legal education. A computer terminal will, as the saying goes, soon be found upon every lawyer's desk. It will be used to retrieve information as to the state of the law by interrogating enormous databases. It will be used to call up clients' accounts. It will be used to facilitate transactions, to prepare and transmit legal documents and perhaps even to formulate legal advice. The pressure to adopt work practices which make full use of the new technology will be very great. It may drastically change the number and kinds of staff involved in legal offices. It will undoubtedly assist in sweeping away cherished but costly and otiose practices.

It used to be said in teaching law that there were two great eras of law reform. (You will discover when these were during your study of law.) The contemporary period has become one of continuous and all-embracing law reform. No area of substantive law and practice is sacred from critical investigation and sweeping renovation, renewal or replacement. This can only mean that, once embarked upon, your study of law will be never-ending. It is to be hoped that you will learn a great deal of value as a law student but accept nothing unquestioningly, and the habit of proceeding by way of knowledge and understanding to critical analysis will continue to inform your professional life.

Appendices

Contents

Law courses available

The reader is asked to note that new courses are developed every year so an accurate picture cannot be presented. The short description of each law department or college is not intended to provide a comprehensive quality guide. Be cautious about choosing or disregarding a law school on the basis of the kind of judgments of standing so prevalent in the media and elsewhere. Visiting the place you hope to study is advisable if it is practicable to do so. Talking to current students on such a visit is very illuminating.

The short description of each college was contributed either by the college or the author. The length of the entry is not to be taken as a sign of merit or demerit, approval or disapproval. It is hoped simply to capture a little of the essence of each college.

University of Wales, Aberystwyth

Courses offered:

1 LLB;
2 BA (Law);
3 LLB with French;
4 LLB with German;
5 LLB with Italian;
6 LLB with Spanish;
7 BA Law with French;
8 BA Law with German;
9 BA Law with Italian;
10 BA Law with Spanish;
11 BA Law with Accounting;
12 BA Law with Economics;
13 BA Law with Business Studies;

14   BA Law with Information Management;
15   BA Law with Politics;
16   BA Law with International Policies.

The Law Faculty at Aberystwyth was founded in 1901, and is one of the oldest in the UK. It boasts many distinguished alumni, particularly in the areas of legal practice, politics, and academic life, and retains its long-established commitment to excellence in teaching and research. The degree programmes on offer include the traditional LLB which consists almost entirely of law subjects, and various major, minor schemes, in which the study of law can be combined with that of a number of other subjects. These subjects include politics, accounting and business to name but three. The Faculty prides itself on its friendly atmosphere and excellent staff student relations, and welcomes applicants from a wide variety of backgrounds. Aberystwyth's library facilities, which include a separate Law Library on campus and the National Library of Wales (one of only five copyright libraries in the UK) only a few minutes' walk away, are among the best there is. Aberystwyth's attributes led the most recent edition of the Potter Guide to Higher Education in Britain to describe it as 'one of the luckiest universities in Britain'.

Anglia Polytechnic University

Courses offered:

1   LLB (Hons);
2   BA (Hons) Business law – subject to validation;
3   BA/BSc Law (Combined Honours);
4   LLB (Hons) 2-year Senior status law degree – subject to validation. It is expected that this will be available from 1998. If not will be available from 1999;
5   Common Professional Examination;
6   LLM/MA Sports Law – subject to validation.

Courses offered at Cambridge:

1   BA/BSc Law (Combined Honours);
2   MA/LLM International and European Business Law;
3   Legal Practice Course (in partnership with Cambridge University Board of Continuing Education and De Montfort University);
4   BA/BSc Criminology (Combined Honours) – subject to validation;
5   BA (Hons) Criminology – subject to validation from 1999.

The Anglia Law School offers a wide range of under-undergraduate, post graduate and professional/vocational, programmes of study at both the

Chelmsford and Cambridge Campuses. Degree level courses have been taught since 1963 and in September 1998 the Law School expects to admit about 300 new undergraduate students. The aim of the School is to provide a friendly, supportive and stimulating environment in which to study.

The School has over 25 full-time academic members of staff supported by visiting professors and fellows and by part-time specialist lecturers and research students. Most of the academic staff are involved in research/writing articles for academic journals/writing books but perhaps the main area of research is in sports law.

The Anglia Sports Law Research Centre is a part of the Anglia Law School. It was opened in 1997 in response to the growing demand for specialisation in the field of Sport and the Law. The Centre has quickly established itself at the cutting edge of this most important and developing area of law, with its members arranging conferences, delivering papers, writing articles and producing Sports Law Bulletin six time per year.

At Chelmsford the Law School is located on APU's Central Campus which is in the middle of the county town of Essex, close to the railway and bus stations and to the shopping, cultural and social facilities of Chelmsford. The Law School occupies the Law Building which contains lecture and seminar rooms. Virtually all law teaching takes place in this building. Central campus is a few minutes walk away from the newly built Rivermead campus where, inter alia, the library and student village are located. The Cambridge Campus is located close to the city centre, near to Parker's Piece. The theatres, museums, art galleries and other cultural and social facilities that Cambridge offers are a few minutes walk from the campus.

As well as having access to the well-stocked campus libraries and the campus wide open-access computing facilities, law students have the use of IT rooms which are only available to law students. These rooms have PCs running a range of packages. E-mail and the Internet are available to all students.

The School considers it important that all of its students develop a range of skills that are not only valued by lawyers but also by a wide range of employers. The School has developed an excellent reputation for mooting/debating/client counselling, having competed successfully in national and international competitions.

Most of the programmes offer the opportunity for the student to play a significant part in designing the make-up of his/her programme of study and in particular to choose modules from a wide range of law options as well as having the opportunity to study modules from outside the School, for example computing, business studies or languages. The latter is particularly encouraged. Many students wishing to take advantage of the opportunity to study abroad for a semester take language modules to improve their proficiency.

Contact information:

Sheila Byrne
Law School Admissions Tutor
01245 493131 x 3338
e mail: s.s.byrne@anglia.ac.uk

Birbeck College London

Course offered:

1   LLB (part-time)

The Department of Law is a newly established department within the College. It has been established as part of an expansion drive with a view to providing a distinctive University LLB programme for part-timer students in London.

The Department of Law has now been established with a complement of nine full-time staff, five part-time staff and an initial intake of 75 students on the inaugural year of the LLB programme. The initial funding of the Law Department staff and Law Library has been entirely through external sponsorship. The Corporation of London sponsored a founding Chair in law. The Rudolph Palumbo Charitable Foundation and the City Solicitors' Education Trust both established named Lectureships, supplemented by funds from British Telecom. Additional support for staffing and services has been received from British Telecom, Lord Mishcon, Lovell White Durrant (Solicitors), Digital Equipment Co Ltd, Unilever plc and Phillips Electronics UK Ltd.

This is the first London University evening degree programme in law and being newly inaugurated it is in an ideal position to reflect contemporary developments in the legal profession.

The degree programme will pay considerable attention to the integral role of European law in the English legal system and in the substantive disciplines of common law. In the light of recent changes in the legal profession and in the perceived need for a response to legal services, the LLB will also pay particular attention to developing skills in legal writing and in lawyer–client relations. In broader terms, this also means approaching the analysis of law with a critical awareness of the social and institutional context of legal practice and of the development of legal rules.

The course is designed to encourage student participation and to foster the oral and argumentative skills necessary to professional success. Oral presentation of points of law, fact finding, drafting of legal documents and the uses and techniques of negotiation will play an important role in the teaching and assessment of the LLB course.

Attendance will be required on three evenings per week during term time and assessment will be a mixture of conventional unseen examinations and assessment of coursework.

Contact information:

The Law Department
Tel: 0171 631 6510
Fax: 0171 631 6506

University of Central England in Birmingham

Courses offered:

1 LLB;
2 LLB with Politics (planned for 1998;
3 LLB with Psychology;
4 LLB with Sociology;
All available full-time (3 years) and part-time (5 years).

The LLB programmes at UCE are distinguished by the emphasis on participative learning methods, including law clinic, mooting, role play activities and workshops, where students have the opportunity to practise legal skills such as advocacy, counselling and document drafting. Students can participate in our community legal advice bureau which provides free advice and legal representation for the general public. Students can select courses from a wide range of legal and non-legal options, including language studies. Students who study options in Psychology, Politics or Sociology may qualify for the degree of LLB (Law with Psychology, Politics or Sociology). Law options which may be selected include Employment Law, Family Law, Law & Medicine, Law and Consumer, Commercial Law, Company Law, Law & Pensions, Revenue Law, Law of the Single Market, Law & Education, Law & Children, Welfare Law & Practice, Law & Immigration, Law and Sport, Law & Psychology, Public International Law and US Supreme Court

In addition to its LLB programmes, the School of Law at UCE offers a range of postgraduate law studies including PgDip in Legal Studies (CPE), PgDip in Legal Practice (Legal Practice Course) and MA in Legal Practice. Also offered, in conjunction with the other Departments in the Faculty of Law and Social Sciences, are MA Criminal Justice and the MA Welfare Policy, Law & Practice. School staff provide supervision for MPhil and PhD research students. An LLM European Legal Studies degree is planned for 1998-99.

The School of Law has its own purpose-built court room and a law resources centre with extensive IT facilities.

Contact information:

Dan Shaffer
Faculty of Law and Social Sciences

University of Central England in Birmingham
Perry Barr
Birmingham
B42 2SU
Tel: 0121 331
Fax: 0121 331
e mail: Dan.shaffer@uce.ac.uk
Website: http://www.uce.ac.uk

University of Birmingham

Courses offered:

1   LLB;
2   LLB (Law with French);
3   LLB (Law with German);
4   LLB (Law and Business Studies);
5   LLB (Law and Politics);
6   LLB (Senior Status);
7   Diploma in Legal Studies (Common Professional Examination);
8   LLM by research (postgraduate only);
9   LMur by research (postgraduate only);
10 LLM by advanced study (postgraduate only);
11 PhD.

The University is set on a large, attractively landscaped site about two miles from the centre of Birmingham, which has excellent social and cultural facilities. It thus combines the advantages of a city centre campus university. The Faculty of Law (celebrating its 70th anniversary in 1998) is committed to achieving the highest quality in teaching and research. It has approximately 650 member undergraduate and 75 postgraduate students, with 37 full-time academic staff and a further 20 part-time and honorary staff. The Faculty admits about 210 full-time undergraduates annually. Most follow the single honours LLB but some take joint degrees in Law and Business Studies or Law and Politics The Faculty also offers four year degrees in Law with French and Law with German for students who study French or German Law as well as English Law in their first two years and spend their third year studying Law in a French or German University. All the undergraduate Law programmes are 'qualifying' degrees, offering successful candidates exemption from the first stage of the professional examinations for the Law Society and the Bar. The Faculty also offers a one year CPE and a two year 'senior status' degree for graduates in non law subjects.

The subjects in the curriculum cover the full range of legal fields, particular strengths of the Faculty include commercial, comparative, European and public law, human rights, criminal law and theory, and empirical studies of the justice system. Teaching methods are varied. While the most usual pattern involves about 36 lectures and six small group discussion classes for each 20 credit module, some modules operate entirely through seminars or a mix of seminars and problem or project classes. Assessment is by way of a mixture of unseen written examinations, group and individual project work, extended essays and research dissertations. The degree is classified on the basis of a combination of second and final year performances. Students benefit from staff who are leaders in their fields, from the excellent Harding Law Library, combining a large collection of texts, monographs and periodicals with access to CD ROM and on line legal data bases, and dedicated computer clusters for student use, offering internal and internet access.

Students have a personal tutor, whom they meet regularly to discuss academic progress and career plans. Pastoral care is co-ordinated by the Student Welfare Co-ordinator, with specialist back up when needed from the University's Student Support and Counselling Service. The many extra curricular activities, mainly organised by the Holdsworth Club (the student law society celebrating its 70th anniversary in 1988) and other specialist societies, offer a wide range of social and academic opportunities. A mooting programme is organised by the Faculty, and distinguished outside speakers regularly visit. Assistance with regard to post graduation planning is provided through the University's careers service, the careers liaison officer within the Faculty, and personal tutors, in applying for placements, training contracts and other employment.

Contact information:

Mrs M Fisher
Admissions Officer
e mail: Fishermj@law.bham.ac.uk
Tel: (0121) 414 6290
fax: (0121) 414 3585

Bournemouth University

Courses offered:

1   LLB (Hons) Business law;
2   Common Professional Examination.

Bournemouth University School of Law works closely with the School of Accounting and Financial Services with the Departments of Finance and Law. The LLB (Hons) Business Law is a qualifying law degree which offers the traditional 'core' subjects within the context of law as it relates to business. The course is a four-year programme including (in the third year) a sandwich placement in legal practice or business.

University of Bristol

Courses offered:

1 LLB Law;
2 LLB European Legal Studies (transfer possible at end of first term);
3 LLB Joint Honours in Law & French and Law & German;
4 Bsc Joint Honours in Chemistry & Law.

The Faculty of Law at Bristol is recognised as being one of the leading law schools in the United Kingdom. It is housed in the Wills Memorial Building at the heart of the University campus just north of the city centre. In the Wills Memorial Building there is a law student common room and a dedicated law library containing approximately 35,000 volumes. The teaching staff numbers over 40. The main undergraduate programme is the three year law degree. Compulsory units are studied in the first two years and a wide variety of options are available for the third year of studies. Students may be admitted to the Law/French and Law/German programmes, permitting a third year of study in a French or German university. Students on the three year law programme may apply in their first year for transfer to the Law with European Legal Studies programme which also permits a third year to be studied at a university in Europe. The B.Sc joint honours in Chemistry and Law is a four year programme studied completely at Bristol involving two years' study of Chemistry followed by two years' study of Law.

The Faculty offers excellent postgraduate opportunities to a wide range of students from the United Kingdom, other member states of the European Union and from overseas. We have over 100 postgraduate students at any one time, the majority of whom are taking a one-year postgraduate taught course. The taught LLM programme is designed to give students maximum choice and flexibility in their postgraduate studies. Students may choose to specialise and take an LLM in Commercial Law, in Public Law, in European Legal Studies and in International Law as well as taking a general LLM programme in a variety of subjects. The LLM can be studied part-time through the Certificate programme and the Weekend Certificate, whereby students who are otherwise employed attend classes on six Saturdays a year, is a very popular way of part-time study for a LLM. The Faculty offers the Diploma in Intellectual Law and Practice, designed for practitioners, with the support and encouragement of the English Intellectual Property Lawyers Association. This diploma is accepted as the equivalent of two modules towards the LLM degree. The Faculty also offers an MA in Legal Studies, which is a postgraduate two-year degree programme designed especially for British non-law graduates and for law graduates from universities overseas who wish to acquire a thorough grounding in English law. It is an alternative to the CPE programme offered in other universities.

Contact information:

UNDERGRADUATE ADMISSIONS:
Mrs Louise Bennett
Department of Law
University of Bristol
Wills Memorial Building
Queen's Road
Bristol BS8 1RJ.
Tel: 0117 928 7435.
Fax: 0117 925 1870.
E-mail: law-ug-admissions@bristol.ac.uk

POSTGRADUATE ADMISSIONS:
Ms Tania Kinane, Department of Law, University of Bristol, Wills Memorial Building,
Queen's Road,
Tel: 0117 928 7435.
Fax: 0117 925 1870.
E-mail: law-pg-admissions bristol.ac.uk

University of West of England Bristol

Courses offered:

1 LLB;
2 LLB with French;
3 Common Professional Examination;
4 Legal Practice Course.

This Law School is established on a large campus on the edge of Bristol. It is a very large Law School providing a wide range of professional and academic law courses. It has most modern facilities. The attractive student city of Bristol is easily accessible.

Brunel University

Courses offered:

1 LLB (3-year and 4-year work placement);
2 LLB Business & Finance Law (3-year and 4-year work placement;
3 LLB Law and French;
4 LLB Law and German;
5 LLB English and American Law (3-year and 4-year);
6 LLM Child Law;
7 LLM Criminal Justices Studies;
8 LLM EU Law .

Brunel's law school occupies a high position on the academic legal hierarchy. Every law lecturer at Brunel is firmly engaged on the front line of legal scholarship. Our lecturers and professors are all deeply involved in original or applied legal research. They are all producing new ideas: they are all challenging established orthodoxies: they are all in the business of convincing judges and legislators that existing laws need to be changed or refined. Brunel's law department is at the cutting edge of legal scholarship. Equally importantly, we are all committed to feeding our research interests into the courses that we teach to our students. This invariably means that the intellectual and academic experience we can offer our students is rich, stimulating, and dynamic. In this law school, you will find that we see our teaching as a learning process not just for you, but also for us.

There are around 25 lecturers in Brunel's law department. We are a heterogeneous group. Many of us have practised as barristers or solicitors in Britain and abroad. Others of us have always specialised exclusively in the academic branch of the legal profession. We have different interests within the law. We hold different political views. We span a wide range of ages. We come from a variety of countries and intellectual traditions. Some of us are eminent scholars in our fields, others are at the start of our careers. All of us see the primary purpose of a law school as fostering a rich academic environment in which both lecturers and students can stretch their intellects to the full.

We have some 500 students in all, studying on undergraduate, Master's and Doctoral programmes. Our standard LLB offer is BBB (ABB for English/US law). They come from Britain, continental Europe, and a number of Asian and African countries. They live and study on a campus location well served by rail, air and road links. We offer students the chance to undertake work placements in legal practice, to study abroad in Europe and the USA, and, because of our location on the edge of London, to have access to all the cultural and intellectual benefits the capital can provide.

Contact information:

LLB courses; Michael Lobban; Alison Diduck
LLM courses; Jenny Deiches

University of Buckingham

Courses offered:

1   Single Honours Law;
2   Law with Business and Finance;
3   Law with French or Spanish;
4   Law and Politics;
5   Single Honours Law Part-time;
6   Access Course for Law;

7   LLM in International & Commercial Law.

Buckingham Law School offers qualifying law degrees in 2 years by operating a 4 x 10 week terms a year and a 3 term taught masters course. As a private institution Buckingham continues to offer undergraduates small tutorial groups (average size 5 students) a well stocked law library and computer teaching facilities. The University is situated in spacious grounds in a small country town, but with easy access to London and Oxford.

Contact information:

UNDERGRADUATE ADMISSIONS
Irving Stevens (e-mail irving.stevens@buck.ac.uk)
Gillian Skelton (e-mail gillian.skelton@buck.ac.uk)

PART-TIME ADMISSIONS
Olga Thomas (e-mail Olga.thomas@buck.ac.uk)

POSTGRADUATE ADMISSIONS
Damian Carney (e-mail damian.carney@buck.ac.uk
Telephone Number 01280 814080
Fax: Number 01280 828206
Website http://www.buck.ac.uk

University of Cambridge

Courses offered:

1   BA;
2   LLM;
3   MPhil in Criminology;
4   Mlitt;
5   Diploma in Legal Studies;
6   Diploma in International Law;
7   Certificate of Postgraduate Study in Legal Studies.

The Faculty of Law currently has 15 professors, 7 readers and nearly 60 other University, Faculty and college teaching officers. Almost every area of legal interest is represented. There are around 710 undergraduates and over 250 postgraduate students in the Faculty. Within the Faculty there is an Institute of Criminology, a Research Centre for International Law, a Centre for European Legal Studies, an Intellectual Property Unit, a Centre for Public Law, and a Centre for Corporate and Commercial Law. The Faculty is also associated with the Centre for Business Research which is an ESRC-designated research centre within the University.

The Squire Law Library

The Squire Law Library is one of the largest university law libraries in the United Kingdom, housing around 130,000 volumes and providing seats for over 500 readers. It maintains a strong collection from the major common law jurisdictions including the United Kingdom, United States, Australia, Canada, and New Zealand. There are also extensive collections in International Law, Comparative Law, Conflict of Laws, the European Union, and the laws of many European countries. The University Library has a somewhat smaller law collection, important for its official publications and rare books. It houses the depository collection of publications of international organisations such as the UN. Most colleges also have law collections (of varying extent) in their own libraries.

Contact information:

Faculty of law
University of Cambridge
10 West Road
Cambridge CB3 9DZ
Tel: 01223 330033
Fax: 01223 330055

Cardiff Law School

Courses offered:

1   LLB;
2   LLB (with French, German, Italian, Spanish or Japanese);
3   LLB (with politics, Sociology or Social Policy);
4   Legal Practice Course;
5   Bar Vocational Course.

Long-established law and languages programme with extensive ERASMUS links with other European law schools. Highly specialised taught Masters programme. Centre for Professional Legal Studies part of Law School, providing the new Legal Practice Course.

Coventry University

Courses offered:

1   LLB Business Law, European Business Law, Legal Studies;
2   Common Professional Examination;
3   Legal Practice Course.

Coventry University Law School places particular emphasis on business law. It is long established in this area. The University is situated in attractive modern buildings adjacent to the Cathedral.

University of Central Lancashire

Courses offered:

1   LLB (full- and part-time);
2   LLB and Languages (full-time);
3   Law on Combined Honours (full-time).

Department of Legal Studies
Contact information:

Admissions Tutor
Department of Legal Studies
University of Central Lancashire,
Preson
PR1 2HE
Tel: 01772 893060/893062

City University

Courses offered:

1   LLB (Honours);
2   LLB (Honours) Business Law;
3   LLB (Honours) Postgraduate entry;
4   Diploma in Law/a CPE course;
5   LLM in Environmental Law.

City University is located close to the legal heart of London and within walking distance of the Royal Courts of Justice, the Inns of Court and the Central Criminal Court. City was founded in 1894, and it has long standing links with the City of London and with the professions.

Unusually, almost half of the students at City are studying for a postgraduate qualification. The relevance of City's degree programmes leads to excellent opportunities for its graduates. City has consistently maintained one of the highest graduate employment records in the country.

The Department of Law at City University has a total of 27 members of staff and about 350 students enrolled on its LLB and Diploma courses, all of which are recognised by the Bar and the Law Society of England and Wales.

LLB Honours Degrees: 70 places a year are available on the three year courses leading to an LLB degree. Lectures, seminars and tutorials in core and elective subjects occupy between 10-14 hours a week. In addition to core law courses students registered for the LLB degree in Business Law take courses in Economics, Accounting; business electives are available in year 3. Assessment is based on a mixture of examinations, course work and projects.

Diploma/CPE: this is a one year full-time (or 2 years, part-time) course for non-law graduates who wish to start training for a career at the Bar or as a solicitor. City was the first institution to offer the CPE. The course has an unrivalled reputation with the profession for the quality of its teaching and the ability of its students.

The seven foundation subjects are taught by lectures, classes and tutorials which occupy 17-19 hours each week. Instruction in the use of legal materials and in legal research methods (including use of electronic retrieval systems) is an integral part of the course.

Holders of City University's Diploma in Law may obtain an LLB degree by taking additional course units by part-time study; alternatively, the Diploma may be converted to an MA degree by completion of a thesis. Five CPE scholarships are available each year.

Graduate Entry LLB Honours Degree: this is a two year, full-time course taken over the normal University terms. The course is designed to provide both a general knowledge of the central areas of law and to allow special interests to be developed. Students follow courses in the seven core legal subjects which are found in most undergraduate law programmes. In addition, in the second year, students choose electives from a range of options.

The academic work and examinations are of first degree standard: the course is taught jointly with the Department's three year undergraduate LLB degree. Lectures and tutorials together occupy 10-14 hours a week. Separate tutorials, tutors and a course director give this course its own special identity in the Department. Successful candidates are awarded a classified LLB honours degree and are eligible for admission to the Bar Vocational Course (intending barristers) or a Legal Practice Course (intending solicitors).

LLM in Environmental Law: this is a one year postgraduate course which is intended to develop special expertise in UK, European and international planning and environmental law. It is taught by specialists by means of lectures, seminars and presentations. Assessment is based on examinations and a substantial piece of written work.

Contact information:

LLB: Jane Davies Tel: 0171 477 8000 x 3302
LLB (Postgraduate): Dr Yvonne Jacobs Tel: 0171 477 8306
Diploma: Christine Trinder Tel: 0171 477 8301
e mail: CPE@city.ac.uk

University of Dundee

Courses offered:

1   LLB (English Law);
2   LLB (Scottish Law);
3   LLB English Law and Accountancy);
4   LLB (English Law) and a modern language;
5   LLB (Scottish Law) and a modern language.

Department of Law, please note all degrees accredited by relevant Law Society(ies) and LLB English Law and Accountancy is fully accredited by both the accounting and legal profession in England and Wales.

Contact information:

Ms D Middleton
Admission Secretary for Law
Admissions and Student Recruitment
University of Dundee
DD1 4HN
Tel: 01382 344028

Derby University

Courses offered:

1   LLB (Hons) with European Studies;
2   LLB (Hons) (Business Law);
3   LLB (Hons) (International Law);
4   LLB (Hons) (Social and Public Law).

Core subjects and law based electives covering the equivalent of 72/96 credits. The European Studies pathway covers 24/96 credits.
    Core subjects and law based electives, covering equivalent of 64/96 credits. The specialist (predominantly law) covers 32/96 credits.
    BA (Hons) (Combined Subjects) Law
    Principles of Law and a maximum of 64 additional credits in law subjects.
    Students on the BA (CS) programme cannot take certain cores (Property I and 2 and Obligations) and thus cannot obtain a qualifying law degree. They are eligible to apply for exemption from subjects within the CPE syllabus which they have successfully studied at degree level.

University of Durham

Courses offered:

1   LLB. Honours in Law;

2   Law with European Legal Studies;
3   Law with Politics;
4   Law with Economics;
5   Law with Sociology;
6   BA Joint Honours in Law & Sociology;
7   Law & Politics;
8   Economics & Law.

The University of Durham, founded in 1832, is the third oldest university in England. Its teaching buildings and colleges are located on a number of sites in this ancient city. The Law Department is to be found at the heart of the historic centre of Durham, almost literally in the shadow of the Norman Cathedral and the Castle (University College), high on the peninsula carved out by the winding River Wear. The Department's premises, in North Bailey, are in the midst of the older colleges and the Law Library is nearby, on Palace Green. The Law Library has a large and airy Law Reading Room housing a comprehensive collection of Law materials, many of which are also held in the main University Library and in college libraries. The Library is a European Documentation Centre.

The Department has its own lecture and seminar rooms, and most tutorials are held in the rooms of members of staff in the Department. The largest lecture classes are held either on Palace Green or in lecture halls in the Elvet Riverside buildings on New Elvet. The University has well-equipped computer classrooms, to which students have access both for research and for computer-based learning. The Department has played a pioneering role in the development and use of computer-based law tutorial packages, to which students have generous access in order to consolidate the skills and knowledge acquired through more conventional forms of teaching and learning. Students are encouraged to acquire or increase their familiarity with word-processing, and are offered instruction in accessing legal databases. The University's Centre for Law and Computing is based in the Department.

The Department is also host to the Durham European Law Institute, and has a dedicated Chair in European Law, generously sponsored by the international law firm Allen & Overy. The Department has also received special funding from the European Commission for a Jean Monnet Chair in European Law, in recognition of the work undertaken in this field by the Department. The Department was one of the first in England to offer a specialist course in European Community Law to its undergraduates. We offer four distinct courses in European Law on our undergraduate programme, and we make provision for graduate students through the LLM. in International and European Legal Studies (for which a separate prospectus is available). The Department also encourages graduate students wishing to pursue the degrees of MJur and PhD by research, further details of which can be obtained from the Adviser to Postgraduate Students.

Contact information:

Francis Pritchard
Law Admissions Tutor, at the Department of Law
50 North Bailey,
Durham, DHI 3ET,
Tel: 0191 374 2045
e mail: Francis.Pritchard@durham.ac.uk

University of East Anglia

Courses offered:

1   LLB (3-year programme);
2   LLB Law with European Legal Studies (4-year programme with year 3 at continental university);
3   Law with French Law and Language (4-year programme with 3rd year at French university);
4   Law with German Law and Language (4-year programme with 3rd year at German university);
5   LLM (Family Law & Policy);
6   LLM (International Business & Commercial Law);
7   Diploma in Law (recognised by the Common Professional Examination Board).

The Norwich Law School, which has been established for some twenty years, is housed in the historic Earlham Hall on the edge of the University campus. This is situated in parkland on the outskirts of the mediaeval city of Norwich. In addition to the core subjects required for purposes of professional exemption, the School offers a variety of optional subjects including not only options in traditional areas such as Company Law and Family Law, but in new areas such as Animal Welfare Law and Pensions Law. There is also an optional unit in Mooting as well as a Mooting competition. The School is within easy reach of Northern Europe and has strong contacts with many universities on the European mainland and a substantial SOCRATES programme.

Contact information:

UNDERGRADUATE ADMISSION:
Ms Sue Leared
Tel: 01603 592835
e-mail: S.Leared@uea.ac.uk

POSTGRADUATE ADMISSION:
Ms Kerry Pottle
Tel: 01603 592520
e-mail: K.Pottle@uea.ac.uk

University of East London

Courses offered:

1 LLB;
2 BA (Honours) Law, Culture and Society;
3 BA (Honours) Criminology and Criminal Justice;
4 MA Legal Studies (Child Law);
5 MA Legal Studies (Crime and Society);
6 LLM (International Legal Studies);
7 LLM (Modular).

The Law School is committed to ensuring a high quality experience in teaching and learning. Particular attention is paid to the wider curriculum beyond the classroom with skills training and visits by distinguished speakers. Law is taught in its social, political and historical context and all the degrees are offered in full and part-time modes.

Contact information:

Fiona Fairweather
Tel: 0181 590 7000 ext 2048 or 0181 590 7722

University of Essex

Courses offered:

1 3-year LLB in English Law;
2 4-year LLB in English and French Law;
3 4-year LLB in English and European Law;
4 LLM in European Community Law;
5 M in International Human Rights Law;
6 LLM in International Trade Law;
7 LLM in Law in Transition in the 'New Europe';
8 LLM in Public Law;
9 MPhil/PhD Research Degrees.

The Department of Law, founded in 1980, is a lively and innovative department with an international reputation for its research (receiving a '5' in the most recent Research Assessment Exercise). The Department's teaching was rated as 'excellent' by the Higher Education Funding Council for England in 1993, in line with its commitment to providing a legal education of the highest quality. The Department is a relatively small one compared with other university law departments, creating a friendly and informal atmosphere. The Department offers a wide choice of Law and non-Law options for undergraduates and postgraduate students, and offers students on the 4-year programmes the opportunity for study abroad in their third year

There are 28 full-time members of staff and approximately 400 undergraduate and 90 postgraduate students. The students come from many different backgrounds and the Department has a strong tradition of accepting mature students and applicants with non traditional qualifications. Good relations exist between staff and students and a warm welcome is given to students from home and abroad.

Contact information:

Admissions Officer – Bob Watt
Undergraduate Director – Peter Luther
Graduate Secretary – Maria Alcayaga
Dept of Law
University of Essex
Wivenhoe Park
Colchester
Essex
CO4 3SQ
Tel: 01206 872587 undergraduate
(01206) 872585 postgraduate
e mail: law@essex.ac.uk

University of Exeter

Courses offered:

1   LLB Honours;
2   LLB Honours with European Study (four years);
3   LLB Honours (European) (four years);
4   BA Honours (Law);
5   BA Interdepartmental Single Honours in law and Society (in conjunction with the Department of Sociology);
6   Bsc Combined Honours in Chemistry and Law (Faculty of Social Science);
7   Diploma in English Law for International Students;
8   Diploma in Law;
9   Diploma in Legal Practice.

Exeter is a well established Law School in a most attractive campus. It has a particular strength in European Law. Recently it has embarked on professional legal education.

Contact information:

School of Law- Sandra Hammond 01392 263371
Centre for European Studies – Nicola Symons 01392 263380
Centre for Legal Practice – Jenny Cook 01392 263157

University of Glamorgan

Courses offered:

1   LLB Honours (full and part-time);
2   LLB Honours (fast track – 2 years);
3   HND in Legal Studies;
4   HNC in Legal Studies;
5   Legal Practice Course;
6   Graduate Diploma in Law;
7   LLM in European Law.

The Law School is located on specially adapted off-campus facilities,
offering a wide range of academic and vocational courses. Established in
1995 and headed by Professor M Griffiths. The School offers a wide range
of academic and vocational courses including LLB (Hons) and the LPC.
Since 1993 the School has offered HND/C in Legal Studies which is now
franchised throughout Wales and England. The HND in Legal Studies,
besides being a stand alone qualification, is recognised by the Law Society
as constituting the equivalent of the first year of study of a qualifying law
degree. Such students may complete their qualifying LLB in two years. The
School recently established a distance learning in LLM in European law
and intends to further develop commercially orientated Masters
programmes to start in September 1998.

   The School also enjoys mature, international links with Malaysia and
Honk Kong.

Contact information:

Karen Counsell
Associate Head (Academic)

Greenwich University

Course offered:

1   LLB.

This is a newly established law degree programme. It is established in a
university with a strong tradition of business education.

London Guildhall University

Courses offered:

1   LLB;
2   Common Professional Examination;
3   Legal Practice Course;
4   Law as part of a joint degree.

This is a very large law school with a range of academic and professional courses. It is situated in Moorgate in the city of London.

University of Hertfordshire

Courses offered:

1   LLB (Hons) 3-year full-time;
2   LLB (Hons) 2-year accelerated full-time;
3   LLB (Hons) evenings part-time;
4   LLB (Hons) daytime part-time;
5   MA (Health Law) full and part-time;
6   Diploma in Legal Practice part-time day time only;
7   LLM (Medical Law) full-time and part-time;
8   LLM (International Law) full-time and part-time;
9   LLM (Business law) full-time and part-time;
10 LLM (Gender & the Law) full-time and part-time;
11 LLM (Legal Practice) full-time and part-time.

The Faculty of Law is located in purpose built premises at the St Albans campus. The attractive and historic location is close to the courts and local legal firms of solicitors and is ideal for the study of law.

Contact information:

Frances Kay, Admissions Tutor
Tel: 01707 286219
Fax: 01707 286205

Professor D Tribe
Dean, Faculty of Law
7 Hatfield Road
St Albans
Herts
AL1 3RS

University of Huddersfield

Courses offered:

1 LLB;
2 LLB Business Law;
3 LLB European Legal Studies;
4 Postgraduate Diploma in Law (Common Professional Examination);
5 Postgraduate Diploma in Legal Practice (Legal Practice Course;
6 LLM;
7 LLM European Business Law (subject to validation).

There are 21 full-time staff in the Department of Law at Huddersfield, meaning that it is a relatively small department where students and staff get to know each other well. We pride ourselves on providing a friendly, supportive environment which enables students to achieve their full academic potential. All our courses can be taken on a part-time as well as a full-time basis.

LLB/LLB Business Law/LLB European Legal Studies

All LLB routes lead to a qualifying law degree recognised by the Law Society and the General Council of the Bar. The Business Law route enables students to specialise in commercially connected options, including non-Law options such as management and accounting, and is felt by graduates to have given them a particular edge in the market. The European Legal Studies route is a three-year programme where the second year is spent at one of our partner universities in the European Union. Competence in another language is not essential for this.

In addition to a wide range of taught options, students can get credit towards their degrees for activities such as placements in the working legal environment, which is a popular choice for many students because of the networking opportunities which can be created.

Postgraduate Diploma in Law (Common Professional Examination)

This is a one-year full-time or two-year part-time course for graduates in disciplines other than Law who wish to qualify professionally. Completion of the Diploma enables students to undertake professional training on a par with Law graduates. At Huddersfield, the full-time course is scheduled over three days only, to allow effective use of blocks of time for private study. From September 1998, it will be possible to undertake the part-time course by Open or Distance Learning via the Internet.

Postgraduate Diploma in Legal Practice (Legal Practice Course)

This is a one-year full-time or two-year part-time course for intending solicitors. Consistently rated 'good' by the Law Society, this highly professional course is ideal for those aiming at provincial High Street practices as well as commercial firms.

LLM by dissertation

Holders of the Postgraduate Diploma in Legal Practice or equivalent can gain the degree of Master of Laws by submitting a dissertation and making a presentation based on it to a panel of examiners. This is an open/distance learning degree, usually taken over one or two years.

LLM European Business Law

Aimed at graduates in Law or with mixed Law degrees, this course consists of seven subjects over two semesters (full-time) or four semesters (part-time) and a dissertation to be prepared over the summer for autumn submission. Attendance is required on two days a week (full-time) or one day a week (part-time).

Contact information:

Admission Tutor
Department of Law
University of Huddersfield
Queensgate
Huddersfield
HD1 3DH
Tel: 01484 472192
Fax: 01484 472279

University of Hull

1   LLB Law;
2   Law with French;
3   Law with German;
4   Law with Philosophy;
5   Law and Politics;
6   Law and Sociology.

Law degree courses as offered in Britain's Universities are not all the same. Most do have some common features, particularly to the extent that they offer the core requirements of the legal professions. However, these requirements themselves allow for some flexibility, and beyond them university law schools will offer modules which reflect their views of the nature of a modern law degree. Often the course is the product of careful and critical evaluation over a number of years, taking into account the views of past generations of students. So what makes the Hull Law degree distinctive? The Hull Law School offers a wide range of programmes in order to suit students' interests and strengths. The LLB programmes have been designed so that students receive a thorough introduction to the skills and areas of substantive law that will allow them to specialise and pursue their own interests, both later in the programme and in life, whether or not they enter legal practice. Thus, for example, we aim to give students an introduction to computer skills such as word-processing and the use of legal databases in the first year, with subsequent refresher courses available. As regards matters of substance, the required subjects form a foundation for all later study of law. For example, in semester I students are taught the basic elements of the law of Contract, an understanding of which is necessary for modules which might be taken later, such as Employment Law.

At the Law School we consider that the study of law cannot be separated from its social, moral and political context. Therefore, in both the Introduction to Law and the Jurisprudence modules we try to set the study of law in this wider context examining, among other things, particular theories of the nature of law and legal obligation. These considerations are also raised in the substantive modules. For example, Criminal Law looks at the historical and social foundations of criminal law and its institutions, practices and procedures, as well as the substantive law. As a Law School, Hull has particular areas of expertise: Public Law, International Law, European Community Law, Information Technology Law, Family Law, Employment Law and Sociology and Philosophy of Law. Staff are active in research in all these areas, which influences their teaching and enables them to acquaint students with the latest ideas.

All the degree programmes offered by the Law School are fully modularised. This means that in each year you must take modules worth 120 credits. There are two 15 week semesters each academic session. Each semester consists of a 12 week teaching period and a 3 week assessment period. The LLB Law Programme is taught entirely within the Law School, subject to students wishing to take advantage of optional modules offered on other Schools within the University in their second and third years. All the Law degrees are qualifying law degrees and provide the necessary exemptions for the purposes of the professional bodies. With the exception of the Law with Languages degrees and our SOCRATES programmes, which take four years, all the degrees take three years.

Contact information:

Admissions Secretary
Law School
University Of Hull
HU6 7RX

Keele University

Undergraduate Degrees

BA AND LLB
The Law course at Keele appeals both to prospective lawyers and to those willing to follow other careers– The Keele Dual Honours Degree allows Law to be combined with over 30 other subjects and can qualify for exemption from the Law Society's Common Professional Examination – thus providing considerable career flexibility.

Law may be combined with one of the following:

American Studies, Ancient History, Applied Social Studies, Biochemistry, Biological and Medicinal Chemistry, Biology, Business Administration, Chemistry, Classical Studies, Computer Science, Criminology, Economics, Educational Studies, Electronics, English, Finance, French, Geology, German, History, Human Resource Management, International History, International Politics, Latin, Management Science, Marketing, Mathematics, Philosophy, Physics, Politics, Psychology or Sociology.

Keele Law Department

The Law Department offers a stimulating environment in which to study Law; students may take advantage of seminars given by leading academics and practising lawyers; participate in our annual mooting programme; attend careers talks given by leading law firms, participate in client interviewing contests, and many other activities. Keele also hosts a Critical Legal Studies Group which provides a forum for debating controversial legal issues; and a very active Student Law Society which arranges social events, visiting speakers, outings to barristers chambers etc and arranges a mock trial every year.

Objectives of the Law course

The law course has three objectives. The first is to give you an understanding of the conceptual framework of the main areas of law. These areas, property law, criminal law, contract, torts and public law are each a bit like a mosaic in which the individual rules, cases, statutes, principles etc fit together to make the overall picture. To understand the significance of a particular rule you need a broader version of the conceptual design of the area of law. Secondly, we aim to develop your analytical skills and to that end you will be given plenty of practice at applying legal rules to fact situations and producing reasoned answers Thirdly, we will encourage you to adopt a critical approach to your law studies. Whether considering a broad issue of law reform or a narrow point concerning the meaning of a judgment, it is important for the lawyer and the law student to take a critical and independent view. In tutorials, you will be encouraged to examine the law from different critical viewpoints and reach your own conclusions.

Teaching Methods

Most modules will be taught by a combination of 20 lectures and 4 tutorials or seminars. One of the characteristics of the Keele Law degree is small group teaching. We aim to limit the numbers in any tutorial to about 7 students to facilitate small group discussion of the issues and problems set for that tutorial. Numbers in seminars will be about 15 students and the work set will be designed for larger group discussion. The work for a typical first year tutorial or seminar would involve some text book reading, study of some cases or perhaps an article, and preparing oral answers to problem questions and theoretical issues.

Contact information:

Undergraduate admissions
Department of Academic Affairs,
Keele University,
Keele, Staffs.
STS 5B6.
Tel: 01782 584003

Kent University

1   LLB three year single honours programme;
2   Three years joint honours with another subject.

Kent Law School has been at the forefront of innovation in legal education, pioneering new approaches to the study and teaching of law. While our courses and programmes are fully committed to the enunciation of doctrinal rules of law, much of the teaching at KLS is socio-legal in orientation and seeks to address the social, historical, economic and political contexts within which law operates. The Law School offers a legal education that is of value both to those who intend to practise law and to those who have other, non-legal, careers in mind. In particular, it is one which encourages students to develop an independent intellectual position of their own.

Law can be studied as a three year single honours programme, or as a three years joint with another subject. The extensive range of four year programmes which include studying law in another language in France, Germany, Italy or Spain. European Legal Studies is for students without another language, and the year abroad is spent at a university where the law of other European countries is taught in English eg at Amsterdam. A three-year programme combining Law with French or German is available and does not involve study abroad.

Part I (First Year)

Single honours students take four law courses: Introduction to Law, Obligations I, Legal Process and Constitutional and Administrative Law. Joint Honours students take at least two of them (including Introduction to Law). Students on the four-year European programmes take a course in the relevant language instead of Legal Process, except for those taking English and French Law who take a module on French Law taught in French (Droit Constitutionnel et Administratif).

Part II (Second and Final Year)

In addition to the remaining professional exemption courses – Obligations II, European Law, Equity and Trusts, Criminal Law, and Property Law – there is also a wide range of options which usually includes commercial, international, family, environmental, human rights, labour law, evidence, medical ethics, mental health law, comparative law, policing, punishment, law and the modern state, law and literature, armed forces and the law, legal history and philosophy of law.

Kent Law Clinic

This is an advice and representation service provided free to members of the public. It is staffed by a solicitor who supervises students, in association with members of the academic staff, local solicitors and barristers. Some option courses have scope for clinical work (Labour Law, Mental Health Law) and there is a clinical option course in Part II. More experienced students are able to represent clients before tribunals.

Entry requirements

Three A levels (exceptionally, two may be considered) or the equivalent. Two AS levels will be accepted as an alternative to a third A level.

We encourage applications from mature students with less educational qualifications on the basis of other relevant experience.

For further course information or admissions enquiries please contact the Office for Undergraduate Admissions, The Registry, University of Kent at Canterbury, Canterbury, Kent, CT2 7NZ.

King's College London

Courses offered:

1 LLB (3 years);
2 LLB in English and French Law (2 years at King's, 2 years at Paris I, resulting in Maitrise en Droit qualification);
3 LLB with German Law (years 1, 2 and 4 at King's, year 3 in Passau;

4   LLB with European Legal Studies (years 1, 2 and 4 at King's, year 3 in Strasbourg or Ferrara);
5   An extensive and distinguished variety of postgraduate courses.

The School of Law is one of six within the University of London. Nationally, the School enjoys a considerable reputation for teaching and research and is regarded as one of the leading law schools in the country. The student body consists of about 800 undergraduate and about 300 postgraduates. The school hosts several specialist centres, such as the Centre of European Law, the Centre of Medical law and Ethics, the Civil Liberties Research Unit, the International Centre for Prison Studies and the Institute for the Study and Treatment of Delinquency.

Contact information:

Ms Aileen McColgan, Deputy Associate Head
Undergraduate Admissions, School of Law

Kingston University

Courses offered:

1   LLB (Hons.);
2   LLB (Hons.) with German Law;
3   LLB (Hons.) with French Law;
4   BA Accounting and Law;
5   Post-Graduate Diploma in Law;
6   LLM in Dispute Resolution;
7   LLM in Business Law;
8   LLM in Employment Relations and Law;
9   English Law for lawyers From Foreign Jurisdictions.

LLB (Hons.)

The LLB course has as objectives the provision of a liberal legal education and a rigorous academic discipline for both prospective practitioners and those who intend to make careers in other areas, such as business, industry or administration. The course is designed to equip students with knowledge of the foundation subjects – such as the Law of Contract, European Community Law, Land Law etc, which provide the essential education for any lawyer, and to provide a variety of optional subjects from which students choose four in the final year which best suit their plans for the future.

We emphasise not only the skills needed to study for a law degree – where and how to find the law, how to read cases, to research, to write, how to solve legal problems, but also skills which are important to non-lawyers, such as the ability to assimilate detailed information, the ability to reflect productively upon your experiences, to communicate effectively, to work well (and efficiently) with others and on your own.

LLB with French or German law

The LLB with French or German Law are four year degrees which, as well as the elements of a full law degree, also contain an introduction to French or German Law (taught in the relevant language) and a specialist language teaching, with an emphasis on legal French or German. Students spend their third year studying with French or German law students at a French or German University.

BA in Law and Accountancy

The course provides an introduction to the core disciplines of the professions of accountancy and the law. The integrated programme offers an understanding of the legal and financial implications of business activities. The course provides foundations for careers in accountancy, law, and business, drawing on the resources of the Kingston Business and Law Schools.

It is possible to take a range of courses which ensure exemptions from later professional examinations. By selecting the required options students can obtain either a qualifying law degree or foundation exemptions of the various accountancy bodies. The flexible nature of the course enables students to select a variety of electives and different career pathways.

Contact information:

The Law School
Kingston University
Kingston Hill,
Surrey, KT I 3QR
Telephone No. 0181 547 7323
Website – http://polaris.king.ac.uk:8080/business/ugadmit.htm
e–mail – K.Mcnab@kingston.ac.uk

Lancaster University

Courses offered:

1   LLB 3 years;
2   LLB (European Legal Studies) a 4–year course with year 3 being spent at a Continental University. In the 1997/98 academic year students are attending the Universities of Nancy, Trier, Lausanne, Saarlands and Salamanca.

The Law Department is relatively small (at 16 staff) and has an annual intake of about 90 students. It is situated in the middle of this campus University. First year students are normally guaranteed a room on campus if they apply for one by dates set by the University. All students may take non-Law subjects as part of their degree. There are opportunities for third year LLB students to spend one term at a Continental University. In 1997/98, for example, three students spent a term at Uppsala University in Sweden and three in Maastricht.

Contact information:

The Departmental Officer
Law Department
Lancaster University
Lancaster
LA1 4YN
Tel.: (01524) 592478
Fax: (01524) 848137
E-mail: a.turner@lancaster.ac.uk

University of Leeds

Courses offered:

1   3-year LLB (second year can be spent at European University through SOCRATES programme);
2   2-year LLB (for graduates of another discipline);
3   Law/French;
4   Law/Chinese Studies;
5   Law/Japanese Studies.

1999 marks the centenary of the Law Department at the University of Leeds. The modern department has around 500 undergraduate students and 25 full-time members of staff. The department houses a separate Law Library with over fifty thousand books covering English, European, Commonwealth, and American Law. There are fifty networked computers within the School buildings as well as access to open clusters across the campus. There is an active mooting programme within the department, and in 1998 for the third successive year a team of Leeds students won the UK national championship of the Jessup Moot Court competition.

All the programmes of study offered by the department are designed to allow students to obtain maximum exemption from the academic stage of training of both the Bar Council and the Law Society of England and Wales. The three year single honours degree in law seeks to develop understanding of the general principles and features of law as a social institution and of the common law in particular and to develop legal research and presentation skills within that tradition. Anyone on the three year course can spend their second year abroad at one of the fifteen other European universities with whom we have links through the SOCRATES programme. Students who go to our partner institutions in the Netherlands, Belgium or Sweden can study in English but otherwise some language ability (about A-level standard) is recommended.

The joint degrees with French, Chinese and Japanese are four year courses and provide a qualifying law degree with a language qualification. On these programmes around half the courses are taken in the law department and half in the chosen language specialisation. Law-Chinese and Law-Japanese students may be offered the opportunity to spend their second year abroad, studying the language and culture of their host country, while Law-French students take courses on French law at a French university.

There is a variety of teaching and learning methods within the department. Formal instruction can take the form of lectures, case-classes, tutorial groups, or seminar classes and can be supplemented by interactive computer-based packages and materials and exercises placed on the world wide web. In the second semester of level one, single honours students take part in a legal skills project, researching a case based on actual legal documents, and developing practical skills of negotiation and advocacy.

The majority of Leeds law students go on to take professional examinations with a view to entering the legal profession and the department has entered into an agreement with the College of Law at York to provide places for our graduates who obtain a lower second class degree or better. However, all law graduates leave Leeds with a set of highly transferable personal and intellectual skills which will be valuable to them both in their professional lives and more generally as educated and reflective citizens.

Contact information:

Further information including the departmental prospectus and video can be obtained from:
The Admissions Secretary, Department of Law, University of Leeds, Leeds LS2 9JT.
Tel: 0113 233 5020 Fax: 0113 233 5019
e-mail: C.J.Wigley@leeds.ac.uk.

Leeds Metropolitan University

Courses offered:

1   LLB full and part-time;
2   Postgraduate Diploma in Law full-time and part-time;

3   Postgraduate Diploma in Legal Practice full-time and part-time;
4   LLM full-time and part-time;
5   ILEX.

The University has a long, established reputation in the teaching of undergraduate and professional Law courses, The School of Law is one of five faculties within Leeds Business School and has offered Final Professional Law Society courses for many years.

The city of Leeds is widely acknowledged to be the largest legal centre outside the capital and the School has close links with the thriving local legal community. Practitioners contribute to the development of courses, a great many give talks to the students and some teach regularly on the courses. These links enhance the quality of education offered and are of immense benefit to students seeking to enter the legal profession.

The School of Law offers the LLB, Postgraduate Diploma in Law, Postgraduate Diploma in Legal Practice, LLM courses together with arrange of paralegal and technical courses

When assessed by the Law Society monitoring team in December 1997, both the full-time and part-time delivery of the Legal Practice Course was accredited good. This reflects the high quality of education delivered by our dedicated and professionally qualified teaching team, many of whom still work in practice.

The School has a lively student law society and an active mooting society. In 1997 a team of LLB students won the Allen & Overy Negotiating Competition triumphing over 45 universities in England & Wales.

The School of Law is situated in Cavendish Hall on the Beckett Park campus in Headingley, The campus has attractive period building surrounding a large grassy quadrangle ('The Acre') adjacent to an area of unspoilt parkland. The campus has its own Student Union including a newly refurbished refectory, bar and leisure facilities. Beckett Park is home to the Carnegie Regional Sports Centre and students can take advantage of impressive sporting facilities, gymnasiums and a swimming pool.

Leeds, one of the most popular student destinations in Britain, offers a huge variety of culture and entertainment combined with a vibrant night life and is surrounded by beautiful countryside. There is a wide variety of good quality student accommodation available including Leeds Metropolitan University's award winning Kirkstall Brewery Complex, and a vast stock of private rented accommodation.

Contact information:

Rachel Walton
Associate Senior Lecturer
Tel: 0113 2832600 ext 4617

University of Leicester

Courses offered:

1   LLB;
2   LLB degree in Law with French Law and Language;
3   BA in Economics and law.

This is a large and cosmopolitan Faculty characterised by a good student personal welfare system, small group teaching, and the approachability and supportiveness of staff. It is also highly rated for its research and teaching, having been awarded an 'Excellent' rating for its teaching in the 1993 Teaching Quality Assessment Exercise, and a 4A rating for its research in the 1996 Research Assessment Exercise. It has also been rated highly by the Times Good University Guide. The Faculty offers two undergraduate courses. The three year LLB degree, and the four year LLB in Law with French Law and Language. It also collaborates with the Department of Economics in offering a BA in Economics and Law. There are opportunities for students to convert the three year LLB degree into a four year degree programme with one year being spent abroad at one of our partner institutions in Modena in Italy, Frankfurt am Main in Germany, San Sebastian in Spain and Singapore. The size of the Faculty allows it to offer an exceptionally wide range of optional courses', ranging from socially-orientated subjects such as Law and Medicine, Family Law and Criminology, to commercially orientated subjects such as Intellectual Property Law, Company Law and Competition Law. Most teaching is undertaken by a combination of lectures and tutorials, tutorials being taken in groups of between seven and nine. A wide variety of assessment methods are adopted, ranging from the traditional three hour unseen examination format to assessed course work and take-home examination papers. The law library is located in the Main University Library, situated conveniently next-door to the Faculty of Law. Open access computer facilities are available in various parts of the campus, including in the Main Library and in the Faculty. The Faculty organises a number of extra-curricular activities, such as mooting and client interviewing competitions and the students run their own legal advice centre. There is also a highly active Student Law Society, which organises a variety of social occasions, including the annual Law Society Ball, staff/student cricket match and trip to London to visit the Houses of Parliament and Royal Courts of Justice. There is a special careers tutor in the Department who provides valuable advice to students about legal careers.

Approximately 50% of our graduates undertake further training so as to enter the legal profession. The rest embark on postgraduate degree courses or take up work in areas as diverse as teaching, accountancy, publishing, financial services, the police service, journalism, management, computing, and government service.

An undergraduate brochure, available from the Faculty, provides further details.

Contact information:

Faculty of Law
University of Leicester
University Road
Leicester
Tel: 0116 252 2363
Fax: 0116 252 5023
e-mail   law@le.ac.uk

De Montfort University

Courses offered:

1   LLB (Hon) Full-time;
2   LLB (Hons) Part-time;
3   LLB (Hons) Law with French Full-time;
4   LLB (Hons) Law with German Full-time;
5   BA Law/Marketing;
6   BA Law/Public Policy;
7   BA Law/Human Resource Management;
8   Legal Practice Course Full-time;
9   Legal Practice Course Part-time open Learning;
10 Postgraduate Diploma in Law Full-time;
11 Postgraduate Diploma in Law Part-time by Distance Learning;
12 LLM Agriculture Law Part-time by Distance Learning;
13 LLM in Advanced Legal Practice Part-time by Distance Learning;
14 LLM in Business Law Part-time by Distance Learning;
15 LLM in Environmental Law Part-time by Distance Learning;
16 LLM in Food Law Part-time by Distance Learning.

The School of Law is one of the largest University Law Schools in England and Wales. The School is housed in its own building adjacent to the university's city centre campus in Leicester. The building has recently been extended and refurbished to a high level.

Our principal objective is the provision of the highest quality legal education, relevant to both personal and professional development and to the needs of the 21st century, Our well qualified staff take pride in the achievement of their students and in the fulfilment of that objective.

The School prides itself on the quality of its teaching and on the range of its research and consultancy in the field of law. In this, it mirrors the wider thrust of the University, strongest performers amongst the new universities in the last HEFCE research assessment exercise.

Although the size of the School of Law brings considerable benefits in terms of the human and physical resources which it can offer to students, its size does not mean that it is an impersonal institution. As a matter of policy, the various courses available are not large by modern standards, with the result that staff and students involved in a particular course know each other and students feel that they 'belong'. Class sizes are small. The emphasis in teaching is on active learning through the medium of seminars and tutorials.

Contact information:

Details of the entry requirements for courses are available on application to the Admissions Tutor for the course concerned. Applications from mature students are welcomed, whether or not they satisfy the normal entry requirements. The relevant Admissions Tutor may be contacted by writing to

The School of Law
De Montfort University
The Gateway,
Leicester LEI 9BH.
Tel: 0116 2577177
Fax 0116 2577186.

University of Liverpool

Courses offered:

1 LLB;
2 LLB (Law and German);
3 LLB (Law and French).

The Faculty of Law celebrated its Centenary in 1992/93 with a large programme of events. From its former staff and students it can list a number of senior and other judges. The Faculty has 24 full-time staff and around 400 students. It is housed in its own building, which contains the Moot Room and Law Library. The LLB (Law and German) and LLB (Law and French) each span four years of study, including a year at a German or French University. German or French Law is taught in the medium of the respective language.

In the first year of the LLB students are required to take Criminal Law, Constitutional and Administration Law, Law of Contract and Legal Methods and Legal Systems. In the second year Equity and Trusts and Law of Torts are compulsory and students can choose from a wide variety of options for their remaining two subjects (or a combination of two or one unit courses), whilst in the third year all subjects are optional. In the academic year 1993/94, 35 optional subjects were offered to students. Students may also choose non-law subjects as part of their curriculum for years 2 and 3.

Liverpool John Moores University

Courses offered:

1   Full-time and Part-Time LLB/LLB (Hons);
2   BA Law – Joint Honours (with Criminal Justice, Business, Languages);
3   Postgraduate Diploma in Legal Practice (Part-Time);
4   MA Criminal Justice (Part-Time);
5   MA European Law for UK Businesses (Part-Time);
6   Legal Executives Part II.

The Law Courses are delivered within the School of Law and Applied Social Studies. The School has a broad interdisciplinary base, providing undergraduate, postgraduate and professional courses in Law, Social Work, Criminal Justice and Youth and Community Work. Approximately half of the School's 1,200 students are undergraduates on the modularised full-time and Part-Time LLB degrees, which provide full qualifying status for professional legal purposes. Students studying on a Joint Honours Programme have the flexibility of deciding to transfer to the LLB in the second year following successful completion of their first year joint programme.

There are twenty four full-time staff teaching wholly or predominantly on Law Courses in the School, as well as a number of part-time and sessional staff. The staff have long experience in delivering modularised courses, and particular features of the LLB degrees are the pervasive nature of legal skills as well as the creation of several discrete modules dealing with legal material not frequently studied at undergraduate level, eg sexual offences, medical law and ethics, and animal law. In addition, the unique interdisciplinary academic mix within the School (especially in relation to Criminal Justice and Social Work) has enabled a range of innovative options to be developed on the LLB degree. These include options in Mental Health Law, Community Care Law, Youth Justice and Welfare Law.

Law students are encouraged to participate in a wide range of extra curricular legal activities. The School has an excellent recent record in external mooting competitions (including being runner-up in the 1997 Observer National Moot), and also submits teams to external debating and client-interviewing competitions. Students are given training in, and then are actively involved in the running of the School's Free Legal Advice Unit; Court Martialling sessions are organised in conjunction with local courts; and there are a number of educational trips eg to the European Courts.

Contact information:

FOR GENERAL QUERIES ON UNDERGRADUATE PROGRAMMES:
Ms Susan Haimes
tel: (0151 231 3906) or
Mr Robert Platt
tel: 0151 231 3957.

FOR LEGAL PRACTICE COURSE INQUIRIES:
Ms Sophie Cockram
0151 231 3977

London School of Economics and Political Science

Law Courses offered

1 LLB;
2 LLB with French Law;
3 BA Anthropology and Law;
4 LLM;
5 M.Sc Regulation.

The Law Department at the School is the second largest department with, in the session 1997/98, 11 professors and 28 other full-time academic staff. In addition, a number of emeritus and visiting professors and other teachers drawn from legal practice participate in teaching and research. The Department prides itself on its international reputation in legal scholarship and research. It was graded 5A in the last Research Selectivity Exercise, and received the highest grade in all previous exercises. Although the research of members of the Department is diverse, there is a particularly strong tradition of drawing upon the position of the Department in a school of social sciences in order to develop interdisciplinary work.

The Law Department admits approximately 100 undergraduates each year to read the LLB degree, and there are also other degrees in which the Law Department is heavily involved, namely Law with French Law and Anthropology and Law. The Department plays a major part in the taught Master's programme, the LLM, which is an inter-collegiate degree taught in co-operation with four other schools in London University. The Department admits about 200 students per annum to this postgraduate degree. Members of the Department are also involved in the teaching of several interdisciplinary masters degrees including M.Sc. Criminology, M.Sc. Criminal Justice, M.Sc. Regulation, M.Sc. Media and Communication. There are plans to introduce more interdisciplinary masters' degrees including an LLM in Labour Law and one in Law and Accountancy. In addition, the Department hosts approximately 35 research students who are preparing M.Phil./PhD theses. The Department was rated 'excellent' by the HEFCE Quality Division with respect to its teaching.

Contact information:

Undergraduate admissions or Graduate admissions.

University of North London

Courses offered:

1   LLB (Hons) Full and Part-time;
2   Postgraduate Diploma in Legal Studies (CPE);
3   Postgraduate Diploma in Legal Practice (LPC);
4   MA Public Policy and Public Law;
5   MA/Postgraduate Diploma in Advice and Para-legal Work;
6   LLM International and European Law.

The School has been teaching its own undergraduate LLB course since 1975 so it is a long-established provider of legal education, but it has also for many years been associated with progressive teaching practices. In its 1993 quality assessment by the Higher Education Funding Council the Law School was praised for several elements of best practice: the lively and vigorous approach seen in its teaching; the effectiveness of its systems for pastoral care; the rigour and integrity of its assessment practices; and its commitment to effective staff development. Throughout the School's extensive portfolio of courses, there is considerable emphasis not only on hard legal study, but also on many associated skills: information technology; research techniques; concise writing; advocacy and interviewing.

An essential element of the School's personality is its policy of broad access to students with different study needs. This means that the LLB is offered in both full and part-time modes: part-timers can study in the day or the evening (or a combination of the two), Again, the Postgraduate Diploma in Legal Studies (CPE) course is offered to both full and part-time students, as is the MA Public Policy and Public Law. The Postgraduate Diploma in Legal Practice (a collaborative venture between this University and South Bank University) is offered only to part-timers.

The School's main responsibility is the LLB (Hons) degree. The course starts with a module in Legal Methods which teaches the techniques needed for handling complex legal rules, and it also emphasises research, information technology and drafting skills. The LLB is able to capitalise on the School's particular expertise in the Public Law area (Constitutional Law, Administrative Law, Civil Liberties, Media Law Social Security, Housing, Collective Employment, Public International Law), but the LLB also offers modules in Family Law and Evidence and in business areas such as Consumer Law, Company Law and Intellectual Property. 'State-of-the-art', skills-oriented modules include Legal Interviewing and Counselling, and Tribunal Representation.

Contact information:

Admissions Office
University of North London, 166 Holloway Rd, London N7 8DP
tel: 0171 753 3355
e mail: admissions@unl.ac.uk

University of Luton

Courses offered:

1 LLB (Hons);
2 BA (Law);
3 BA (Law and Combinations).

Contact information:

Department of Law
Lynda White
Law Department Administrator
University of Luton
Faculty of Humanities
Park Square
Luton
LU1 3JU
Tel: 01582 743105

The University of Manchester

Courses offered:

1 LLB (Hons);
2 LLB (Hons) English Law and French Law;
3 BA (Hons) Accounting and Law;
4 BA (Hons) Government and Law;
5 LLM International Business Law;
6 LLM Law and Economics;
7 LLM European Law and Policy;
8 MA Health Care Ethics & Law;
9 Diploma in Legal Studies Master of Philosophy.

Contact information:

Ms Jean Metcalfe (after Sept 98)

Manchester Metropolitan University

Courses offered:

1   LLB Full-time;
2   LLB Full-time with French and German;
3   LLB Distance Learning;
4   Legal Practice Course Full-time;
5   Legal Practice Course Part-time (from 1994);
6   Bar Examination Course;
7   Common Professional Examination Distance Learning;
8   Diploma in Personal Injury Litigation.

The School of law at the Manchester Metropolitan University has 50 academic staff and an extensive portfolio of courses, accommodating approximately 1,100 students in a variety of modes. The School has a vigorous continuing education policy, organising conferences and short courses, and an active programme of research activities, including the Institute of Law and Popular Cultures, and the British Association for Sport and the Law. Extensive links have been set up with European universities, in terms of staff and student exchanges, and there is a franchise agreement with the University of Hong Kong.

Middlesex University

Courses offered:

1   LLB (Hons) full-time;
2   BA (Hons) Law Major full-time;
3   BA (Hons) Minor full-time;
4   Common Professional Examination full-time;
5   Common Professional Examination distance learning in partnership with Wormy Hall, Oxford.

Modularisation at Middlesex University facilitates flexibility in programme planning and modes of study. The LLB (Hons) programme is recognised as a qualifying law degree by the professional bodies, providing a grounding in skills and a range of specialist options. LLB graduates with a lower second honours award (or above) are guaranteed a place if desired on the Legal Practice Course at the College of Law. Law may also be studied as a major or minor with another subject area. A policy of widening access has resulted in a significant proportion of students who are female, mature, or from ethnic minorities.

University of Northumbria at Newcastle

Courses offered:

1   LLB (three year);
2   LLB (four year) Exempting graduates from BVC and LPC;
3   LLB (four year) Exempting Law Degree with French Law;
4   Common Professional Examination;
5   Common Professional Examination Distance Learning;
6   LLB Part-Time;
7   LLB (Distance Learning);
8   Legal Practice Course;
9   Legal Practice Course Part-Time;
10   Bar Vocational Course;
11   Various LLM Programmes.

The University of Northumbria in Newcastle runs the only undergraduate degrees which exempt graduates from the Bar Vocational Course or the Legal Practice Course. These four year degree programmes (there is also a traditional three year programme) integrate the academic study of law with legal practice from the beginning. All students take part in advising live clients through the School Law Office and a small number complete their training as trainee solicitors in the Student Law Office.

The school is housed in a large city centre building with its own law court video and computer libraries and specialised legal practice library (in addition to the main law collection in the University library).

There are approximately 60 academic members of staff and an intake of 120 students onto the full-time law degree. The grades expected are BBB but lower offers are sometimes made to highly motivated students.

Contact information:

School of Law
Sutherland Building
University of Northumbria
Newcastle upon Tyne
NE1 8ST
Tel: 0191 2274494
Fax: 0191 2274557
web address: http://www.unn/ac.uk/~lux5
e mail lawgen@unn.ac.uk

Nene College Northampton

Courses offered:

1   LLB;
2   BA Combined Honours.

Contact information:

School of Law
Mike Cuthbert
Tel: 01604 735500
Fax: 01604 721214

University of Newcastle upon Tyne

Courses offered:

1   LLB (Hons) Law;
2   BA (Hons) Law with French;
3   BA (Hons) Accounting and Law.

Newcastle Law School is situated in buildings on the edge of the campus and city centre. We have our own lecture and seminar rooms, student common rooms and staff rooms. The Law section of the University Library is situated in the School and the University Library is close by. Computing facilities are available within the Law School and in clusters around the University.

Relations between staff and students are relaxed and friendly. Each student is allocated to a personal tutor who monitors their academic progress and will give support and confidential advice on any matter. There is a staff-student committee which meets regularly to discuss matters of mutual interest and concern. Our students run their own society, the Eldon Society, which organises moots, talks by outside speakers, sporting and social events.

All of the courses offered by the Law School can provide exemption from Stage 1 of the Solicitors and barristers professional examination in England and Wales provided the seven foundation modules are taken. Also, it is possible for LLB students to take the additional subjects required in order to seek training at the Institute of Professional Legal Studies. Most of the teaching centres on lectures giving the basic framework. In addition there are seminars which are small classes held once or twice a week to work through legal problems and discuss legal issues. Individual preparation for these is very important and occupies much private study time. Computer assisted learning packages are available to supplement personal study. Emphasis is also placed on the acquisition of transferable skills, such as written and oral communication, teamwork, conducting legal research and computer literacy.

Traditional end of year examinations form a large part of the assessment but in some of them books, notes and statutory materials can be used so that understanding as well as memory can be tested. Compulsory course work counts for one third of total assessment in Stages 2 and 3.

We currently admit about 125 students each year, including 15 on the Law with French degree. As with other Law Departments, competition for entry is fierce and we normally ask for ABB at A level (BBC for Accounting and Law). Any mixture of subjects will be considered and two AS levels may be substituted for one A level. Applicants with equivalent qualifications, such as Scottish Highers (AABBB usually required), CSYS, BTEC, the International Baccalaureate and other overseas qualifications are also welcome. Students with other qualifications should contact the Law School before applying.

Contact information:

Admissions Tutors
Newcastle Law School
University of Newcastle
Newcastle upon Tyne
NE1 7RU
Tel: 0191 222 7558
Fax: 0191 212 0064

The Nottingham Trent University

All Law Courses offered

* Full-time LLB
* Sandwich LLB
* LLB Europe
* LLB Distance Learning
* Full-time Post Graduate Diploma in Law (Graduate Conversion Course)
* Distance Learning Post Graduate in Law
* Legal Practice Course full-time
* Legal Practice Course by block mode
* LLM in Corporate Law, full-time
* LLM in Corporate Law, distance learning
* LLM in Advanced Litigation
* MBA in Legal Practice

Nottingham is the largest University Law School in the United Kingdom. It enjoys a national and international reputation for delivering high quality education and training across a broad range of academic and professional law programmes. There are over 100 full-time law lecturers in the Law School supporting over 2,000 undergraduate and post-graduate students. Professorships are sponsored by major Nottingham and London law firms and leading legal publishers.

The electronic law library and vast collections of law reports and materials are accessed in the Boots library on the city centre site of the Law School campus.

Contact information

Mrs Jean Bunn, Marketing Officer.
Telephone direct line: 0115 9486043

University of Nottingham

Courses offered:

1. LLB;
2   BA (Law);
3   BA (Law and Politics).

Each of these may be converted into a fourth year degree with American Law or with South East Asian Law or with European Law with the addition of a year abroad;
4   BA (Law with French);
5   BA (Law with German).

The Department is committed to achieving excellence in both teaching and research. Its undergraduate degree programmes are flexible, allowing, but not requiring, students to take subjects from other disciplines, this being facilitated by the University's modular degree programmes. A variety of teaching methods are employed, including lectures, discussion groups, seminars, tutorials and moots. A number of modules are explicitly skills-based. Applications from mature students and students with disabilities are welcome. A detailed undergraduate Admissions Brochure and information concerning postgraduate programmes is available from the Department.

Oxford Brookes University

Courses offered:

1   BA;
2   LLB.

Oxford Brookes University was the first institution to offer a modular course of study and this has now been established for 20 years. Flexibility of student choice are key features of the study of law at Brookes. Our admissions policy is similarly encouraging of diversity, with some 25% of our law intake classified as mature and 10% international.

Oxford University

Courses offered:

1   BA Law;
2   BA Law with Studies in Europe;
3   Diploma in Legal Studies;

4   Bachelor of Civil Law;
5   M Stud.\M. Litt.\D.Phil.

The Law Faculty welcomes applications from students of the higher calibre for its courses. For undergraduate degrees, applications must be made to individual Oxford Colleges. Graduate programmes are dealt with through the Graduate Studies Office, Wellington Square, Oxford OX1 2JD. A full prospectus can be obtained from the Admissions Office, at the same address.

Contact information:

Oxford Colleges Admissions Office
University Office
Wellington Square
Oxford
OX1 2JD

University of Plymouth

Courses offered:

1   LLB (Honours);
2   BSc (Honours) Law Major.

The Law Department is part of the Plymouth Business School. It is headed by Peter Shears and staffed by twelve Senior Law Lecturers.

   The LLB programme has been designed to meet both educational and vocational aims and it encourages the acquisition of skills as well as high quality academic work. Study of the Foundation Subjects required for entry to the Legal Practice Course/Bar Vocational Course, is spread over the three year programme. A number of optional modules are available in the second and third year. These are subject to change but may include Employment, Consumer, Company, Environmental, Media and Family Law. Skills modules are included in each year: Legal Method in the first stage; Lawyers Skills in the second stage which includes negotiation, advocacy and drafting skills and the Free Representation Unit in the Final Stage. The latter is an optional module and involves the student handling their own client caseload and representing the client at Tribunal if necessary.

   The BSc(Hons) Law, (Law Major) programme aims to provide a challenging opportunity to study law and to ensure an understanding of the main principles and analytical methods underlying the study of law. This programme is not a qualifying degree for Legal Professional Exemption purposes. In the first year students are required to study English Legal system and Legal Method. The remainder of their law modules are selected from a number of options, including Contract or Constitutional Law. There are no compulsory law subjects in stages two and three, but students are encouraged to select law modules which are complementary to one another and/or their minor programme. Options include those mentioned above.

Contact information:

Donna Treneary
Plymouth Business School
University of Plymouth
Drake Circus
Plymouth
Devon PL4 8AA
tel: 01752 232804
fax: 01752 232853

University of Reading

Courses offered:

1   LLB;
2   LLB (Law with French Law)
3   LLB (Law with Legal Studies in Europe);
4   LLM (General);
5   LLM (Property Law);
6   LLM (Construction Law);
7   LLM (by research);
8   M.Phil (by research);
9   PhD (by research).

The University of Reading received its charter in 1926 and the Law School admitted its first undergraduates in 1974. Currently we have an intake of approximately 90 students onto the three undergraduate programmes and about 15 postgraduates enter onto taught masters' programmes. There are 17 full-time and 2 part-time academic staff. We feel fortunate in that we have retained a relatively small intake of good quality students and have a staff student ration which has permitted the retention of small group teaching.

The first year at Reading covers two academic terms with examinations after Easter. During the first year students study, after an introductory programme on legal method, contract, tort, criminal law and one non-law subject. The non-law subject can be one of a wide range on offer – languages (including Japanese), social sciences and traditional humanities are available as are courses in mathematics, biology and geology. After the first year examinations students can opt to transfer to their non-law subject if they so wish (very few do) and those who have not passed law at an appropriate level may also transfer to their non-law subject (transfer is dependent on passing that subject at an appropriate level). First year marks do not count towards the degree classification.

After Easter, students embark on their final degree course which consists of 38 modules (18 in year 2 and 20 in years 3 or 4) broken down into 2 and 4 module units. The second year consists largely of compulsory units (6 optional modules) while the final year consists largely of optional units. There is a wide range of options within the law department and it is also possible to take 4 modules in another subject area. In both the second and final year there are 2 compulsory module units which are assessed by means of an extended essay. In other units, examinations are taken at the end of the second and final years and the combined results of these examinations and assessed work determine degree classification. It is not possible to proceed to the final year of the degree until one has passed all previous examinations and assessments.

For those taking the four-year degree, the third year is spent at a European university. For those taking Law with French law there is an intensive French law course taught principally in French during the second year at Reading. We have links with universities in many European countries and have sent students to France, Spain, Germany, Italy, Holland and Sweden (in the last two countries our partner university teaches law in English). A number of students enter for the three-year degree but transfer to the four-year programme while they are with us.

The majority of teaching in the compulsory units is by means of lectures and tutorials (first year groups average six students, subsequently group sizes rise to an average of ten). In optional units a wide variety of teaching methods are employed apart from lectures and tutorials and some units assess students partly by assessed work as well as examinations.

Contact information:

Undergraduate: Professor R A Buckley
Mrs S E Murdoch

University of Sheffield

Courses offered:

1　LLB Law;
2　BA Law with Criminology;
3　BA Law with Languages;
4　BA Law.

The Department successfully combines almost a century of traditional legal scholarship with a dynamic and innovative approach to teaching and research. With over 60 staff and 1000 students from over 20 countries, the environment is truly European and international. Our top rankings for teaching and research bear testament to the work of international excellence that is carried out here.

Contact information

Department of Law
University of Sheffield
Crookesmor Building
Conduit Road
Sheffield
S10 1EL
Tel: 0114 222 6771
Fax: 0114 222 6832
Website: http:\\www.shef.ac.uk.academic\I-M\law
e mail: UGLAW@Sheffield.ac.uk

Sheffield Hallam University

Courses offered:

1   LLB (Hons);
2   LLB (Hons) part-time;
3   BA Honours International Financial and Legal Studies.

Contact information:

Division of Law
School of Financial Studies and Law
Mr Douglas Smith Admissions Tutor.

Southbank University

Courses offered:

1   Law degrees with qualifying status
    LLB Full-time (150)
    LLB part-time (4 years – evenings and weekends) (50)
    Combined Honours Law Major Programme (Law can be studied in conjunction with approximately 15 other academic disciplines
2   Non-qualifying law degrees
    Combined Honours Joint Honours Law Programme (60)
    Combined Honours Law Minor programme (60)
3   Postgraduate Courses
    Part-time PG Dip in Legal Practice –LPC (2 years, offered in conjunction with University of North London) (60)

Full-time PG Dip in Legal Studies – CPE (3 5)
Part-time PG Dip in Legal Studies – CPE (2 years – evenings) (3 5)
LLM in Legal Practice (Full-time and Part-time) (25)
MA in Legal Studies (Full-time and Part-time) (25)
4   Post-experience courses
Certificate in Applied Advice Work (day release 1 day per week) (50)

The Law Division is one of 8 divisions forming the South Bank Business School. It provides a range of full-time and part-time courses, at undergraduate and postgraduate levels, including a part-time LPC. The Law Division comprises 18 teaching staff most of whom are qualified lawyers, many with practice experience and postgraduate qualifications. The Division is committed to the provision of effective up-to-date teaching to enable students to cope with the rapidly changing conditions in the legal profession, and related occupations.

The Division has a lively research record, a matter it considers essential for effective teaching. Recent major projects include research into equal opportunities, access to the legal profession, clinical legal education, legal aid, judicial review, possession proceedings by local authorities, and help on arrest schemes. Staff have also published a wide range of student texts in the areas of Company Law, Commercial Law, Housing Law, Family Law, Criminal Law and Public Law.

The LLB course provides a structured an challenging undergraduate legal education, with students being offered an interesting range of options including Women and the Law, Medical Law and Ethics, and Environmental Law. The Combined Honours scheme allows student to combine the study of law with disciplines such as accounting, economics, history, English, modern languages, sports science, psychology and, from September 1998, forensic science. Students who major in law on the combined honours scheme will graduate with a qualifying law degree.

Contact information:

The Law Division
South Bank Business School
South Bank University
103 Borough Road
London SE1 OAA

COURSE ADMINISTRATOR FOR LAW UNDERGRADUATE PROGRAMMES
Ms. Helen Edge
Tel: 0171 815 5739

COURSE ADMINISTRATOR FOR LAW POSTGRADUATE AND POST-EXPERIENCE
PROGRAMMES
Ms. Jill Denham
Tel. 0171 815 7856

University of Surrey

Courses offered:

1 BSc Hons French and Law, German and Law, Russian and Law;
2 LLB Law with French, or German or Russian (1999 plan);
3 LLB Law with Professional English (1998 plan).

School of Language and International Studies.

We specialise in the combination of modern languages and a professional subject eg law; particular features of the degrees are a course on the national law of the foreign jurisdiction, and a final year dissertation on a topic of European or foreign law.

Contact information:

Admissions Secretary
Mrs L Fox
School of Language and International Studies
University of Surrey
Guildford
GU2 5XH
Tel: 01483 259950
L.Fox@surrey.ac.uk

University of Sussex

Courses offered:

1 LLB;
2 LLB with a Language Diploma;
3 LLB in European Commercial Law;
4 BA in Law;
5 BA in Law with a Language;
6 BA in Law with North American Studies ;
7 BSc (Chemistry and Law);
8 BSc (Physics and Law);
9 BSc (Environmental Sciences and Law);
10 CPE (Postgraduate;
11 LLM in International Criminal Law;
12 MPhil;

13 LLM in International Commercial Law;
14 DPhil;
15 LLM. .

Each of the undergraduate degrees includes all 7 core courses as required for exemption from the Bar and Law Society professional examinations.

The various degrees are, to a greater or lesser extent, devised with the University of Sussex' fundamental aim of interdisciplinary education in mind. Thus with the BA in Law, for example, students are registered either in the School of European Studies or the School of English and American Studies and supplement the core law courses (which are taught simultaneously with the core law courses to LLB students registered in the Centre for Legal Studies) with courses devised around the subjects studied in those two Schools.

In the case of the degrees BA in Law with North American Studies, LLB Law with a Language and BA in Law with a Language, the degree is four years with the third year in each case spent either in the country of the appropriate language or on the campus of a North American University.

The three joint degrees with Chemistry, Physics and Environmental Science will have their first intake of students in Autumn 1999 and apart from the inclusion of the core law courses and the fundamental science courses, these degrees will contain specialist options in Intellectual Property and Forensic Science and the Legal Process, which will have been devised and which will be taught by faculty from both the Centre for Legal Studies and the School of Chemistry, Physics and Environmental Science.

Whereas the LLMs in International Criminal and International Commercial Law are suitably restricted in the range of courses which can be selected, the newly-established generic LLM permits students an unrestricted choice both from the courses available for the two specialist LLMs and others specially devised. The twenty-strong faculty at the Centre for Legal Studies span a wide range of research interests and supervision can be offered to most well-qualified, serious-minded students wishing to engage in research,

Contact information:

Professor H. H. Rajak,
Director,
Centre for Legal Studies,
Arts Building E,
University of Sussex,
Falmer,
Brighton, BNI 9QN
Tel: 01273 678532

Fax: 01273 678466
E-mail: H.H.Rajak@sussex.ac.uk

Southampton Institute

Courses offered:

1   LLB (Hons);
2   BA (Hons) Business and Law;
3   BA (Hons) Legal Studies;
4   LLM.

Contact information:

Faculty of Law
Susan Barbor
Southampton Institute
East Park Terrace
Southampton
SO14 OYN
Tel: 01703 319501
Fax:01703 235948

University of Southampton

Courses offered:

1   LLB;
2   LLB (European Legal Studies);
3   Accounting and Law*;
4   Politics and Law**;
5   Politics with Law**;
6   LLM;
7   MA (Criminal Justice);
8   MPhil/PhD.
* operated by Department of Management
** operated by Department of Politics

The Faculty of Law at the University of Southampton strives for excellence both in teaching and learning and in research. The Faculty was rated as Grade 5 in the 1996 Research Assessment Exercise, confirming its position in the top rank of UK law schools. The quality of the University of Southampton law degree is widely recognised by solicitors firms (especially in the City of London). The Faculty places great importance on the link between research and teaching: members of staff are actively involved in the development of law at both national and international levels, whether it be company law or criminal justice, shipping law or social security law. This activity leads back into teaching. Similarly, the Faculty has a strong tradition of developing innovative options in both the undergraduate and postgraduate curricula (e.g. Information Technology Law and the Law relating to Ethnic Minority Customs). A key part of the undergraduate LLB degree is the compulsory third-year dissertation, which counts as a full course. This represents an important opportunity for students to hone their research and writing skills.

The Faculty has established research and teaching centres in the Institute of Maritime Law, the Institute of Criminal Justice, the Centre for Environmental Law and the Law and Behavioural Sciences Network. However, much of the Faculty's teaching and research is conducted in other areas and outside these organisational frameworks.

The Faculty has some 500 undergraduates following the LLB or LLB (European Legal Studies) degrees. It also participates in joint honours degrees operated by the Departments of Management (Accounting) and Politics. It has a thriving community of postgraduate students on both taught and research degree programmes. The Faculty's teaching and learning is supported by the university's Hartley Library, which houses the Law Collection and the specialist Ford Collection of Parliamentary Papers. In addition, the Law Building houses a dedicated Law Computer Laboratory providing access to legal databases and the university network. Access to the Internet is also available and all students are encouraged to register as E-mail users. A number of undergraduate courses integrate the use of on-line course materials into the teaching programme.

The students in the Faculty of Law organise and run two societies: the Law Faculty Society and the Inns of Court Society. Each society arranges social events during the year, as well as evening events directed towards careers. The Law Faculty Society (LFS) provides invaluable support in showing applicants around the campus on visiting days. LFS representatives also attend meetings of the Staff Student Liaison Committee which are held on a regular basis to discuss matters of mutual interest. Year representatives also attend meetings of the Law Faculty Board.

As regards careers, the Faculty has its own experienced Careers Tutor, a member of the academic staff with particular responsibility for co-ordinating the overall careers programme. The Faculty has an agreement with the College of Law that all our students graduating with at least a lower second class honours degree are guaranteed a place on the Legal Practice Course at the College.

Contact information

UNDERGRADUATE ADMISSIONS TUTOR:
Mr Mike Newark

UNDERGRADUATE ADMISSIONS SECRETARY:
Mrs Margaret Newton
Tel: 01703 592596
E-mail: M.B.Newton@soton.ac.uk

School of Oriental & African Studies

Courses offered:

1 LLB;
2 BA LLM & Another subject.

The Department of Law at SOAS, founded in 1947, offers both an LLB degree course and two-subject BA degree courses in Law and another discipline or a language. The single-subject Law degree (the LLB) has been recognised by the Law Society and the Council of Legal Education for the purpose of the completion of the academic stage of legal training, provided students have taken the seven 'core subjects'.

Law courses at SOAS are taught on a comparative or international basis and with an emphasis on the way in which law functions in society. Thus the LLB at SOAS is essentially broad, comparative and theoretical in its orientation. All students undertake some study of African and Asian laws and it is possible to take specialised courses in the laws of selected geographical areas or countries in Asia and Africa as well as to study legal issues in a trans-regional context. The existence of a wide range of two subject degrees (BA degrees) also makes it possible for a student to study law in an interdisciplinary fashion (i.e. law and another discipline) or to study law and to develop linguistic skills at the same time (i.e. law and a language).

The Department also has an expanding and varied LLM programme which provides a number of advanced courses both on comparative and international law, and on aspects of the legal systems of Asia and Africa. The association with the Foundation for International law and Development (FIELD) and the growth of environmental law expertise in the Department also mean that the Department is now one of the major international centres for the study of environmental and sustainable development law.

In 1989 the School established a Centre of Islamic and Middle East Law (CIMEL) and an East Asian Law Centre (EALC). Both Centres are located in the Department of Law and are responsible for formally promoting the study of Islamic, Middle Eastern and East Asian Laws by organising conferences and public lectures, producing publications, and other activities. The Group on Ethnic Minority Studies (GEMS) and the Malaysian Legal Studies Group (MLSG) are also located in the Department. The Law Reports of the Commonwealth, the Journal of African Law and the Review of European Community and International Environmental Law are all edited within the Department. In addition, the Department participates in the University of London Law and Development Programme together with the Institute of Advanced Legal Studies and four other London Law Schools. In addition to its very close link with FIELD, it has links with several other universities and institutes with similar interests in Europe, the United States, Africa and Asia.

Although the Department has expanded considerably in the last decade, it remains relatively small in terms of both student and staff numbers. During 1996/7 121 students were registered for the LLB, 57 registered for the BA, 73 registered for the LLM and 47 registered for the MPhil/PhD. At present there are 20 full-time members of academic staff and 12 visiting members including 5 members of FIELD.

Contact information:

Ms Cathy Jenkins
Law Department
SOAS
Thornhaugh Street
Russell Square
London
WC1H OXG

Staffordshire University

Courses offered:

1   LLB Full-time and Part-time;
2   Undergraduate awards in Law and in Legal Studies (Major or Combined BA Hons)
3   The Graduate Diplomas in Law (Common Professional Examination);
4   The Postgraduate Diploma in Legal Practice Course;
5   LLM (Names Routes);
6   MA in Legal Studies.

The Law School has a strong tradition of teaching law at degree level and has a 55 full-time staff. Approximately 1,100 students are enrolled each year on undergraduate, postgraduate and professional programmes. The School is also actively involved in Continuing Education for Solicitors and other Professional groups.

It is our firm belief that our courses, while placing full emphasis on developing the skills which are essential to the modern lawyer, provide a well rounded education through the medium of legal study.

Contact information:

Jo Bradbury

Admissions Co-ordinator
Tel: 01782 294551

University of Wales, Swansea

Courses offered:

1   LLB Single honours full-time;
2   LLB Joint honours full-time;
3   M.Phil (by research only);
4   PhD.

The Law Department is now 6 years old and accepts about 160 undergraduate students each year. It also supervises about 10 postgraduate students per year. It is an academic department with an interdisciplinary bias.

Contact information:

Professor of Law
Jennifer Levin.

Swansea Institute of Higher Education

Course offered:

1   LLB.

This is a newly-established degree programme within an established College of Higher Education. Swansea is a City on the very attractive Gower peninsula.

University of Teesside

Course offered:

1   LLB.

This is a quite newly established law degree programme in a college with a long tradition of teaching for the LLB London External degree. It provides a qualification for entry to both the solicitor's and barrister's professions.

Thames Valley University

Courses offered:

1   LLB full-time;
2   LLB Evening;

3   LLB with French/German/Spanish;
4   Law and Language full-time;
5   BA European Law full-time;
6   BA Criminal justice full-time;
7   BA Criminal justice Evening;
8   BA Accounting and Law full-time;
9   Common Professional Examination full-time and evening.

The Law School at Thames Valley has in recent years developed a specialism in Criminal Justice and in greater European orientation. Thus the School offers a range of courses offering the student a choice of taking either a conventional LLB course or a course which enhances the student's knowledge of a European language (coupled with spending a year abroad and learning some continental law) or a course which will expressly prepare the students for a choice of careers in the criminal justice system. The School is now looking to develop closer links with the practising profession and runs flourishing full-time and evening CPE courses. It has for some years maintained close links with the Far East from where students come to take the Bar Examination course.

University College London

Courses offered:

1   LLB
2   A large range of taught LLM programmes and research opportunities

The Faculty was the first in England too offer a systematic university education on the common law. It seeks to offer its students an excellent liberal legal education. It now has over 460 undergraduates, 300 postgraduates, 38 full-time staff (including 15 professors) and about 30 part-time teachers, many of them distinguished practising and academic lawyers. The Faculty achieved a top grading in the Research Selectivity Exercises conducted in 1985, 1989 and 1992 by the universities funding body. In 1993, a three-day Quality Assessment visit designed to test the strength of the Faculty's teaching was carried out and the assessors rated it as excellent. Through a diverse range of teaching methods, critical studies and active interest in law reform, the Faculty of Law promotes the values of its founders – justice, liberty and equal rights for all. The programmes provide both a liberal legal education and a basis for careers in many fields.

Contact information:

Faculty of Law

University College London
Bentham House
Endsleigh Gardens
London
WC1H 0EG

GRADUATE
Tel: 0171 391 1441/1425
Fax: 0171 209 3470
e mail: m.mark@ucl.ac.uk

UNDERGRADUATE
Tel: 0171 391 1414
Fax: 0171 391 1414
e mail: uctlaet@ucl.ac.uk

University of Warwick

Courses offered:

1   three-year programme leading to an LLB degree;
2   four-year, rather broader programme also leading to an LLB degree;
3   four-year European LLB degree with a year spent at a French, German or Italian University;
4   four-year joint honours programme leading to a BA (Law and Sociology);
5   three or four year honours programme leading to a BA Law and Business Studies.

Research degrees include:

1   LLM by Research: This involves a thesis of up to 40,000 words. Duration one year;
2   MPhil: This involves a thesis of up to 60,000 words. Duration two years;
3   PhD: This involves a thesis of up to 80,000 words. Duration three years.

The School with 37 full-time members of staff is able to offer research supervision over a wide range of legal topics. The School has particular strengths in the areas of International Economic and Development Law, Criminal Justice, Public Law and Local Government, Children and the Law, Environmental and Housing Law, Law and Technology, European

Law, Modern Equity, Employment Law, Gender and the Law, and Commercial Law. However, supervision can be offered in other subject specialisms.

Instead of concentrating on the study, analysis and memorising of legal rules, the Schools aim is to widen the scope of legal studies to include the social context in which law and lawyers operate. Students cover those aspects of the law which are closely related to major social problems in areas such as crime, housing, consumer protection, labour relations, companies, human rights, the family, sport and the environment. In addition, the School has a special interest in international legal problems, European legal systems and, mainly at the graduate level, law and development and International Economic law.

One of the assumptions behind the courses has been that law is an interesting subject to study in its own right both as a discipline and as an important aspect of society. At the same time the School is well aware that many students choose to read law with a view to practising as a solicitor or barrister. A further aim of the courses has therefore been to lay a foundation for those who wish to go on to practise and at the same time provide a course of study which will be of value if students go on to do something else. The School felt that the kind of preparation traditionally provided for future practitioners needed to be broadened in essentially the same direction that made law worth studying by students who did not eventually go on to practise. This is achieved by putting law in its context, studying the role of law and lawyers in society at the same time as studying the way in which they go about their tasks, and giving students the opportunity of reading more than purely legal materials

A distinctive feature of the School of Law at Warwick is that an effort is made to encourage in every course an approach which is both broadly gauged and critical and which examines the contribution of law and other disciplines to the diagnosis and handling of contemporary social and economic problems.

The School of law's teaching was rated 'excellent' in the most recent Teaching Quality Assessment by the HEFCE.

Contact information

Further information on undergraduate and postgraduate study is available at the website: http//www.warwick.ac.uk/law/

For fuller details of undergraduate degrees, please request a copy of the Law School's own Prospectus by sending an A5 size stamped addressed envelope to Carol Hughes, School of Law, University of Warwick, Coventry CV4 7AL

FOR A COURSE BROCHURE
Tel: 01203 523075
E-mail: June.Green@warwick.ac.uk

FOR A POSTGRADUATE PROSPECTUS
Tel: 01203 523079
E-mail: Margaret.Wright@warwick.ac.uk

University of Westminster

Courses offered:

1   LLB;
2· Common Professional Examination;
3   Legal Practice Course.

This Law School is long established in Red Lion Square in the heart of 'Legal London'. It has strong links with the legal profession and has recently embarked upon solicitors' professional legal education with the commencement of the Legal Practice Course.

Queen Mary and Westfield College, University of London

Courses offered:

1   LLB;
2   LLB in English and European Law;
3   LLB in Law with German;
4   BA in Law and Politics;
5   BA in Law and Economics.

The Faculty of Law was established in 1965 and comprises the Department of Law and the specialist Centre for Commercial Law Studies. Situated on the outskirts of the City of London the Faculty has strong links with the practising profession and with legal advisers in international organisations, government and industry. The Faculty fosters a strong sense of community within which the Student Law Society plays an enthusiastic and active part. Close relations exist with a number of overseas law schools as a result of which the Faculty can offer exciting opportunities for study abroad as an integral part of QMW law courses. The Faculty does not prescribe any particular A-level subjects and conditional offers will usually require BBB or BBC. The Faculty encourages applications from mature students and the LLB may be completed in two years by those who are already graduates of a recognised institution.

University of Wolverhampton

Courses offered:

1 LLB [Honours] Full-time;
2 LLB [Honours] Part-time;
3 LLB [Honours] Distance Learning;
4 BA [Honours] Criminal justice Full-time;
5 BA [Honours] Combined Studies. Law Major, Full-time and Part-time;
6 LLDip (CPE) Full-time;
7 LLDip (CPE) Part-time;
8 Legal Practice Course Part-time;
9 Legal Practice Course Full-time;
10 LLM Full-time;
11 LLM, Part-time;
12 LLM, Distance Learning;
13 MA (English Laws) Full-time;
14 MA (Legal Studies) Full-time;
15 MA (Legal Studies) Part-time;
16 M.Phil;
17 Ph.D;
18 FILEX, Part-time.

All Distance Learning Awards offered jointly with Holborn College London.

The staff of the School currently consists of one Dean of the School, two Associate Deans and some 43 other academic staff at Principal/Senior/Lecturer levels. There are four graduate Research Assistants in post and 13 part-time staff are employed by the School. There are, in addition, 11 administrative, secretarial and technical staff in the School.

The School runs a full-time LLB Hons degree course with about 400 students, a part-time LLB and LLB Hons degree course with about 350 students, the Legal Practice and CPE courses with 175 students altogether, FILEX with about 60 students and a very successful taught LLM programme has been developed which is delivered on a full-time, part-time and distance learning basis.

As regards other courses, the School is responsible for the teaching of law throughout the University. Law is taught on degree courses such as BA (Hons) Modular degree, BA (Hons) Economics, BA (Hons) Business Studies, and on subdegree courses such as BTEC. It is also taught on a wide variety of professional courses including accountancy, education, engineering, management, and nursing.

Additionally, the School has collaborative links with Wigan & Leigh College, Holborn College, London, and National Law Tutors.

The staff of the School of Legal Studies currently occupy modern, purpose built premises and the teaching accommodation is good. There is an excellent Law Library with a specialised library staff, and computerised information retrieval facilities are available. Some computer assisted learning programmes are already available and many other computer applications, including inter-active video, are under active development. The School is due to be networked during the course of this academic year.

The staff of the School are well-motivated and enthusiastic. Excellent staff-student relationships have been built up over the years.

There is a wide range of consultancy and research carried out within the University including activities in association with industry, commerce and the professions. All staff are encouraged to participate in research and consultancy projects and it is expected that the level of this activity will continue to grow.

The School is committed to the development of information technology in all aspects of its work, and is currently involved in a major multi-media project.

Contact information:

DEAN'S OFFICE:
Tel: 01902 321519
Fax: 01902 321567

ADMISSIONS OFFICE:
Tel: 01902 321999
Fax: 01902 321570
E-mail: in5070@wlv.ac.uk

Appendix 2
Citation of legal sources

Cases

1 Always cite the more prestigious series of reports. The hierarchy is the Law Reports, Weekly Law Reports, All England Law Reports, other series. In other series, generally, the fullest report is the most satisfactory.

2 Note the proper use of round and square brackets for the date in citing law reports. The rule (with reports in this jurisdiction) is that square brackets are used if the date is an essential part of the reference and round brackets if the date is not. The correct mode of citation is given in each volume of the law reports.

3 If referring to a particular page of a report, then cite it as follows:

R v Butterwasser [1948] 1 KB 4, 9

Thus showing that you refer the reader to page 9 of the report.

4 To refer to a particular statement in a judgment place your quotation in the text, eg 'the evidence of a police officer who knows the prisoner and his habits, and has seen him in the streets, is, no doubt, very proper evidence' and in your reference cite *R v Butterwasser* [1948] 1 KB 4, 9 (per Lord Goddard LCJ). Alternatively, as follows: 'As Mr Justice Veale said in *Halsey v Esso Petroleum Co Ltd*, setting the tone for the rest of his judgment, "This is a case, if ever there was one, of the little man asking for the protection of the law against the activities of a large and powerful neighbour" (see [1961] 2 All ER 145, 149).'

5 If words are omitted from a quotation, this is indicated by a short row of dots. Words you insert to make sense of a quotation in your text are shown in brackets. Words in a quotation which may seem incorrect or

ungrammatical or shocking to a reader may be followed by the word *sic* in brackets (ie the Latin for 'thus'). The following is an example of the modern usage to indicate an unacceptable or shocking train of thought: '… society can prevent those who are manifestly unfit from continuing their kind. The principle that sustains compulsory vaccination is broad enough to cover cutting the Fallopian tubes … Three generations of imbeciles are enough.' (sic) (per Holmes J in *Buck v Bell* 274 US 200 (1927), a now discredited (?) decision of the United States Supreme Court.

6   Once a case has been cited in the text, it may be referred to afterwards by an abbreviated name as follows: 'The sentiment expressed in *Butterwasser* is typical of the English judiciary. That expressed in *Halsey's* case is not. As for *Buck v Bell* decided before the holocaust we can now see with hindsight the danger of the eugenic beliefs it endorsed.'

Statutes

1   There are two conventional methods of citation. By short titles and by regnal year, ie by the number of an Act of Parliament within a parliamentary session – the year of that parliamentary session being denoted by the year or years of the monarch's reign. So, 26, 7 Will 4 & 1 Vict, refers to the 26th Act of Parliament passed during the parliamentary session which straddled the seventh or last year of King William IV's reign and the first year of Queen Victoria's. This Act is now more commonly known as the Wills Act (1837).

   Since 1962, Acts have not been arranged chronologically in regnal years but only in calendar years. Even in respect of older Acts of Parliament it is now a quaint anachronism to use regnal years. The short-title will invariably be used unless it is an Act for which there is none.

2   It is important to learn the correct name for each division of an Act. References to an Act should be as follows. A number of sections may be grouped in a *part*, eg Law of property Act, Pt I (ss 1-39). A section may be divided into sub-sections and sub-sections into paragraphs. For example: 'An estate in fee simple absolute in possession may exist as a legal estate in land (see Law of Property Act 1925 (s 1(1)(a)).' This refers to paragraph (a) of sub-section (1) of section 1 of that well-known Act.

3   Schedules to Acts of Parliament are divided into paragraphs and sub-paragraphs and cited as follows. The Theft Act 1968 (Sch 1, para 192) provides that unlawfully killing a deer in enclosed land where deer are usually kept is an arrestable offence.

4   In an essay an Act referred to often may be referred to by a clear abbreviation, eg the LPA 1925. In a more formal work. abbreviations may still be used, eg referring for the second time to the 'Prevention of Fraud (Investments) Act 1958', you may say 'the 1958 Act' or 'the Prevention of Fraud etc Act' as appropriate to the context.

Statutory instruments

These are normally divided into *rules* and *paragraphs* and *sub-paragraphs*. Occasionally longer instruments are divided into *sections*, *paragraphs* and *sub-paragraphs* see, eg Land Registration Rules 1925. They are cited by their short title and the correct citation is now invariably given in rule 1 of each instrument. In more formal works it is customary to cite the number as well as the name, eg 'For this purpose the definition of "Qualifying Student" is found in rule 2(2) (see Rent Rebates and Rent Allowances (Students) (England and Wales) Regulations 1976 (SI 1976 No 1242)).' Further on in your text, an abbreviated reference may be used, eg 'Part-time teacher training courses seem to be excluded (see the Rent Rebates etc Regulations 1976, r 2(2))'.

Textbooks

1   Try to avoid references to textbooks unless the reference adds something of substance to your argument.

2   Use the author's surname and cite the necessary bibliographic detail, as follows: Treitel *An Outline of the Law of Contract* (3rd edn, 1984) p 254.

Journals

1   Each journal states in each issue the recommended form of citation. Use this.

2   In short essays an exact reference is not necessary, eg 'Wilkinson in his recent article (1984 Conveyancer) examined the case concerning the application of the Misrepresentation Act 1967 to sales of land ... '

3   In a longer piece of work, place your reference in a footnote - the first citation should give the whole reference: 'Wilkinson *Exemption Clauses in Land Contracts* 1984 Conv 12.' Future references may be, provided there is no ambiguity, much foreshortened, eg '*Wilkinson* (op cit) p 14.'

Members of the judiciary

1   Use their correct full titles before their name or the conventional
    abbreviation after their name.
        These are correct:

    The Lord Chief Justice, Lord Parker ...

                                or

    Lord Parker LCJ

    The President, Sir Jocelyn Simon ...

                                or

    Simon P

    The Lord Chancellor, Lord Gardiner

                                or

    Lord Gardiner LC

    Mr Justice Veale

                                or

    Veale J

    For a Crown Court Judge:
    His Honour Judge Cohen

                                or

    Judge Cohen

    For a magistrate:
    Dr S Marsh JP

2   Do not use familiar names, Christian names or slovenly abbreviations.
    Even when referring to legal authors, avoid the use of Christian names
    unless this is the author's own usage - many still find this practice a
    vulgar Americanism.
        Finally, in your use of citation aim for unambiguity, neatness and
    consistency. If you achieve these three goals you will have achieved
    enough.

Appendix 3
Suggested method of typing headings

<u>This is a principal A heading</u>

This principal 'A' heading is typed in upper and lower case and centred on the page. The following text begins on a new line.

This is a second grade B heading.

This second grade 'B' heading is typed in upper and lower case and starts at the left-hand margin. The following text begins on a new line.

<u>This is a third grade C heading</u>

This third grade 'C' heading is typed in upper and lower case; it is underlined and starts at the left-hand margin. The following text begins on a new line.

<u>This is a fourth grade D heading</u>. This fourth grade 'D' heading is typed in upper and lower case: it is underlined and starts at the left-hand margin. The text, however, continues in the same line.

Appendix 4

The Gobbledygook Test*

This test measures the approximate level of difficulty of a piece of writing. It is a rough measure because it deals only with word length and sentence length: many other variables, like sentence structure and size of print, help to make reading easy or difficult. Never write just to please the test: a low score does not guarantee simplicity or clarity. Follow the instructions to work out the level of difficulty of the text, remembering that:

- Numbers and symbols are counted as short words
- Hyphenated words are counted as two words
- A syllable, for the purpose of the test, is a vowel sound. So *advised* is two syllables, *applying* is three.

Instructions		Sample A	Sample B	Sample C	
1	Count a 100-word sample				2
2	Count the number of complete sentences in the Sample A column.				
3	Count the total number of words in all the complete sentences and note it in the sample A column.				3
4	Find the average sentence length by dividing the answer for instruction 3 by the answer for instruction 2.				4
5	Count the number of words of three or more syllables in the full 100 words. This gives the percentage of long words in the sample.				5
6	Add the answers for instructions 4 and 5. This gives the test score for the sample.				
7	Repeat with two more samples, B and C.				
8	Add the three test scores.	Test scores A + B + C =			
9	Divide by three to get a final average score.	Average of A, B & C =			
10	Compare your score with the results below. (The lower the score, the more comprehensible the material is likely to be.)				

(The calculations on newspapers were made on 14 July 1980.)

*   Adapted from R. Gunning's *FOG* (frequency of gobbledygook) formula. The formula is considered best for testing material for adult readers.

*   The Gobbledygook Test is reprinted with the permission of the Plain English Campaign, Vernon House, Whaley Bridge, Stockport SK12 7HP

Appendix 5
Addresses of professional bodies

The Bar Council
3 Bedford Row
LONDON
WC1R 4DB

The Council of Legal Education
4 Gray's Inn Place
LONDON
WC1R 5DX

The Under-Treasurer
Lincoln's Inn
LONDON
WC2A 3TL

The Sub-Treasurer
Inner Temple
LONDON
EC4Y 7HL

The Under-Treasurer
Middle Temple
LONDON
EC4Y 9AT

The Under-Treasurer
Gray's Inn
LONDON
WC1R 5EU

The Secretary
The Senate of the Inns of Court and the Bar
11 South Square
Gray's Inn
LONDON
WC1R 5EL

The Institute of Legal Executives
Kempston Manor
Kempston
BEDFORD
MK42 7AB

The Law Society
The Law Society's Hall
113 Chancery Lane
LONDON
WC2A 1PL

John Stuart Colyer Esq, QC (for details of chambers granting pupillage)
11 King's Bench Walk
Temple
LONDON
EC4

The Secretary
Institute of Taxation
3 Grosvenor Crescent
LONDON
SW1X 7EL

The Secretary
Association of Certified Accountants
29 Lincoln's Inn Field
LONDON
WC2A 3EE

The Chartered Institute of Arbitrators
75 Cannon Street
LONDON
EC4N 5BH

Appendix 6

Information: sources of postgraduate finance

The Grants Register (issued annually)
Macmillan Educational Commission
United States – United Kingdom
Student Adviser's Office
6 Parker Street
LONDON W1M 1 HR

(Postgraduate study in the United States and details of current awards)

Secretary
Association of Commonwealth Universities
36 Gordon Square
LONDON
WC1 OPF

(Book *Scholarship Guide for Commonwealth Postgraduate Students* published every two years)

British Council
65 Davies Street
LONDON
W1Y 2AA

(Booklet *Scholarships Abroad*)

The British Academy
Burlington House
LONDON
W1V 0NS

(Grants for research)

Economic and Social Research Council
1 Temple Avenue
LONDON
EC4Y 0BD

(Grants for research in sociolegal fields, criminology, economics and law)

DES
Room 1127
Elizabeth House
York Road
LONDON
SE1 7PH

(State studentships for Postgraduate Awards in Humanities)

Sources of Funding for Research and Publication
(A useful booklet published by University of Leicester Primary Communications Research Centre.)

Graduates Studies (issued annually) - The Guide to Postgraduate Study in the UK (CRAC) contains a comprehensive survey of available courses.

Register of Educational Research in the UK (includes information on sources of finance).

Research in British Universities, Polytechnics and Colleges, Vol 3, Social Sciences - a survey of current research projects.

Appendix 7
Bibliography

Bird *A Guide to Articled Clerks and Trainee Legal Executives* (1989) Sweet & Maxwell

Butterworths Property Law Handbook (1994) Butterworths

Cheshire, Fifoot & Furmston's Law of Contract (13th edn, 1996) Butterworths

Clignet *Liberty and Equality in the Educational Process* (1974) Wiley

Dane and Thomas *How to Use a Law Library* (1987) Sweet & Maxwell

Harris *An Introduction to Law* (3rd edn, 1988) Weidenfeld & Nicolson

Harvard Law Review Association *A Uniform System of Citation* (Gannet House, Cambridge, Massachusetts 02138, USA)

Kenny *Sweet & Maxwell Law File/Cohabiting Owners* (1984) Sweet & Maxwell

Lloyd *The Idea of Law* (revised edn, 1981) Pelican

Lowe and Woodroffe *Consumer Law and Practice* (3rd edn, 1991) Sweet & Maxwell

Megarry and Wade *The Law of Real Property* (6th edn, 1993)

Miers and Twinning *How to Do Things with Rules* (3rd edn, 1991) Butterworths

Miller and Parlett *Up to the Mark* (1973) University of Edinburgh Centre for Research in the Educational Sciences Occasional Paper 13

Murphy and Clark *The Family Home* (1983) Sweet & Maxwell

Newman *The Bar Finals Guide* (2nd edn, 1987) Sweet & Maxwell

Smart *The Ties That Bind* (1984) Routledge & Kegan Paul

Smith and Hogan *Criminal Law* (8th edn, 1996) Butterworths

Smith and Thomas *A Case Book on Contract* (9th edn, 1992) Sweet & Maxwell

Stevens, Miers and Page *Legislation* (1990) Sweet & Maxwell

Street *Freedom, the Individual and the Law* (6th edn, 1990) Pelican

Street *Torts* (10th edn, 1998) Butterworths

Sweet & Maxwell's *Property Statutes* (6th edn, 1993) Sweet & Maxwell

Treitel *The Law of Contract* (8th edn, 1991) Sweet & Maxwell
Weir *Casebook on Tort* (7th edn, 1992) Sweet & Maxwell
Williams *The Proof of Guilt* (3rd edn, 1963) Sweet & Maxwell
Wiliams and Marsh *A Second Survey of Legal Education in the United Kingdom, Supplement No 1* (1981) Institute of Advanced Legal Studies
Winfield and Jolowicz *Tort* (13th edn, 1989) Sweet & Maxwell

Appendix 8
Sample law report

Mullin v Richards and another

COURT OF APPEAL, CIVIL DIVISION

BUTLER-SLOSS, HUTCHISON LJJ AND SIR JOHN VINELOTT

6 NOVEMBER 1997

Negligence - Duty to take care - Foreseeable harm - Child - Test of foreseeability - 15-year-old plaintiff injured during game with defendant of same age at school - Game not considered dangerous or prohibited by school authorities - Whether accident foreseeable to 15-year-old child - Whether defendant negligent.

M and R, two 15-year-old schoolgirls, were fencing with plastic rulers during a class when one of the rulers snapped and a fragment of plastic entered M's right eye, causing her to lose all useful sight in that eye. M brought proceedings for negligence against R and the local education authority. The judge, dismissed the claim against the education authority, but found that both M and R had been guilty of negligence of which M's injury was the foreseeable result and, accordingly, that M's claim against R succeeded subject to a reduction of 50% for contributory negligence. R appealed, contending, inter alia, that the judge had erred when considering foreseeability by omitting to take account of the fact that R was not an adult.

Held - Although the test of foreseeability in negligence was an objective one, where the defendant was a child the question for the judge was not whether the actions of the defendant were such as an ordinarily prudent and reasonable adult in the defendant's situation would have realised gave rise to a risk of injury, but whether an ordinarily prudent and reasonable child of the same age as the defendant in the defendant's situation would have realised as much. Since the judge in his judgment had referred to M and R's age, it followed that he had had in mind the correct principles and had approached the matter in the correct way. However, there was insufficient evidence to justify his finding that the accident was foreseeable, since there was no evidence as to the propensity or otherwise of such rulers to break or any history of their having done so, nor that the practice of playing with rulers was banned or even frowned on in the school, nor that either of the girls had used excessive or inappropriate violence. What had taken place was nothing more than a schoolgirl's game which was commonplace in the school and there no justification for attributing to the participants the foresight of any significant risk of the likelihood of injury. The appeal would therefore be allowed and judgment entered for R (see p 924 *e* to *j*, p 926 *c* to *e j*, p 927 *b* to *j* and p 928 *a* to *j*, post).

McHale v Watson (1966) 115 CLR 199 adopted.

Notes
For the standard of care required of children, see 33 *Halsbury's Laws* (4th edn) para 621.

Cases referred to in judgments
Bolton v Stone [1951] 1 All ER 1078, [1951] AC 850, HL.
Gough v Thorne [1966] 3 All ER 398, [1966] 1 WLR 1387, CA.
Hughes v Lord Advocate [1963] 1 All ER 705, [1963] AC 837, [1963] 2 WLR 779, HL.
McHale v Watson (1966) 115 CLR 199, Aust HC.

Cases also cited or referred to in skeleton arguments
Carmarthenshire CC v Lewis [1955] 1 All ER 565, [1955] AC 549, HL.
Draper v Hodder [1972] 2 All ER 210, [1972] 2 QB 556, CA.
Latham v Johnson & Nephew Ltd [1913] 1 KB 398, [1911-1913] All ER Rep 117, CA.
Mahon v Osborne [1939] 1 All ER 535, [1939] 2 KB 14, CA.
Staley v Suffolk CC (26 November 1985, unreported), QBD at Norwich.
Vacwell Engineering Co Ltd v BDH Chemicals Ltd [1969] 3 All ER 1681, [1971] 1 QB 88.
Wieland v Cyril Lord Carpets Ltd [1969] 3 All ER 1006.
Williams v Humphrey (1975) Times, 20 February.
Wilson v Pringle [1986] 2 All ER 440, [1987] QB 237, CA.

Appeal
The first defendant, Heidi Richards, appealed from the decision of Judge Potter on 14 November 1995 in the Birmingham County Court whereby he awarded the plaintiff, Teresa Jane Mullin, damages of £27,500 for personal injury caused by the first defendant's negligence, but ordered that the damages should be reduced by 50% because of the plaintiff's contributory negligence. The judge dismissed the plaintiff's claim against the second defendant, Birmingham City Council, and the council took no part in the appeal. The facts are set out in the judgment of Hutchison LJ.

Richard Lee (instructed by *Cobbold & Gailey*, Lichfield) for the first defendant.
Michael Stephens (instructed by *Sehdev & Co*, Birmingham) for the plaintiff.

HUTCHISON LJ (giving the first judgment at the invitation of Butler-Sloss LJ).   On 29 February 1988 at Perry Beeches Secondary School in Birmingham two 15-year-old schoolgirls, Teresa Jane Mullin and Heidi Richards, who were friends and were sitting side by side at their desk, were engaged in playing around, hitting each other's white plastic 30 cm rulers as though in a play sword fight, when one or other of the rulers snapped and a fragment of plastic entered Teresa's right eye with the very unhappy result that she lost all useful sight in that eye, something that must be a source, I am sure, of great distress to her and her family.

Teresa brought proceedings against Heidi and the Birmingham City Council, who were the education authority, alleging negligence.   It is worth noting that her pleaded case involved facts quite different from those that I summarised a moment ago.   My summary reflects the learned judge's unchallenged findings of fact as well as the case pleaded by Heidi in her defence.   The judge dismissed the claim against the authority, holding that the mathematics teacher, Miss Osborne, whose class was coming to an end when the mishap occurred, had not been guilty of negligence and the plaintiff does not appeal against that decision.   The case against the local authority was based only on lack of proper supervision in the classroom on the day in question.   However, the judge having rejected Teresa's and accepted Heidi's version of how the accident occurred, concluded that each had been guilty of negligence, that Teresa's injury was the foreseeable result and that, accordingly, her claim against Heidi succeeded subject to a reduction of 50% for contributory negligence.

From that decision Heidi now appeals to this court.   I have referred already to the fact that it was not the plaintiff's case that the accident happened in the way the judge found and it is worth just taking a moment to see how things stood on the pleadings.

The plaintiff in her particulars of claim had alleged facts which involved that the first defendant, her friend Heidi, had tapped her from behind on the arm on a number of occasions with her ruler.   She alleged that she had at some stage stood up and had been minded to go and speak to the class teacher to have this conduct stopped but had refrained from doing that, and there came a time when Heidi hit her again and she put up her arm to shield herself and the ruler broke against her arm, that she turned to the front and then, turning back again, felt some pain or discomfort in her eye, the inference being that at that moment it was that she was injured.   The important feature of her account was that she was not doing anything or participating in anything with Heidi and that her accident resulted from the unwelcome attentions of Heidi and her use of the ruler.

In answer to that case, the first defendant by her pleading had denied the account given by the plaintiff and she had said in the particulars of contributory negligence:

'(i) The Plaintiff was a willing participant in a game in which the Plaintiff was fencing with the First Defendant, with rulers, during the course of which one of the rulers broke. (ii) If, which is denied, the Plaintiff suffered any injury, the First Defendant will aver that it was caused by a piece of plastic, detaching itself from the broken ruler and hitting the Plaintiff in the eye.'

It would have been open to the plaintiff, had she wished to do so, to amend her particulars of claim and allege an alternative case based upon the possibility that the judge might accept the case being advanced by the first defendant, but her advisers chose not to do that, probably for tactical reasons because they thought it would weaken her primary case about which she was resolute and maybe also because they thought that it was a case that was unlikely to be successful, one knows not. But the important thing is that there was no amendment and therefore those two versions were before the judge. No one was advancing a case of negligence based upon Heidi's version of what occurred.

Most of the judgment of the learned judge was devoted to resolving the dispute as to whether Teresa's or Heidi's account of what happened was the correct one, a task which the judge made clear, and I have to say I understand why he said this, and I sympathise with him, was made much more difficult by the fact that the trial was in November 1995, many years after the accident which occurred.

Having rejected Teresa's account the judge also held that Mrs Osborne, the class teacher, did not really see what had happened. She had said in evidence: 'Heidi and Teresa were playing with rulers, playing at a sword fight.' Heidi's account was that contained in her pleadings and the judge said of that:

'I was not willing to accept the evidence of the twins on the matter [the twins being a reference to Heidi and her twin sister, who gave evidence to the same effect] simple though it was, merely because they repeated it so many times with such enthusiasm. I have had to examine the notes they both wrote close to the event ... I think these ... are far more valuable ... The first defendant's note is very interesting: "Me and Teresa were playing around, hitting each other. I hit her with the ruler. It snapped out, went in her eye. It was a pure accident." Her sister wrote a similar note: "Heidi and Teresa were messing around, hitting each other. Heidi['s] ruler snapped and accidentally went into Teresa['s] eye. It was a complete accident."'

When he came to make his findings as to what happened, the judge, who plainly gave the matter very careful consideration, said:

' ... I conclude on the balance of probabilities that the plaintiff has not correctly stated ... what occurred and that in the concluding stages of the rough play between these two girls it is probable that what was going on was more like what is described by the first defendant and her sister than what is described by the plaintiff.'

Neither defendant argued volenti non fit injuria, though the particulars of contributory negligence, as will be recalled from my citation, referred to the plaintiff being a willing participant in the game. The judge adverted to the absence of any such contention in terms which suggest that he thought it would not have been a possible defence, something as to which I express no opinion. I simply note that it does not arise because it was never raised. The judge therefore had to determine whether negligence had been proved against either defendant; if so, whether the plaintiff's injury was foreseeable; and whether there was contributory negligence on the part of the plaintiff. What he said on these matters in so far as it relates to the position between Teresa and Heidi was:

'... I do not think any doubt was raised as to this, that if on the balance of probabilities the two girls were participating on equal terms, or both as free agents participating in an event of horseplay which, as they must both have appreciated became in its concluding stage dangerous because it involved rulers being used with some violence, if those are the findings I make, and they are the findings which, as I say, on the balance of probabilities I feel driven to, then however surprising it may be to the lay mind, the result must be that both were negligent. One cannot describe it as a lawful assault so one could also say that they were mutually engaging in assault, although that does not matter to my mind, and their joint mischievous efforts produced a particular total of unintended damage which happened to fall entirely on one participant rather than both.'

The judge went on to refer to defence counsel's argument on foreseeability, saying:

'The point was raised by Mr Lee in his helpful argument as to whether what happened was foreseeable or whether I should put it down to something that leads to no liability as between them because it was a totally uncovenanted and unforeseeable event. Having considered that, I do not think that it is the view that I take. In fact it is not, because as the matter ended, these girls were playing with a degree of misdirected and dangerous force sufficient to produce the physical and mechanical result that it did, and at 15 I am satisfied they must both have appreciated that to play like that was dangerous and although the precise injury would not have been foreseen, the danger of physical injury, including injury of this type, must have been readily foreseeable. So on that part of the case the plaintiff succeeds but only as to half.'

By her notice of appeal the first defendant contends, first, that there was no or no sufficient evidence for the judge's finding that she must have appreciated that what she was doing was dangerous; second, that there was no or no sufficient evidence for the judge's finding that it was readily foreseeable that her conduct might cause injury of the type that the plaintiff sustained; thirdly, that the judge erred when considering foreseeability by omitting to take account of the fact that the first defendant was not an adult but a 15-year-old schoolgirl. What he should have done, it is contended, was to consider objectively what a normal and reasonable 15-year-old schoolgirl would have foreseen. Fourthly, it is asserted that the judge's finding that Heidi must have appreciated that this sort of conduct was dangerous was inconsistent with his finding that it was common in the school and with his conclusion that it was comparatively innocent and the absence of any evidence of prohibition or previous injuries. Finally, it is said that there was no evidence on which the judge could find that the shattering of the ruler was foreseeable.

So far as negligence is concerned, the relevant principles are well settled and I do not understand there to be any real difference between the views of counsel for the parties to this appeal. I would summarise the principles that govern liability in negligence in a case such as the present as follows. In order to succeed the plaintiff must show that the defendant did an act which it was reasonably foreseeable would cause injury to the plaintiff, that the relationship between the plaintiff and the defendant was such as to give rise to a duty of care, and that the act was one which caused injury to the plaintiff. In the present case, as it seems to me, no difficulty arose as to the second and third requirements because Teresa and Heidi were plainly in a sufficiently proximate relationship to give rise to a duty of care and the causation of the injury is not in issue. The argument centres on foreseeability. The test of foreseeability is an objective one; but the fact that the first defendant was at the time a 15-year-old schoolgirl is not irrelevant. The question for the judge is not whether the actions of the defendant were such as an ordinarily prudent and reasonable adult in the defendant's situation would have realised gave rise to a risk of injury, it is whether an ordinarily prudent and reasonable 15-year-old schoolgirl in the defendant's situation would have realised as much. In that connection both counsel referred us to, and relied upon, the Australian decision in *McHale v Watson* (1966) 115 CLR 199 esp at 213-214 in the judgment of Kitto J. I cite a portion of the passage I have referred to, all of which was cited to us by Mr Lee on behalf of the appellant, and which Mr Stephens has adopted as epitomising the correct approach:

'The standard of care being objective, it is no answer for him [that is a child], any more than it is for an adult, to say that the harm he caused was due to his being abnormally slow-witted, quick-tempered, absent-minded or inexperienced. But it does not follow that he cannot rely in his defence upon a limitation upon the capacity for foresight or prudence, not as being personal to himself, but as being characteristic of humanity at his stage of development and in that sense normal. By doing so he appeals to a standard of ordinariness, to an objective and not a subjective standard.'

Mr Stephens also cited to us a passage in the judgment of Owen J (at 234):

' … the standard by which his conduct is to be measured is not that to be expected of a reasonable adult but that reasonably to be expected of a child of the same age, intelligence and experience.'

I venture to question the word 'intelligence' in that sentence, but I understand Owen J to be making the same point essentially as was made by Kitto J. It is perhaps also material to have in mind the words of Salmon LJ in *Gough v Thorne* [1966] 3 All ER 398 at 400, [1966] 1 WLR 1387 at 1391, which is cited also by Mr Stephens, where he said:

'The question as to whether the plaintiff can be said to have been guilty of contributory negligence depends on whether any ordinary child of 13 can be expected to have done any more than this child did. I say "any ordinary child". I do not mean a paragon of prudence; nor do I mean a scatter-brained child; but the ordinary girl of 13.'

I need say no more about that principle as to the way in which age affects the assessment of negligence because counsel are agreed upon it and, despite the fact that we have been told that there has been a good deal of controversy in other jurisdictions and that there is no direct authority in this jurisdiction, the approach in *McHale v Watson* seems to me to have the advantage of obvious, indeed irrefutable, logic. Then, even if the requirements that I have so far summarised are satisfied with the consequence that negligence has been proved, the defendant will not be liable if the injury actually sustained is not foreseeable, that is to say is of a different kind from that which the defendant ought to have foreseen as the likely outcome of his want of care (see in that regard *Hughes v Lord Advocate* [1963] 1 All ER 705, [1963] AC 837).

Applying those principles to the facts of the present case the central question to which this appeal gives rise is whether on the facts found by the judge and in the light of the evidence before him he was entitled to conclude that an ordinary, reasonable 15-year-old schoolgirl in the first defendant's position would have appreciated that by participating to the extent that she did in a play fight, involving the use of plastic rulers as though they were swords, gave rise to a risk of injury to the plaintiff of the same general kind as she sustained. In that connection I emphasise that a mere possibility is not enough as passages in the well-known case of *Bolton v Stone* [1951] 1 All ER 1078, [1951] AC 850, to which Mr Lee helpfully referred us, make clear. I cite some of the passages on which he relied. Lord Porter said ([1951] 1 All ER 1078 at 1080, 1081, [1951] AC 850 at 857, 858):

> 'The question however remains: Is it enough to make an action negligent to say that its performance may possibly cause injury or must some greater probability exist of that result ensuing in order to make those responsible for its occurrence guilty of negligence? ... It is not enough that the event should be such as can reasonably be foreseen. The further result that injury is likely to follow must also be such as a reasonable man would contemplate before he can be convicted of actionable negligence. Nor is the remote possibility of injury occurring enough. There must be sufficient probability to lead a reasonable man to anticipate it. The existence of some risk is an ordinary incident of life, even when all due care has been, as it must be, taken.'

Lord Reid said ([1951] 1 All ER 1078 at 1084, [1951] AC 850 at 864):

> 'My Lords, it was readily foreseeable that an accident such as befell the respondent might possibly occur during one of the appellants' cricket matches. Balls had been driven into the public road from time to time and it was obvious that if a person happened to be where a ball fell that person would receive injuries which might or might not be serious. On the other hand, it was plain that the chance of that happening was small.'

Lord Radcliffe made this observation ([1951] 1 All ER 1078 at 1087, [1951] AC 850 at 868):

> 'I can see nothing unfair in the appellants being required to compensate the respondent for the serious injury that she has received as a result of the sport that they have organized on their cricket ground at Cheetham Hill, but the law of negligence is concerned less with what is fair than with what is culpable, and I cannot persuade myself that the appellants have been guilty of any culpable act or omission in this case.'

I have omitted to cite two further passages which were referred to in the speeches of Lord Normand and Lord Oaksey which are to the same effect (see [1951] 1 All ER 1078 at 1082-1083 and 1083-1084, [1951] AC 850 at 860-861 and 863).

I do not propose, in the light of the conclusion to which I have come without hesitation in this case, to deal individually with all the grounds of appeal, though I should mention in relation to the third ground, which asserts that the judge treated the first defendant as an adult and not as a 15-year-old child, that I reject that contention. It seems to me that his reference to the age of the two girls in the passage which I have cited from his judgment shows that he had in mind the correct principles. Accordingly I would hold that he approached the matter in that respect in the correct way.

However the question of actual foreseeability (that is to say the application of that correct approach in law to the facts) raises, in my judgment, great difficulties. First, there certainly was no evidence as to the propensity or otherwise of such rulers to break or any history of their having done so. There was evidence which the judge does not say he rejects and which he may, since it was an admission against interest, be taken to have accepted, that ruler fencing was commonplace. That is to be found in the evidence of Heidi herself, who said when she was asked:

'*Q.* As far as this business of fencing with rulers is concerned, was this the only time you had ever done that? *A.* No, it was a popular game at school.'

Miss Osborne, the teacher, was asked questions to the same effect:

'*Q.* ... Had you seen this game going on around the school? *A.* Yes, I knew it was a common game with pupils.'

While I am dealing with her evidence I should mention an answer on which Mr Stephens places particular reliance. The judge asked her:

'*Q.* ... did you think perhaps it was a thing to stop because it might be dangerous? *A.* Yes, and it was also unacceptable behaviour in the classroom.'

It seems me that though she assented to the judge's proposition that she would stop it because it was dangerous, the point she was really making was she would stop it because it was unacceptable conduct in the classroom. There was no evidence at all that the practice was banned or even frowned on. There was no evidence that it was discouraged in any way. The question of foreseeability therefore has to be judged against that background, the prevalence of the practice, the absence of prohibition, the absence of warning against it or of its dangers and the absence of any evidence of there having been any previous injury as a result of it. The further point can be made, which is that the judge's finding, if that is the right description of it, that excessive violence was used by either girl is not supported by any evidence so far as I can see. It has to be remembered that he had rejected Teresa's account which did involve a relatively heavy blow on her forearm and there is no reason to think that in rejecting it he had, as it were, preserved and resurrected that one part of it: and the passages in which Heidi gives her account of the mock fencing do not bear the construction that any degree of violence was being used. Indeed there are passages in the evidence elsewhere that indicate that the two girls were not even trying to knock the rulers out of each other's hands but merely to touch rulers, as it were, in mock fencing.

There was, therefore, as it seems to me, no evidence to support the finding that these two girls were guilty of using misdirected and dangerous force, which is one of the judge's phrases, or that there had been a violent clash of rulers or that the rulers had been used with some violence, which are other phrases that he used. This had not been said by the first defendant in her evidence. It had not been suggested to her at any stage. I pause to interpolate that not only was that case never put, but it is at least doubtful whether it was urged in argument as an alternative basis for a finding of negligence, though for present purposes I shall assume that it may have been. Mr Stephens was not present at the trial and has no instructions on the matter.

The judge, it seems to me, found negligence without there being material on which he could properly do so. He seems indeed from the language he used to have regarded it as axiomatic that if there was a fight going on, such as he found there was, a play fight, that imported that injury was reasonably foreseeable and from his finding that the ruler broke that there was necessarily dangerous or excessive violence. For my part, I would say that in the absence of evidence one simply does not know why the ruler broke, whether because it was unusually weak, unlike other rulers; whether because it had been damaged in some way; or whether because rulers of this sort are particularly prone to break; one does not know. What certainly one cannot infer, and the judge was, I consider, not entitled to infer, was that there was here excessive violence or inappropriate violence over and above that which was inherent in the play fencing in which these two girls were indulging. This was in truth nothing more than a schoolgirls' game such as on the evidence was commonplace in this school and there was, I would hold, no justification for attributing to the participants the foresight of any significant risk of the likelihood of injury. They had seen it done elsewhere with some frequency. They had not heard it prohibited or received any warning about it. They had not been told of any injuries occasioned by it. They were not in any sense behaving culpably. So far as foresight goes, had they paused to think they might, I suppose, have said: 'It is conceivable that some unlucky injury might happen', but if asked if there was any likelihood of it or any real possibility of it, they would, I am sure, have said that they did not foresee any such possibility. Taking the view therefore that the learned judge—who, as I have said, readily and almost without question accepted that on his findings of fact there was negligence on the part of both these young ladies—was wrong in his view and there was no evidence on which he could come to it, I would allow the appeal and direct that judgment be entered for the first defendant. I have to say that I appreciate that this result will be disappointing to the plaintiff for whom one can have nothing but sympathy, because she has suffered a grave injury through no fault of her own. But unfortunately she has failed to establish in my view that anyone was legally responsible for that injury and, accordingly, her claim should have failed.

SIR JOHN VINELOTT. I agree. It seems to me that, in the passage which Hutchison LJ has cited at length, the learned judge at the very end of his judgment comes very close to saying: 'This accident happened. It must therefore be the case that these young ladies were playing with these rulers with a degree of misdirected and dangerous force sufficient to cause a ruler to break or splinter as a result of which injury was caused; it was and must have been an injury which was reasonably foreseeable.' That is an inappropriate approach. There was in fact no evidence that the ruler broke because the mock fight was carried on with dangerous force and, equally, there was no evidence that physical damage would be likely to result if a ruler broke or splintered in the course of that activity. In the absence of any sufficient evidence on those two points, it seems to me that the conclusion that the learned judge reached was unfounded.

BUTLER-SLOSS LJ. I agree with both judgments and since there has been little earlier authority on the proper approach to the standard of care to be applied to a child, I would like to underline the observations of Hutchison LJ and rely upon two further passages in the persuasive judgment of Kitto J in the High Court of Australia in *McHale v Watson* (1966) 115 CLR 199 at 213):

> 'In regard to the things which pertain to foresight and prudence experience, understanding of causes and effects, balance of judgment, thoughtfulness—it is absurd, indeed it is a misuse of language, to speak of normality in relation to persons of all ages taken together. In those things normality is, for children, something different from what normality is for adults; the very concept of normality is a concept of rising levels until "years of discretion" are attained. The law does not arbitrarily fix upon any particular age for this purpose, and tribunals of fact may well give effect to different views as to the age at which normal adult foresight and prudence are reasonably to be expected in relation to particular sets of circumstances. But up to that stage the normal capacity to exercise those two qualities necessarily means the capacity which is

normal for a child of the relevant age; and it seems to me that it would be contrary to the fundamental principle that a person is liable for harm that he causes by falling short of an objective criterion of "propriety" in his conduct—propriety, that is to say, as determined by a comparison with the standard of care reasonably to be expected in the circumstances from the normal person to hold that where a child's liability is in question the normal person—to be considered is someone other than a child of corresponding age.'

I would respectfully indorse those observations as entirely appropriate to English law and I would like to conclude with another passage of Kitto J (at 216) particularly relevant to today—

'... in the absence of relevant statutory provision, children, like everyone else, must accept as they go about in society the risks from which ordinary care on the part of others will not suffice to save them. One such risk is that boys of twelve may behave as boys of twelve ...'

—and I would say that girls of 15 playing together may play as somewhat irresponsible girls of 15. I too would allow this appeal.

Appeal allowed.

Dilys Tausz Barrister.

Index